DATE DUE

Constituency Labour Parties in Britain

Published for
The Foreign Policy Research Institute
UNIVERSITY OF PENNSYLVANIA

EDWARD G. *adrial* JANOSIK

Constituency Labour Parties in Britain

FREDERICK A. PRAEGER, *Publishers*

NEW YORK · WASHINGTON · LONDON

FREDERICK A. PRAEGER, *Publishers*
111 Fourth Avenue, New York, N.Y. 10003, U.S.A.
77–79 Charlotte Street, London W.1, England

Published in the United States of America in 1968
by Frederick A. Praeger, Inc., Publishers

Copyright 1968 in London, England,
by Edward G. Janosik

Library of Congress Catalog Card Number: 68–19853

Printed in Great Britain

Contents

successful. However, constituency independen...
...ates may be the means of affording certain mem...
...Party who hold a particular point of view a status...
...might not otherwise possess.
...the Labour Party have virtually ignored the appoi...
...ating of delegates to the Annual Conference. The ca...
...t stems from widely held opinions of the unimportan...
...al Conference as a policy-making body, and from t...
...ct that constituency parties cast only about 17 per ce...
...l vote of the conference. Since it was assumed that th...
...ity of the remaining 83 per cent of the vote was cast b...
...ons in favour of moderate or right-wing resolutions, ther...
...investigation into the nature of the constituency party vote...
...ill true that constituency delegates cast only a sixth of the...
...he Annual Conference, but it is no longer the case that the...
...l Executive Committee can automatically depend on a...
...y of the trade union vote in support of its conference actions...
...before the replacement of Arthur Deakin as head of the...
...-strong Transport and General Workers Union by Frank...
...ns, leader of the unilateralist forces at the 1960 and 1961...
...al conferences, the assured approval by the trade unions of...
...proposals had been brought to an end.
...lthough the Annual Conference does not determine Labour...
...ty policy nor control the Parliamentary Labour Party, it cannot...
...held that conference decisions have an impact only upon the...
...ternal affairs of the Labour Party, if indeed this was ever the case.
...he approval of a resolution at the 1960 conference calling for the...
...nilateral renunciation of the manufacture, stockpiling and basing...
...of nuclear weapons in the United Kingdom created a crisis of...
...historic proportions within the Labour Party. There was no indica-
...tion that Hugh Gaitskell and other leaders would ever have accepted
...the unilateralist position, and it is difficult to say what the future
...would have held for the Labour Party had not the 1961 conference
...reversed the unilateralist policy. Even with the reversal, the effect
...of the unilateralist controversy on the international relations of
...Britain, on the NATO allies, on members of the British Common-
...wealth, and on all major world powers, can only be surmised.
...Considering the fact that trade-union solidarity at the Annual Con-
...ference can no longer be guaranteed and that conference decisions

Acknowledgements

The opportunity to spend the academic year 1962–63 in Britain to gather data for this book was provided by the University of Pennsylvania, which gave me a sabbatical leave for the task. Additional support came from the Social Science Research Council and the Foreign Policy Research Institute of the University of Pennsylvania. The latter organisation made it possible for me to obtain the material on which chapter 3 is based during a four-week visit to Britain to study the General Election of 1964, and also furnished invaluable assistance on a number of other occasions. My special thanks go to Robert Strausz-Hupé for his encouragement of and interest in this study.

My debt to a number of British political scientists is substantial. Many of the questions to which I sought answers grew out of the writings of Robert T. McKenzie of the London School of Economics and Richard Rose of the University of Strathclyde. The entire manuscript was read by Richard Rose and by Peter Calvert of Southampton University, and their comments were instrumental in developing what merit this volume may have. I should also like to thank Derick Mirfin of the Pall Mall Press for his helpful collaboration, and Miss Gillian Mercer for technical assistance.

The study could not have been completed had it not been for the willing co-operation of scores of members of the Labour Party. I am able to identify only H. R. Underhill of the Head Office, W. J. Clarke and W. G. Thom, agents for Kemptown and Reading, respectively, and Albert J. Murray, MP for Gravesend. The leaders of the thirty-six constituency parties who agreed to be interviewed, and the party members who were helpful in many other ways I must thank anonymously, but no less sincerely.

To my wife Ellen, who skilfully played the alternative roles of supporter, critic and editor, I am deeply and lastingly grateful. My dedication of this book to her is small recognition of her contributions to it.

Geneseo, New York
January 1968
E.S.J.

Introduction

A SABBATICAL leave for the aca[...]
the author to organise a research pr[...]
between national and local politic[...]
Party. A number of excellent studies [...]
last decade have dealt largely with su[...]
tribution of power within the Labour [...]
unions in the Labour Party, the Labou[...]
ideological tensions within the Labour [...]
haviour and the Labour Party, the future o[...]
a functional study of the British political syst[...]

Valuable as these studies are, there rema[...]
resolved questions regarding the importance [...]
parties as elements of the Labour Party. W[...]
documentation, a marvellous mythology has e[...]
the selection of parliamentary candidates, and the[...]
and independence possessed respectively by nat[...]
stituency organs over the selection process. This matt[...]
where the socialisation of new Labour MPs by the [...]

[1] R. T. McKenzie, *British Political Parties*, 2nd edn; Mar[...]
Trade Unions and the Labour Party since 1945; A. H. Birch, *Small-[...]
C. A. R. Crosland, *The Future of Socialism*; Ralph Miliband, [...]
Socialism; David Butler and Richard Rose, *The British General [...]
1959; David Butler and Anthony King, *The British General Election[...]
A. J. Allen, *The English Voter*; Mark Abrams and Richard Ros[...]
Labour Lose?; R. H. S. Crossman, *Labour in the Affluent Society*; Richar[...]
Politics in England.

B

1

2 Constituency [...]

Labour Party is[...]
selecting candid[...]
of the Labour [...]
a forum they [...]

Students of[...]
ing and mand[...]
of this negle[...]
of the Annu[...]
empirical fa[...]
of the tota[...]
vast major[...]
trade uni[...]
was little[...]

It is s[...]
vote at [...]
Nationa[...]
majori[...]
Even [...]
millio[...]
Cous[...]
annu[...]
NEC [...]
Par[...]
be[...]
in[...]
T[...]

have an influence far beyond the conference hall, those procedures by which the conference delegate is appointed and mandated deserve more attention than they have heretofore been given.

Concern has been expressed by Labour Party leaders about the social characteristics of the party, particularly in regard to the bias toward maturity among MPs and constituency party leaders. Information is available on the social background of MPs, but there is little public information on the social and political backgrounds of constituency party leaders. This has led to the conclusion that only impressionistic evidence is the basis of the presumption that local party leadership is ageing.

Similarly, empirical information is lacking in regard to the attitudes of constituency party leaders on matters of party and public policy. Until recently, the impression was accepted with few qualifications that trade unionists were almost exclusively on the right of the party and that constituency party leaders were almost exclusively on the left. In current investigations there is less of a tendency to lump all trade unionists under one label and all constituency leaders under another, but the study of the policy views of British party activists has only begun.

Factionalism is so outstanding a characteristic of the national Labour Party that there is little reason to be surprised at the attention it has received in some studies of voting behaviour and the British political system. It is unfortunate that no effort has been made to determine whether the propensity toward factionalism in the national party is equally prevalent in the constituency parties, or whether factionalism is a luxury which only persons operating on the parliamentary level feel they can afford.

One of the most interesting and perplexing aspects of British political studies is the manner in which the British party system is consistently described. There are frequent references to a disciplined, two-party system in Britain; and the Labour Party, which has governed Britain for a total of ten years since the end of the First World War, is depicted as part of a competitive two-party system. At the same time, while the Liberal Party—which has increased its numerical vote by sixteen times and its proportion of the total vote by over four times since 1955—is invariably recognised as a political party, it is apparently not considered to be part of the British party system. In some respects, certainly, it can be argued that Britain has a two-party system, but the continued presence and vigour of the Liberal Party raises the question whether three functioning parties can constitute a two-party system. There is also a question regarding the so-called discipline of the Parliamentary Labour Party, not in voting behaviour in the House of Commons, but in other parliamentary actions and in activities outside the House of Commons. Some constituency parties apparently serve as a protected base of operations for Labour MPs who carry on a running battle with party leadership: a struggle that has aroused doubts of the credibility of the Labour Party as a governing agent in the British political system.

Data for this study were gathered from party leaders in a stratified random sample of thirty-six constituencies. The 618 constituencies of Britain were arranged in rank order based on their electoral support of the Labour Party in the 1959 general election.[2] A random sample of twelve constituencies was taken from each of the highest, the median, and the lowest quintiles in terms of Labour Party strength.[3] The range of support for the Labour Party in the highest quintile was from 57 to 85 per cent; in the median quintile the range was from 40.5 to 48.3 per cent; in the lowest quintile the range was from 9.4 to 31.9 per cent.

The decision to designate the constituencies in the median quintile as marginal constituencies was based on the assumption that the 1959 election results, which were used to determine Labour Party strength, were skewed in favour of the Conservative Party. It was felt that the distortion in the 1959 figures was sufficient to assume that Labour would carry every seat it had won in 1959, as well as every seat in which it had polled more than 48.3 per cent of the vote in straight fights in 1959.[4] The results of the 1964 election completely

---

[2] The twelve Northern Ireland divisions were excluded on the advice of political scholars and practitioners alike, on the grounds that the religious question permeated Irish politics to such an extent that a questionnaire developed for Britain would be irrelevant. The Gallup poll released its results of the 1964 election with two sets of figures, one for Britain, and the second for the United Kingdom.

[3] The total sample comprised 6 per cent of all constituencies; the sub-sample of twelve constituencies comprised 10 per cent of each of the three quintiles.

[4] The latter half of this assumption held in seventeen of eighteen constituencies, the exception being the Lowestoft division of Suffolk.

vindicated the decision concerning marginal divisions. Labour held twenty-four of these constituencies as it entered the 1964 election. One of these seats was lost and thirty-eight were gained, giving Labour control of sixty-one of the 123 constituencies in the median quintile. Furthermore, of the twelve constituencies selected for the sample, six were won by Labour and six by the Conservatives.

Not even this generous concept of marginality was sufficient to cover all Labour gains and losses. Eight constituencies which had polled between 35.8 and 40.4 per cent for Labour in 1959 were carried in 1964, and one of these with but 35.8 per cent of the vote.

TABLE INTRO. 1. *CLP respondents to survey questionnaire*

| | Constituencies | | | |
	All	Strong	Marginal	Weak
MPs	10	9	1	0
Prospective parliamentary candidates	25	2	11	12
Chairmen	35	12	12	11
Secretary-agents	35	11	12	12
Annual conference delegates	31	11	11	9
Others	18	5	6	7
Totals	154	50	53	51

At the other end of the scale, Labour lost three seats in which their 1959 vote was over 50 per cent in straight contests, the strongest of these being Smethwick where Labour, with Patrick Gordon Walker as its candidate, had polled 54.7 per cent of the vote in 1959. Thus, marginality expressed in terms of Labour gains and losses ranged from 35.8 to 54.7 per cent.

A total of 142 questionnaires was completed by constituency party leaders. Table 1 indicates there were 154 respondents in six leadership categories.

The discrepancy is explained by the fact that seven secretary-agents, two parliamentary candidates, one MP, one chairman, and one treasurer were also appointed as delegates to the 1962 conference. One MP and one secretary-agent, both from the same division, refused to grant appointments for an interview or to complete the questionnaire. In one weak constituency the poor state of organisation was suggested by the absence of a chairman of the General

Management Committee. Five constituencies, because of organisational shortcomings and financial problems, sent no delegate to the
1962 conference.

The miscellaneous leadership category used in Table 1 included
constituency party treasurers, *ad hoc* general election agents, and
certain party leaders whose views seemed important within their
respective divisions. The presence of two prospective parliamentary
candidates from strong divisions was due to the retirement of the
sitting members from those constituencies.

The inclusion of General Management Committee (GMC) chairmen and secretary-agents as constituency party leaders requires no
explanation. MPS, prospective parliamentary candidates and conference delegates were selected for two reasons. Some of the information relating to the selection of parliamentary candidates, and the
appointing and mandating of annual conference delegates could be
obtained only from the persons filling these posts. Just as important
was the fact that these persons had been chosen by their General
Management Committees and could be considered to represent a
consensus of the GMC, even though the candidates were not necessarily a resident of the constituency involved.

All but twelve of the 142 questionnaires were completed by the
interviewer in the presence of the respondent. (The remaining
twelve were completed privately and returned by mail.) In cases
where a lengthy answer was given to a question, the entire response
was read back to the respondent to assure accuracy. A promise of
confidentiality was made at the beginning of each interview, not only
between the respondents within the constituency, but also between
constituencies. The same undertaking was given in respect to regional or national party officials, and particularly to newspapers
and journals. Any reluctance to co-operate on the part of Labour
officials stemmed from their concern that the project might be an
elaborate device by the British partisan press to elicit information
embarrassing to the Labour Party. All respondents were told that no
information would be attributed by name to their constituency but
would appear only as part of the total data ascribed to different
types of constituencies or different leadership categories, age groups,
etc.

Length of the interviews varied considerably. The shortest interview, which was of a half-hour's duration, was with a hurried MP in

the cafeteria of the House of Commons. Interviews with two secretary-agents who were also annual conference delegates lasted nearly five hours, as did a meeting with one MP in his London home. Most of the interviews required from an hour to one and a half hours, in addition to the time required to explain the nature and purpose of the study, with appropriate interruptions for tea. Two full days were spent in each division, so that it was possible to meet most of the officials informally before the actual interview session.

Any extra time in the constituencies was devoted to activities which gave additional insight into the operation of the constituency parties. Formal meetings of local government councils were attended, as well as caucuses of the Labour members of local government councils which preceded the formal meetings. Invitations to attend and observe GMC meetings and ward party sessions were extended, and countless exchanges of political views occurred in 'locals' and Labour clubs after the adjourning of the party meeting. The author, after fifteen years' experience in American local politics, has no reason to believe that the data gathered for this study represent other than a candid and honest response on the part of the constituency party officials who participated in the study.

1

Social Background of Constituency
Labour Party Leaders

THERE HAVE BEEN few studies made dealing with the social characteristics of Constituency Labour Party (CLP) leaders or members. In 1959 A. H. Birch noted that such inquiries had only recently been undertaken, and suggested those undertaken were valuable because of the important role played in the British political system by rank and file party members.[1] Unfortunately, too, investigation in this area has not been extensive. Studies which have been made reflect a preoccupation with the political effects of class as opposed to a broad range of social attributes. Birch's own study of political life in the small town of Glossop included questions on age, religion, and occupation, but his data were too limited to be useful for comparative purposes. With the exception of some slight personal information on MPs and parliamentary candidates, there are virtually no data available regarding the people who perform basic political tasks and who bear important party responsibilities. A few of the party members receive modest salaries, but the vast majority work voluntarily, 'psychic' income constituting their only reward for devoting much of their leisure time to party activities. Lack of precise knowledge about the personal characteristics of constituency party leaders has not precluded generalisations on such matters as the age structure of divisional parties and the need for greater involvement of party members in voluntary community organisations.[2]

[1] A. H. Birch, *Small-Town Politics*, London and New York 1959, p. 79.
[2] Morgan Phillips, *Labour in the Sixties*, 1960, pp. 16–18.

8

1. *Length of political activity*

Although slightly more than half the respondents in the study became politically active after the Labour victory of 1945, many veteran leaders were found among constituency leaders. About 28 per cent of the respondents dated their political participation to the period between the General Strike of 1926 and the end of the Second World War. Another 15 per cent traced their political involvement to the years between 1915 and 1926, and 4 per cent were active in trade unionism and politics prior to the outbreak of the First World War.

Distribution of the four categories of length of political activity varied widely among the different types of constituencies. As Table 1.1 shows, there was rather even distribution in strong divisions, but

TABLE 1.1. *Length of political activity, expressed by percentage of constituency type*

| | Constituencies | | | |
	All	Strong	Marginal	Weak
Pre-1914	4	13	2	0
1915–26	15	27	7	10
1927–45	28	29	38	17
Post-1945	53	31	53	73

in marginal districts 91 per cent of the leaders had become active after 1927, while in weak districts 73 per cent had become active after 1945, and 14 per cent after 1956.

Recruitment of constituency party leaders did not come at an even rate, as Table 1.2 demonstrates. There is no ready explanation for these variations.

Certain historical events coincided with some of these periods, but not too much can be made of such fortuitous circumstances. There was a general election in 1923, while the years 1925–6 might be associated with the General Strike. 1931–3 marked the worst years of the Great Depression, and 1936–8 saw the development of international tensions leading up to the Second World War. Party recruitment practically stopped during the political moratorium of the war years, but increased between 1945 and 1956. The high point in attracting new members who ultimately became constituency party leaders came during the four-year period 1948–51, when thirty-one potential leaders joined the Labour Party. The three-year period 1953–6 was also quite productive in leadership recruitment and suggests that newer party members were not denied responsibility, as this group had been in the party ten years or less at the time this study was made.

According to the respondents, 84 per cent of their political work was solely with the Labour Party. About 6 per cent had remained in the Independent Labour Party after the decision of that group in July 1932 to disaffiliate from the Labour Party, but later transferred their membership to the Labour Party.[3] Five per cent had been members of the Communist Party, some of them leaving as

TABLE 1.2. *Accession pattern of CLP leaders recruited to the Labour Party for selected years between 1923 and 1962*

1923	8
1925–26	7
1931–38	13
1936–38	11
1939–44	8
1945–46	10
1948–51	31
1953–56	21
1957–62	9

early as 1924 while others remained in the party until the Hungarian revolution of 1956. Another 5 per cent had belonged to various minor parties, among them Sir Richard Acland's Commonwealth Party. One former Conservative had joined the Labour Party when the Royal Navy withheld his pay after the sinking of his ship in the First World War, holding him responsible for the loss of his gear.

2. *Age of CLP leaders*

Because the relationship between age and length of political activity is necessarily close, a basic similarity is apparent in Tables 1.1

[3] The ILP lost 75 per cent of its membership in three years following its decision to disaffiliate. Cf. Henry Pelling, *The Origins of the Labour Party*, London and New York, 2nd edn, 1954, p. 77; quoted in Ralph Miliband, *Parliamentary Socialism*, London, 1961, p. 195.

and 1.3. The close correspondence of the pre-1914, 1915–26, and 1927–45 categories of length of political activity to the age groups over 65, 56–65, and 46–55 should be noted, as well as the comparison between the three remaining age groups and those leaders who had joined the Labour Party after 1945. The most striking feature of Table 1.3 is the difference in the age structure of CLP leaders in the various types of constituencies. In the strong divisions, 56 per cent of the respondents were between 46 and 65 years of age. Marginal divisions reflected the distribution of the entire sample, but with much larger concentrations in the middle-age groups, with 72 per cent of these respondents in the 36–55 categories. In weak divisions, 60 per cent of the leaders were between 26 and 45 years old.

TABLE 1.3. *Age of CLP leaders, expressed by percentage of constituency type*

	Constituencies			
	All	Strong	Marginal	Weak
Over 65	6	15	2	4
56–65	18	31	9	15
46–55	28	25	42	17
36–45	29	23	30	33
26–35	16	6	13	27
25 or less	3	0	4	4

Presumably it was the age distribution in the strong constituency parties which gave concern to Labour Party leaders like the late Morgan Phillips, for with the exception of one Midlands division having three officials under 45, the leadership of the strong constituencies could fairly be described as ageing. That these parties, which polled between 60 and 75 per cent of the vote in the 1959 general election, have a clear predilection for older officials is supported by the evidence that 71 per cent of their leaders were over 45, while only 6 per cent were under 35. With the thrust of competition lacking, there was a noticeable disinclination in the strong divisions to make extensive changes in office or to bring in new blood to the organisation. Of the twelve, eight indicated the minimum constituency party membership of 800, although in many cases this was not synonymous with minimal activity.[4] In seven of the strong constituencies the parliamentary candidate had been sponsored by trade unions or an affiliated organisation, and there was evidence to indicate that this practice had a depressing effect on constituency activity. The secretary-agent of one such division was asked what proportion of his time was devoted to fund raising. His response was 'None'. He went on to explain that the trade union sponsoring the parliamentary candidate furnished any money needed by the division, which was one reporting a minimal membership to the national party. An operation of this sort, however successful in electing its candidate, required neither youth nor vigour, and was unlikely to attract younger people.

The political environment in marginal constituencies, which polled between 40 and 48 per cent of the vote in 1959, differed radically from that in the strong divisions. Most of the marginal parties thought they had a good chance to win in the coming parliamentary election. While there was a tendency among marginal party leaders to exaggerate the importance of organisation, it was in such constituencies that close elections took place in which party organisation might make the difference between winning and losing.[5] In contrast with the strong divisions, only two marginals reported minimum membership, the remaining ten having between 1,000 and 2,000 on the party rolls. Also, where there was but one paid agent in the strong constituencies, the marginals had on salary five full-time and one part-time agent. The resources the marginal parties had available were almost exclusively indigenous. Only two of the twelve parliamentary candidates were sponsored by organisations affiliated with the Labour Party, which meant that these parties were usually required to raise their own funds, a task they accomplished effectively.[6] Consequently, these divisions strove to recruit, train and organise as many active workers as possible in

[4] Constituency parties pay affiliation fees to the national Labour Party on the basis of size of their party membership. Many vigorous divisions, in order to reduce the size of the payment, report only minimum membership which was set by the national party at 800 in 1962, and increased to 1,000 in 1965.

[5] Less than 1 per cent of the votes cast separated the victor from the loser in twenty-one seats in the 1964 general election, of which Labour won ten.

[6] In the 1964 general election, the marginal constituencies spent 94 per cent of their legal maximum expenses, the strong divisions 71 per cent, and the weak 61 per cent.

order that all necessary activities be done, while the leaders were expected to have the time, experience and energy to give the workers a strong lead. These qualifications were most likely to be found in the middle age groups from which almost three out of four marginal party leaders were recruited.

If it is assumed that the age distribution of the entire populations of all types of constituencies is the same, and there is no evidence to the contrary, the distribution of CLP leaders over the age of 55 would appear to be a matter of conscious choice. Thus only 11 per cent of marginal CLP leaders were over 55, partly because of the high expectations the GMCs had of the time and energy needed for the work. Forty-six per cent of strong CLP leaders were in the two oldest age groups because of the irrelevance of these expectations in a situation where little work was required for Labour to win. Perhaps the reason weak divisions had almost twice the proportion in the two oldest age groups than did the marginals was due to the fact that it seemed that no amount of work could make any difference in divisions that had polled less than 30 per cent of the vote in 1959. It is not easy to suggest explanations for the replacement of the 46–55 group by the 26–35 category in the weak divisions. It could be that the kind of idealism needed for leaders in weak constituencies diminishes rapidly after the age of 45, and that the retirement of discouraged middle-aged leaders creates a vacuum which draws younger party members into positions of responsibility more quickly than would be the case in marginal and strong constituencies.

The age distribution of CLP leaders compares quite favourably with that of the entire British population, even when the highly unfavourable data from the strong divisions are included. With the exception of the 25 or less category, there is a clear bias in favour of younger CLP leaders. The small proportion of CLP leaders under 25 years of age is not inconsistent with the findings of studies of political behaviour in other western democracies. It is apparent that interests of young adults which distract their attention from politics are present in other countries as well as Britain.[7]

---

[7] Julian L. Woodward and Elmo Roper, "Political Activity of American Citizens", *American Political Science Review*, December 1950, p. 877. See Birch, op. cit., p. 80, for partial information on the age of all party supporters in Glossop. See also Mark Benney *et al.*, *How People Vote*, London and New York, 1956, p. 51.

TABLE 1.4. *Age distribution percentage of CLP leaders compared with age distribution percentage of British population, March 1965*[8]

	CLP leaders	British population
Over 65	6	17
56–65	18	17
46–55	28	18
36–45	29	20
26–35	16	18
25 or less	3	10

Age distribution of CLP leaders by leadership category revealed interesting variations, and supported the alarm of some Labourites over the advanced age of the Parliamentary Labour Party. Among incumbent MPs, 80 per cent were in the 45–65 age category, but 72 per cent of the parliamentary candidates were in the 26–45 age groups, with two candidates under the age of 25. Nevertheless, were it not for the parliamentary candidates, the age distribution for all divisions, especially the marginal and weak constituencies, would have been somewhat heavier in the older age groups. It should be remembered that the parliamentary candidates of the Labour Party were not part of the permanent leadership group in the constituencies. After the 1964 general election those in the weak divisions and

TABLE 1.5. *Age of CLP leaders expressed by percentage of leadership category*

	Over 65	56–65	46–55	36–45	26–35	25 or less
MPs	10	40	40	10	0	0
Parliamentary cands.	0	4	16	36	36	8
Chairmen	3	23	34	34	6	0
Secretary-agents	8	13	34	24	18	3
Delegates	16	9	28	34	13	0

[8] British population figures from *Monthly Digest*, Central Statistical Office, London, No. 231, March 1965.

approximately half in the marginal divisions were removed from the party organisation.[9]

3. Involvement with party and public office

Constituency party leaders are extremely busy people, perhaps too busy. The extent of involvement of constituency party leaders in party and public office holding is shown in Table 1.6. About one-third of all CLP officials in strong and marginal divisions held three or more party and public offices, while about one-sixth of the officials in weak districts were so involved, the lesser figure probably due to decreased opportunity for local public office in weak divisions. Whether party officials assumed several responsibilities because of their psychological needs, or simply because there were not enough individuals in the CLP to fill available offices, is impossible to say. Labour Party leaders in Transport House were disinclined to exert more control over the constituencies, but official discouragement of multiple office-holding by key party leaders might be in order, rather than indiscriminately to urge party members to 'increase their interest and activity in the other voluntary organizations in their communities'.[10]

In addition to party and public office, many CLP leaders held elective posts in trade unions as well as in community groups of different types. All of them, with the exception of some of the housewives, had to earn a living for themselves and their families since their political labours were completely honorary. The conditions under which many constituency party leaders work must also be taken into account when demands upon their time are considered. There were many divisions which had no party offices, and their secretary-agents worked without even the rudimentary time-saving devices. In one appalling case, a secretary in a weak marginal division had no office, no typewriter, no telephone and no private transport, even though the constituency was composed of a few small villages and an extensive agricultural area. This official held four party and three public offices, at least three of which were offices of some significance.

[9] Of the seven successful parliamentary candidates who were not incumbents, four were between 41 and 45 years of age. One was in the 51–55 group, one in the 46–50 group, and one in the 31–35 group.

[10] Phillips, op. cit., pp. 18–19.

TABLE 1.6. *Percentage of CLP leaders holding party and public office, by type of constituency*

	Constituencies		
	Strong	Marginal	Weak
Party office			
0	14	17	19
1	55	47	48
2	27	25	31
3	4	11	2
Public office			
0	27	42	67
1	55	43	27
2	14	9	6
3	4	6	0
Total, party and public			
0	6	6	6
1	22	30	52
2	35	32	27
3	25	19	9
4	12	13	6

NOTE: Prospective parliamentary candidates may not hold office in the constituency party.

4. Occupations of CLP leaders

Occupations of CLP leaders (Table 1.7) were fairly evenly distributed among the various categories.[11] The inclusion of MPs and parliamentary candidates caused the professional group to be the largest. White-collar workers and trade-union and party officials were almost equal in size, followed closely by the semi-skilled group.

[11] There is no uniform method of establishing occupational categories followed by political researchers in Britain. The classifications used in David Butler and Richard Rose, *The British General Election of 1959*, London 1960, were followed until the size of the miscellaneous category became so large that it seemed advisable to subdivide it into 'white collar', 'trade-union and party officer', and 'housewife'. White collar included supervisory, sales, clerical, and technical personnel. Official sources of data are not always helpful in establishing lines between groups in the British population. Recently a part of the 1961 Census was published in which people were divided into three groups. Group 3 included unskilled manual workers and farm labourers, the armed forces, including admirals and field marshals, and Persons with Inadequately Stated Occupations, including dukes. See Pendennis, *Observer*, March 7, 1965.

The business and skilled categories equalled one another and house-wives composed the smallest group. Considerably more businessmen and fewer from the professions were found in the weak as opposed to the marginal and strong divisions, but when the two categories were combined, they constituted just under one-third of the respondents in all three types of constituencies.[12]

TABLE 1.7. *Occupations of CLP leaders, expressed by percentage of constituency type*

	All	Strong	Marginal	Weak
Professional	20	21	26	14
Business	12	10	6	19
White collar	17	12	25	14
Skilled	12	16	9	11
Semi-skilled	14	16	7	19
Trade-union and party officials	16	19	21	9
Housewives	9	6	6	14

Slightly less than one-third in the strong and weak divisions were skilled and semi-skilled workers, as against 17 per cent in the marginal divisions. Conversely there were twice as many white-collar workers in the marginal than in the strong and weak con-stituencies. The small proportion of trade-union and full-time party officials in the weak divisions suggests the absence of professional agents and the lack of interest on the part of trade unions in con-stituencies in which the Labour Party is hopelessly outnumbered.

5. *Trade-union membership of CLP leaders*

Conditions of membership as outlined in Clause III of the Labour Party Constitution provide that 'Each individual member must, if eligible, be a member of a Trade Union affiliated to the Trades Union Congress as a *bona fide* Trade Union'. In the face of such a directive it is not surprising that the vast majority of CLP leaders belong to trade unions, as shown in Table 1.8. However, some

[12] See J. Blondel, *Voters, Parties and Leaders*, Harmondsworth and Baltimore, 1964, p. 101.

interesting anomalies appeared in the break-down by type of con-stituency. Somewhat surprisingly, the weak divisions had a larger proportion of their leaders in affiliated unions than did the marginal divisions, which had nearly four times as many unaffiliated trade unionists as did the weak constituencies.

Presumably, there was a relationship between the pattern deve-loped by Table 1.8 and that noted in Table 1.7 which showed that marginal divisions had an appreciably higher proportion of leaders with professional occupations and appreciably lower proportions of leaders with skilled and semi-skilled occupations, when compared to strong and weak divisions. The description of non-political unions

TABLE 1.8. *Trade-union membership of CLP leaders,*
expressed by percentage of constituency type

| | Constituencies | | | |
	All	Strong	Marginal	Weak
No union member-ship	16	8	15	23
Affiliated union membership	71	80	64	71
Unaffiliated union membership	13	12	21	6

by Martin Harrison suggested that this particular sort of union was more likely to have members in divisions with the occupational dis-tribution of marginal constituencies.[13] Members of non-affiliated unions have suffered no loss of status in their divisional parties, and with the gradual growth in affluence of British society the time may come when the Labour Party will understand, without scorn, 'the lack of class consciousness or snobbishness which keeps middle-class unions from taking an active part in politics'.[14] Indeed, if George Woodcock, General Secretary of the Trades Union Congress, had his way, the party might have to accept the disaffiliation of the entire trade-union movement.[15]

[13] Martin Harrison, *Trade Unions and the Labour Party Since 1945*, London and Detroit, 1960, pp. 324–34.
[14] Ibid., p. 333.
[15] Pendennis, "Fighting for the TUC's Soul", *Observer*, September 1, 1963; and Samuel Brittan, "Unsettled at Brighton", *Observer*, September 8, 1963.

6. *Religious affiliation of CLP leaders*

It may be true that, as Morgan Phillips once said, 'The Labour Party past owes more to Methodism than to Marx',[16] but this obligation was not easily established by the religious affiliation of present CLP leaders. Fully two-thirds of them claimed to belong to no organised religious group. The Church of England and the Roman Catholic Church each were acknowledged by 7 per cent of the total sample, the Methodist Church by 10 per cent and other Nonconformists by 9 per cent. Only two of the respondents, or slightly more than 1 per cent of the sample, described themselves as Jews. The question asked the respondents in this study was: 'Do you belong to an organised religious group?' If an affirmative answer was given, the respondent was asked to specify his denomination. In the coding, if an official described himself as 'inactive', he was considered not to belong to an organised religious group. Even had these answers been coded otherwise, the findings would not have been materially affected.

In sharp contrast were the religious affiliations of Labour Party members and leaders reported in other studies. Birch says that 'analysis of the religious affiliations of [in Glossop CLP] members shows that about half of them are Noncomformists, about a quarter of them are Roman Catholic, and the rest are either inactive Anglicans or not religious. . . .'[17] More specifically Benny found that among leaders of the Greenwich Constituency Labour Party in 1949, 62 per cent claimed affiliation with the Church of England, and 17 per cent with Nonconformist denominations; 19 per cent were members of other religious groups, and only 2 per cent had no religious affiliation.[18] Rose quotes a Gallup survey of December 1962, in which 58 per cent of those interviewed stated their religious preference to be Church of England and 21 per cent Nonconformist; Roman Catholics comprised 11 per cent of the sample, 4 per cent other denominations, while only 6 per cent said they had no religion.[19]

[16] Quoted in Abrams and Rose, *Must Labour Lose?*, Harmondsworth and Baltimore, 1960, p. 94.
[17] Birch, op. cit., p. 67.
[18] Benney, op. cit., p. 51.
[19] Richard Rose, *Politics in England*, Boston 1964, London 1965, pp. 21–2.

As Table 1.9 demonstrates, there were no differences among the three types of constituencies in regard to the proportion of respondents in each group disavowing any religious affiliation. Variations among the numbers claiming certain religious persuasions may be attributable to the relatively small number of respondents to be distributed among the four categories. Still, the unusually small proportion of Methodists in the marginal divisions, of other Nonconformists and of Roman Catholics and Jews in strong divisions, and of Anglicans in weak divisions, is worth noting. Also of interest is the fact that of a total of forty-nine respondents claiming a religious connection, thirty-nine were clustered in fifteen divisions, while the remaining twenty-one divisions had but thirteen religiously involved officials. Of course, this analysis cannot be carried too far because of the limited amount of relevant data.

TABLE 1.9. *Religious affiliation of CLP leaders,*
expressed by percentage of constituency type

| | Constituencies | | | |
	All	Strong	Marginal	Weak
None	66	66	64	68
Methodist	10	19	2	11
Other Nonconformist	9	2	13	11
Church of England	7	9	9	2
Roman Catholic	7	4	10	8
Jewish	1	0	2	0

The factor of age had an uneven effect on religious affiliation. In the age group under 25 years of age the sample was not large enough for the low proportion claiming no religious affiliation to be meaningful. However, as can be seen in Table 1.10, those in the oldest age group were almost unanimous in their rejection of formal religion. Those between the ages of 26 and 45 exceeded the figure for all respondents claiming no religious connection, and those from 46 to 65 were under the figure for the total group, with almost half the 46–55 category claiming religious affiliation.

Labour Party activists may not have had many formal religious commitments, but it should not be inferred that they lacked a religious tradition or had no values against which to measure their party, their opposition, and public policies. Unsolicited remarks by many respondents indicated that they had been reared in a religious atmosphere, and some described themselves as inactive members of various denominations. In no case did a respondent volunteer a comment critical of religious groups, although one elderly official related that his activity in the Labour Party had caused him to become so unpopular within his church that he left the congregation. This and other remarks made by respondents lent the impression that the Labour Party, with its highly developed traditions of social conscience and amelioration of the harshness of British society for the poor, had been adopted by some members as a secular religion. No reluctance was encountered in eliciting answers to questions on religion. Every respondent, including the few to whom the questionnaire was sent by mail, replied to these queries.[20]

TABLE 1.10. *Religious affiliation of CLP leaders by age percentage*

	Under 25	26–35	36–45	46–55	56–65	Over 65
None	25	71	76	53	60	90
Methodist	0	4	11	12	18	0
Other Nonconformist	25	4	4	14	11	10
Church of England	25	4	7	7	7	0
Roman Catholic	25	13	2	14	4	0
Jewish	0	4	0	0	0	0

7. *Education of CLP leaders*

Of all the information compiled in this study, that dealing with the formal education of CLP leaders was most revealing of the class distinctions in Britain, of recent relaxations of the class system, and of the basis of class attitudes found in the Labour Party. Americans, with their almost naive belief in the efficacy of education, may be

[20] See K. J. W. Alexander and Alexander Hobbs, "What Influences Labour MPs?", *New Society*. December 15, 1962, p. 11, who suggest that their questions on religion were 'traditionally a dangerous subject politically'. They then relate that even after he had been promised anomymity, one MP wrote a letter particularly asking that he not be identified in this context.

surprised that over half the Labour Party activists in the constituency parties had left school between the ages of 12 and 14 upon completion of elementary school. Table 1.11 shows that about one-quarter of the respondents had completed secondary school, and the remaining one-fifth had some formal education past the age of 18 years.[21]

In strong divisions two-thirds of the officials had completed only elementary school. Marginal constituencies had a large proportion, almost one-quarter, who had received formal education beyond the secondary level. In weak divisions over one-third of the leaders had completed work at the secondary level. The large number of CLP leaders in the marginal constituencies with formal education beyond the secondary level was another manifestation of the deviation

TABLE 1.11. *School-leaving age of CLP leaders,*
expressed by percentage of constituency type

| | Constituencies | | | |
	All	Strong	Marginal	Weak
12–14	54	69	49	46
15–18	26	14	28	35
19 and over	20	17	23	19

already observed in marginal constituencies, namely that these constituencies contained the highest proportions of professional men and of members of unions unaffiliated with the Labour Party.

The effect of recent alterations in the educational patterns of Britain appear in Table 1.12. Of those whose formal education ended with elementary school, the largest proportion was in the 46–55 age group. In this category, undoubtedly affected by the First

[21] The term secondary school is used here to include the British grammar school—which is roughly equivalent to an American academic high school, plus one additional year—and the secondary modern school, which educates, until they reach the school-leaving age (now 15), those youngsters who have completed elementary school but who have failed to qualify for a grammar-school place. Students may elect to continue in the secondary modern schools until they complete the course of work, usually at the age of 18.

World War and the depression which followed, two-thirds had only the minimal education offered in Britain. Time after time when this subject was being explored, a respondent would offer that he had been forced to stop school in order to obtain a job and help the family. Occasionally, with a trace of bitterness, would be added the comment, 'even though I had passed the eleven plus'. It was difficult to imagine what a fourteen-year-old could do to help his family in an economy in which adults could not find employment, although some respondents surmised that the adults were rendered unemployable partly because of the ready supply of fourteen-year-olds entering the labour market each year.

TABLE 1.12. *School-leaving age of CLP leaders by age-percentage*

	12–14	15–18	Over 19
Under 25	25	25	50
26–35	25	37.5	37.5
36–45	57	32	11
46–55	65	21	14
56–65	61	21	18
Over 65	60	10	30

Within the group ranging from 36 to 45 years there was a considerable decrease in the proportion who left school at 14, and a corresponding increase in those who completed secondary school. Among this age group there was found a small decrease in the proportion who were educated past the secondary level, but this can be explained by Britain's massive preoccupation with the Second World War.

The age group from 26 to 35 years showed that only one-quarter of their number had left school at 14 years. Equal proportions in this category had finished grammar or a secondary modern school as had continued formal education past the age of 19. Neither the youngest age group with four members, nor the oldest group with ten, was large enough to furnish reliable information, but the general pattern suggesting the greater educational opportunities of the young as compared to the old is apparent.

In Table 1.13 can be seen the greater amount of formal education enjoyed by MPs and by parliamentary candidates.[22] Despite some minor variations, the other leadership groups were similar in their distribution between the three educational categories.

TABLE 1.13. *School-leaving age of CLP leaders expressed by percentage of leadership category*

	12–14	15–18	Over 19
MPs	30	0	70
Parliamentary candidates	16	40	44
Chairmen	66	28	6
Secretary-agents	63	24	13
Delegates	61	26	13

The education profile of CLP leaders would be incomplete without reference to the high value placed upon education by party workers and by the Labour Party itself. Therefore, while the school-leaving age for 54 per cent of CLP leaders was between 12 and 14 years, about two-fifths of this group could boast of additional education ranging from scholarships at Ruskin College (a college for adults at the University of Oxford supported by the trade unions) to courses in politics and economics and public speaking sponsored by the National Council of Labour Colleges. Many respondents who had been confronted with idleness during the last depression had taken the opportunity to continue their education informally. Some officials took the occasion to remark that adult education was less popular in Britain today than in the period preceding the Second World War. They went on to state that this valuable means of improving oneself had fallen before the pleasures of the 'telly', the car, and the motor-cycle. It was probable also that raising the school-leaving age to its present level of 15 years with the option of staying in school until the age of 18, the proliferation of technical

[22] Parliamentary candidates (including MPs) in 1964 had considerably more formal education than did the 1959 group. The proportion for each year in the three educational categories was:

	1959(%)	1964(%)
Elementary	26	20
Secondary	34	29
University	40	51

colleges, and the increased number of university places had reduced not only the impetus but the need for informal adult education.

The knowledge evinced by respondents of the history and policy of the Labour Party, their skill at organising and presenting argument, their knowledge of international affairs, even if sometimes biased, their pervading confidence and poise, were impressive. While it may be possible to lay this at the door of the untested presumption of the superiority of British education, even when it stops at the age of 14, it is more likely that these characteristics were largely the product of the efforts of the proud, fiercely individualistic, party leaders themselves.

2

Political Attitudes of Constituency Labour Party Leaders

T HE LITERATURE of the Labour Party has long tended to characterise leaders of the constituency Labour parties as left-wing
militants. One of the favourite quotations to support this point of
view is an entry in Beatrice Webb's diary in 1930 relating an account
of a conversation between her and her husband and Oswald Mosley:[1]

> Looking in the future [Mosley] foresees a growing cleavage
> between the constituency parties led by the left-wing enthusiasts,
> and the Trade Unions led by rather dull-witted and conventional
> Trade Union officials. The keenest of the young Trade Unionists
> are in revolt against the Block Vote and the dictatorship of the
> well-established officers of the big Trade Unions. Sidney observed
> afterwards that the constituency parties were frequently unrepre-
> sentative groups of nonentities dominated by fanatics, cranks, and
> extremists, and that *if* the block vote of the Trade Unions were
> eliminated it would be impracticable to continue to vest the
> control of policy in Labour Party Conferences.[2]

[1] Sir Oswald Mosley had joined the Labour Party shortly before the 1929
general election and was appointed to the Labour government formed by
Ramsay MacDonald in June of that year. He remained in the government
until May 1930, when he resigned in protest against what he considered to
be inadequate action by Labour leaders in regard to the unemployment
problem in Britain.

[2] *Beatrice Webb's Diaries*, May 19, 1930, folios 53–4, quoted in R. T.
McKenzie, *British Political Parties*, 2nd edn., London and New York 1964,
p. 505.

Commenting on this observation of Webb's, McKenzie seems to accept Webb's description without qualification by saying that 'there can be little doubt that he accurately reflected the conviction of the great majority of the parliamentary leaders of the Labour Party then *and now*. They would find it intolerable if the conference could be dominated or controlled by those (many of whom they consider "fanatics, cranks, and extremists") who turn up in large numbers as delegates from constituency parties.'[3]

Leon Epstein could as well be discussing the unit of political organisation in any British political party when he writes of Conservative constituency associations: 'The voluntary and amateur nature of these associations ensures that they attract zealots in the party cause, and particularly so at the local leadership level where there are many routine political chores which only the devoted are likely to perform. Principles, not professional careers, are what matter here.'[4] Certainly this is the impression Ralph Miliband creates when, throughout his study of the Labour Party, he refers again and again to the reactions of the 'activists in the constituency parties' in the context of a constant left-wing response to policies of the trade unions or the National Executive Committee.[5] Ultimately, he does take the stand that 'the orthodox trade union leaders never spoke for the whole trade union movement, just as there was always a substantial number of constituency parties who faithfully supported the Labour leadership against its critics on the Left'.[6]

This latter position is supported by Martin Harrison who evaluates the balance between the trade unions and the constituency parties in these terms:

> The unions have never been as thoroughly unprogressive—nor the local parties as fanatically left-wing—as popular legend decreed. Obviously the constituencies are on balance to the left of the unions, but the overlap is considerable. This overlap is one reason why the two wings have held together through all the Party's

[3] Ibid. See also McKenzie's views of the militancy of representatives of constituency associations at Conservative Annual Conferences, pp. 196–7.
[4] Leon Epstein, "British MPs and Their Local Parties", *American Political Science Review*, June 1960, p. 385. See also Rita Hinden, "The Lessons for Labour", in Abrams and Rose, op. cit., p. 102.
[5] Ralph Miliband, op. cit., pp. 105, 107, 110, 173, 252, 319.
[6] Ibid., p. 320.

internal upheavals. However, the constituencies are so divided and unpredictable that beyond doubt the leadership would be forced to move to the left if it could not count on the support of several large unions.[7]

Similarly, Richard Rose reaches the conclusion, based on an analysis of annual conference resolutions submitted by Conservative constituency associations and constituency Labour parties over a five-year period, that 'differences in policy exist within parties, and the conflict is sometimes great, but this is not conflict between a monolithic bloc of activists and a monolithic leadership. Rather, it would seem that factional disputes divide parties vertically, joining some Privy Councillors, MPs, lobbyists, activists, and voters into a faction which is in conflict with another which also contains members drawn from all ranks of the party.'[8]

The following analysis generally supports the Harrison-Rose thesis that all constituency Labour parties are not cut on the same pattern and that discernible policy differences exist among them. However, there is exception to one of the conclusions in the Rose study, namely, the 'policy views are randomly distributed among constituency parties without regard to electoral strength'.[9]

1. Attitudes of CLP leaders toward current Labour Party policy

It is not surprising for Table 2.1 to show that a negligible segment of CLP leaders expressed a wish to see the Labour Party move to the right. The Labour movement's history and tradition, its past and present composition ineluctably tend to preserve the leftist posture of the party. No matter that to some members 'socialism' is a label, to others mere rhetoric, and to only a few a dogma essential to the ordering of societal and personal relations, almost all within the Labour Party agree that it is 'left' and that its activists must be likewise. What Martin Harrison said concerning the annual meetings of trade unions can be applied to other elements of the Labour Party as well, even in private conversation:

[7] Martin Harrison, op. cit., pp. 238–9.

[8] Richard Rose, "The Political Ideas of English Party Activists", *American Political Science Review*, June 1962, p. 371.

[9] Ibid., p. 368.

Whether a union's conference is 'right' or 'left', the attitude to dissenters is broadly similar: left-wing dissent is respectable, right-wing opposition is not. Throughout the movement 'talking left' is listened to tolerantly . . . in most unions a speaker who suggested that living standards had risen under the Conservatives would have run the risk of being shouted down even at the peak of full employment.[10]

TABLE 2.1. *Attitude of all CLP leaders toward current Labour Party Policy, expressed by percentage of constituency type*

| | Constituencies | | | |
	All	Strong	Marginal	Weak
Move right	3	0	2	6
Status quo	43	54	51	25
Move slightly left	46	44	36	59
Move sharply left	8	2	11	10

Taken as a group, constituency party leaders indicated a slight left bias, with 54 per cent desiring a slight or sharp move to the left, while 46 per cent were satisfied with current Labour Party policy or preferred a shift to the right. The weak constituencies were responsible for this overall left bias, as slightly over half the respondents from the strong and marginal divisions were in favour of maintaining a policy *status quo*, as opposed to only a quarter in the weak constituencies.[11] Even though moderate policy views prevailed in the

[10] Harrison, op. cit., pp. 158–9.

[11] The context for these responses changed during the course of the field research. Hugh Gaitskell died on January 18, 1963, by which time twelve divisions had been visited. Six more were completed during the four weeks preceding the election of Harold Wilson as Party Leader, and the eighteen remaining constituencies were interviewed afterwards. A number of respondents in the last group, when asked if and how they would like to see Labour Party policies changed, replied: 'Now that Wilson is Leader, I'm satisfied with the policies as they are.' While Gaitskell was Leader, the response had sometimes been: 'There's not so much the matter with the policies as there is with how they are being applied.' See also Frank Bealey, J. Blondel and W. P. McCann, *Constituency Politics*, London and New York 1965, pp. 286–7, on the popular response to Gaitskell. While he had broad support in the Newcastle-under-Lyme CLP, it was based on his personal qualities rather than his political views.

strong and marginal divisions, there was broad support for a move to the left, particularly in the marginal constituencies where 11 per cent of the respondents favoured a sharp shift to the left. Support for a clearer left orientation was particularly prevalent in the weak divisions, receiving the endorsement of seven out of ten respondents.

The response from party officials in all constituencies lends credence to the popular assertion that the Labour Party can be successfully led only from a left of centre position. It may also explain in part Harold Wilson's success as Leader of the Labour Party, as he interprets left of centre in the context of the Labour Party as opposed to Hugh Gaitskell's application of the term to British politics in general.

TABLE 2.2. *Attitude of CLP leaders toward current Labour Party policy expressed by percentage of leadership category*

	MPS	Parl. Cands.	Chairmen	Sec.– Agents	Delegates
Move right	0	0	0	3	6
Status quo	50	28	51	53	36
Move slightly left	40	64	43	36	45
Move sharply left	10	8	6	8	13

Various categories of party leaders reacted differently to the question of the direction of Labour Party policy. Secretary-agents, chairmen, and MPs were most likely to accept current policy orientation. It is possible that secretary-agents and constituency party chairmen were more tolerant than other respondents because they were directly involved in party administration and in preparatory activities for the imminent general election. The desire for success or to make a good showing may have increased their willingness to accept current party policy, with unity holding a high priority in their scale of values. All the MPs but one came from safe constituencies, and it was the exception from a marginal division who hoped for a sharp move to the left. It is worth noting that those MPs with the longest service were most likely to favour the *status quo*, while those with a lesser period of parliamentary experience thought the party should move slightly to the left.

The differences in regard to policy orientation of the three leader categories discussed above and parliamentary candidates and conference delegates were substantial. Almost three-fifths of the delegates and three-quarters of the parliamentary candidates were in favour of a slight or sharp move to the left. The distribution of the 1962 conference delegates on this question supports the contention that CLP representation at the annual conference is far from monolithic. The delegates had a wider distribution than any other category of party leaders, ranging from 6 per cent who wanted to move to the right to 13 per cent who desired strong left orientation.

Slightly more than half of all respondents expressed a desire that the Labour Party move either slightly or sharply to the left. When asked what particular issues they had in mind, they gave answers which could be categorised under the headings of central control, which included nationalisation and national planning, social

TABLE 2.3. *Frequency of issues mentioned by CLP leaders desiring a move to the left, by type of constituency*

	All	Strong	Marginal	Weak
Nationalisation and National Planning	69	22	22	25
Foreign and defence policy	49	11	16	22
Social services	34	9	12	13
Total mentions	152	42	50	60

services and foreign and defence policy. Of over-riding importance was the issue of nationalisation, which was mentioned almost as frequently as the other two issues combined. Table 2.3 also showed that nationalisation received the same high level of support in all types of constituencies. The same could not be said for social services, and particularly not for foreign and defence policy, which received twice as many mentions in weak than in strong divisions. The preoccupation of the weak constituencies with policy is suggested by the fact that they had the most mentions on every issue, and provided 40 per cent of the total mentions even though they comprised but one-third of the sample.

The strong commitment of CLP leaders to the concept of nationalisation raised the question as to whether this issue, divisive within the party and generally unpopular with the electorate, has been rationalised. There is other evidence than this study to support the statement that nationalisation has a strong grip on the minds of Labour Party activists.[12] It is almost as if the attempt made by Gaitskell to induce the party to modify Clause IV in the Party Constitution had reinforced rather than weakened the attitude of constituency party leaders on this point.

The same could be said of the many studies and analyses on the subject of nationalisation and its impact on the electorate that have appeared since the 1959 general election. Some of these studies have questioned the traditional, inflexible approach to public ownership advocated by the 'red-blooded socialists' in the Labour Party. Thus C. A. R. Crosland proposes a programme of public ownership he readily admits would not 'satisfy the Clause IV Bourbons; for it is based on the underlying assumption that ownership, while it can influence, does not uniquely *determine* the character of society. But, unlike the Utopian programmes of the "Left-wing" traditionalists, it consciously uses the means of public ownership, in a supple, flexible, and relevant manner, to achieve certain definite socialist ends.'[13] Austen Albu, in questioning nationalisation as the panacea for Britain's economic and social ailments, raised the possibility that nationalisation might make more difficult the shift from traditional, declining industries to expanding new ones.[14]

The political impact of nationalisation has received considerable attention. Butler and Rose in their study of the 1959 election cited the *Daily Herald* as reporting that in an East Anglia constituency the Labour candidate was 'trying hard to combat rumours of

---

[12] The 1962 Annual Conference rejected by a margin of only 40,000 votes a resolution to restore the municipalisation of rented property to the party's programme. Even with Anthony Greenwood speaking for the National Executive Committee (NEC) and urging that the resolution before the conference be remitted to NEC because of the discussions it was presently conducting on housing, the margin was slim. The vote for the resolution was 3,052,000 against 3,092,000. See *Labour Party Annual Conference Report*, 1962, pp. 119–26. There is some evidence that CLP leaders draw strong support from their members on this issue; see Bealey, Blondel and McCann, op. cit., p. 283.

[13] C. A. R. Crosland, *The Conservative Enemy*, London 1962, p. 49.

[14] Austen Albu, "Comment on Crossman", *Socialist Commentary*, August 1960, p. 13.

Labour plans to nationalise the factory in the constituency'.[15] The same authors describe the post-election complaint of another Labour candidate as follows:

> I had to spend the first week of the campaign on the entirely negative task of convincing my own party people that we were not planning to nationalize the local engineering firms. We distributed thousands of leaflets denying the 'nationalization of 600' plan (anti-nationalization groups had suggested that Labour planned to nationalize 600 industries if elected) at factory gates, morning, noon, and night.[16]

Post-election surveys conducted by Gallup poll reported that '20 per cent of the electorate regarded nationalisation as one of the major causes of Labour's defeat'. The *Daily Telegraph* poll in the same period reported that 40 per cent of all ex-Labour voters thought that Labour should now drop its nationalisation policy.[17] Still another post-election survey confirmed these findings by showing that 33 per cent of all informants stated that nationalisation was the issue which would have pleased them least in a Labour victory. Even among Labour informants, 16 per cent would have been least pleased with nationalisation had their party won.[18]

The Labour leaders who wished to see a shift to the left felt the party would be strengthened thereby. Of this group 45 per cent thought a leftward shift would render it easier to win elections, and another 13 per cent thought such a reorientation would make no difference. Presumably, this was the group which believed that many previous Labour supporters had been disaffected by the moderation of party policy, but would stream back from self-imposed exile to vote for a Labour Party with a firm radical programme. Another 28 per cent declared that moving to the left might make it more difficult for Labour to win elections, but this group thought that such a move, however sacrificial, was the only way for Labour to retain its identity as a party. Among this group were a few who

[15] Butler and Rose, op. cit., p. 254. The factory under discussion was a branch of ICI, one of the world's largest chemical companies, dominating an important sector of the British economy.

[16] Ibid., p. 254.

[17] Ibid., p. 255.

[18] Abrams and Rose, op. cit., pp. 36–7.

C

thought the question irrelevant, since to them there was no relationship between party policy and winning an election. These were
discreet aspects of politics. Political principles should be foremost,
and if elections were lost this was the fault of the electorate or the
party workers, never of the political principles espoused by the party.
These persons implied that the principles of the Labour Party had
been established when the party was founded, and that changes in
British society since the First World War did not invalidate these
principles.[19] The remaining 14 per cent thought that a move to the
left might make winning elections harder initially but easier ultimately. These respondents suggested that the real problem was one
of communication between the party and the electorate. This group
also held that party principles should remain as originally articulated,
and that party workers needed to become more knowledgeable and
hence enthusiastic about nationalisation. With the Labour Party
unreservedly devoted to nationalisation as a basic precept of
socialism, it was thought that no difficulty would be encountered
in persuading a majority of the electorate to support Labour policy
on public ownership. Although Hugh Gaitskell did not express these
views, the following statement of his made in another context suggested the process by which a move to the left was expected to
redound to Labour's benefit:

> You see, I am a rationalist. I like to think that in a mature demo-
> cracy people reach their conclusions mostly on the basis of actual
> evidence and argument. I do not like to think that they vote as
> they do because something appeals to their unconscious.[20]

This reformist belief in the rationality of men, in their susceptibility
to reasoned discussion, in their familiarity with public issues, in their
objective evaluation of ideas within the reformers' frame of reference,
characterises the position of those who think that the chief problem
of the Labour Party is to contact and convince the British voter.[21]

[19] For a longer exposition, including some highly interesting statements
leading to this conclusion, see R. H. S. Crossman, *Labour in the Affluent
Society*, London 1959, Fabian Tract 325.

[20] Quoted in Butler and Rose, op cit., p. 29, from an interview in the
Daily Mail, July 30, 1959.

[21] See R. T. McKenzie, "The Wilson Report and the Future of the
Labour Party Organisation", *Political Studies*, February 1956.

2. *Attitudes of CLP leaders toward the proscription policy of the Labour Party*

Political parties having a doctrinal basis and formal membership are required to judge the actions of party members and the qualifications of applicants for membership, using as criteria stated party principles and by-laws. This has been a particular problem of the Labour Party, for, since its inception, continuous efforts have been made by many political parties and organisations to infiltrate and gain control of its various elements. The vast majority of these efforts have originated with Marxist or Communist groups, a natural outgrowth of the Labour Party's commitment to parliamentary action as the means of gaining political power, and its policy since the early 1920s of non-coöperation with the Communist Party.[22]

The authority of the Labour Party to take disciplinary action through the National Executive Committee (NEC) against individuals or organisations, or to deny them membership in or affiliation with the party, is found in the Party Constitution.[23] Similar authority for constituency party action in this area is based on provisions of the *Model Rules for Constituency Labour Parties*.[24] The NEC in times past has not been reluctant to use its powers against prominent party figures like Sir Stafford Cripps, Aneurin Bevan, and George Strauss, in addition to other men less well-known outside the party, notably D. N. Pritt, John Platts-Mills, Lesley Solley, and Konni Zilliacus.[25]

[22] The Labour Party rejected proposals for affiliation from the Communist Party in 1921, 1924 and 1935. In 1924 the Labour Party declared that members of the Communist Party were not eligible for endorsement as Labour Parliamentary candidates or for membership in the Labour Party. Suggestions for a Popular Front with the Communist Party were refused in 1934 and 1935. See Miliband, op. cit., pp. 86, 118, 128, 218, 242 and 250.

[23] *Labour Party Annual Conference Report*, 1963, p. 276. Section 4 of Clause II (Membership) states: 'Individual members shall be persons not less than 15 years of age who subscribe to the conditions of membership, provided they are not members of Political Parties or organisations ancillary or subsidiary thereto declared by the Annual Conference or by the National Executive Committee in pursuance of Conference decisions to be ineligible for affiliation to the Party.'

[24] *Model Rules*, Set A, Clause IV, Section (3).

[25] Miliband, op. cit., p. 264, and *Labour Party Annual Conference Reports*, 1940, p. 20; 1948, p. 17; and 1949, p. 17.

For the information of all concerned, the Labour Party publishes a list of proscribed organisations each year in the Annual Conference Report.[26] Appeals from disciplinary decisions of the constituency parties lie to the NEC, while similar action taken by the NEC must be reported to the subsequent Annual Conference at which time the decision of the NEC can be debated and voted on.[27]

Clause II, Section 4, of the Party Constitution and the policies it entailed were accepted by four out of five respondents, although some officials expressed regret over the necessity of it. Many of the respondents were embarrassed that the party published a list of proscribed organisations, since this action seemed to smack of McCarthyism or to resemble the United States Attorney General's list of subversive organisations, both of which were deemed reprehensible. Despite their bias against a practice that limited freedom of political expression and action, there were very few CLP leaders who completely rejected the clause and the policy. Those who did held that infiltration of the party by other groups did not constitute a real problem, and even if the danger existed, the party should not engage in 'witch hunting'. The 17 per cent who did not fully accept the proscription policy were more concerned about the relatively unrestrained power of the NEC to administer the policy than they were with the presence in the Party Constitution of the provision on which the power of the NEC was based. This preoccupation with the implementation of the policy was reflected in the submission of twenty-four amendments to the Party Constitution at the 1962 Annual Conference, all of which would have imposed limitations on the NEC in the administration of its proscription powers. Another amendment would have completely removed from the NEC its authority to apply its power to expel or exclude individuals and

---

[26] *Labour Party Annual Conference Report*, 1963, p. 286. The principle of proscribing all parties or organisations that run candidates against those of the Labour Party is not followed to the extent that the Conservative and Liberal parties appear on the list of Proscribed Organisations. The Communist Party of Great Britain is the only political party appearing on the list that comprised forty-eight organisations in 1963. A few typical examples of the organisations on the list are: British Soviet Society, Scottish USSR Society, Women's Parliament, Welsh Peace Council, British Youth Festival, West Yorkshire Federation of Peace Organisations, and Artists for Peace.

[27] *Model Rules*, Set A, Clause XIV, Section (3), and *Party Constitution*, Clause VIII, Section 2 (b).

organisations from membership in the party, and one amendment that would have abolished the authority entirely.[28]

On the question of proscription, differences among the types of constituency were noticeable. Strong divisions were very slightly more critical of proscription policy than were the marginal constituencies for two reasons. First, respondents in the strong divisions thought that attempts by Communists, Trotskyites and others to penetrate their organisations were infrequent. Second, the strong divisions have long since forgotten the time when the shift of a few hundred votes marked the difference between victory and defeat. Conversely, the marginal divisions were intensely aware of the need for unity, and if the proscription policy enabled them to keep their

TABLE 2.4. *Attitude of all CLP leaders toward Labour Party proscription policy, expressed by percentage of constituency type*

Constituencies	Accepts	Partially accepts	Rejects
All constituencies	79	17	4
Strong	87	13	0
Marginal	92	8	0
Weak	57	31	12

divisional parties free of disruptive influences, the marginal constituencies were willing to support it. In addition, the social and economic characteristics of marginal divisions seemed more likely to make them responsive to extreme political attitudes, whereas the age, educational, and occupational structure of the strong divisions rendered potential infiltration less likely.[29] Table 2.4 also indicates

[28] *Agenda, Labour Party Annual Conference, 1962*, p. 6 and pp. 10–16.

[29] This is not to say that there are not strong divisions which are far left in their ideology. Some leading members of the Labour left wing since the war came to prominence as members for seats so marginal that Labour lost them during the 1950s—Ian Mikardo at Reading and Michael Foot at Devonport come immediately to mind. Both these men have since returned to Parliament as members for strong constituencies, which suggests that, if an MP with any ability really makes a reputation as a left-wing fire-eater and is subsequently defeated, he has good prospects of being adopted by a strong division with a pronounced left bias.

that the reaction of CLP leaders in weak divisions differed greatly from that of strong and marginal divisions. Almost one-third of the weak constituencies were willing to give only partial acceptance to Labour's proscription policy, while two out of five respondents in weak divisions either partially accepted or wholly rejected party policy on this matter. All those who totally rejected the policy came from weak divisions. They included a parliamentary candidate, two CLP chairmen, and two CLP secretaries.

Whereas only half of the MPs favoured the *status quo* in regard to party policy, 90 per cent accepted Labour Party proscription policy. Parliamentary candidates had the largest proportion that only partially accepted Labour policy on proscription, but it should be emphasised that only two marginal division candidates had any reservations on this question, and that the remaining six candidates who had reservations or rejected party proscription policy all came from weak divisions. The response of conference delegates is also worth noting, as this category usually exhibited a left-wing bias on such questions.

TABLE 2.5. *Attitude of CLP leaders toward proscription policy, expressed by percentage of leadership category*

	Accepts	Partially accepts	Rejects
MPs	90	10	0
Parliamentary cands.	68	28	4
Chairmen	77	17	6
Secretary-agents	82	13	5
Delegates	86	14	0

Sharp differences developed in attitudes among various age groups on the question of Labour proscription policy. In the 26–35 age category almost as many had reservations on proscription policy as were willing to accept it. The same attitude characterised the 36–45 age group, but less markedly. In the 46–65 age groups were found the strongest supporters of Labour proscription policy, although respondents over 65 were not far behind. Under the age of 26, the four respondents were unanimous in their acceptance of the policy as it existed.

3. *The proposal to amend Clause II, Section 4*

It is one thing for the vast majority of constituency party leaders to accept a policy of many years standing, as they have done in the case of Labour proscription policy, and quite another to favour amendments making proscription or expulsion easier to invoke. At the 1962 Annual Conference this fact was discovered by the National Executive Committee when it attempted to change the Party Constitution. An amendment to the membership clause was introduced which would have amended Clause II, Section 4, to read: 'Provided they are not members of *or associated with* Political Parties or organisations . . . declared . . . to be ineligible for affiliation to the Party'.[30] Objections to the proposed amendment were many, and its opponents vied with one another in their interpretations of the phrase

TABLE 2.6. *Attitude of CLP leaders toward proscription policy, by age percentage*

	Accepts	Partially accepts	Rejects
Under 26	100	0	0
26–35	54	42	4
36–45	76	22	2
46–55	89	9	2
56–65	86	7	7
Over 65	80	10	10

under consideration. While official discussion of the proposal took place at a private session of the conference, heated arguments developed among the delegates before and after the conference acted on the motion to amend. Some delegates asked if riding to work on a bus with a Communist as a fellow-passenger constituted 'associating with'. Others wondered whether working along side a Communist, or being a fellow trade union official with a Communist would make one guilty of 'associating with'. In fairness it must be said that the NEC very likely would have had no more difficulty interpreting the phrase 'associated with' than some of the objectors would have had in judging a member of the Conservative Party who was seen habitually in the company of members of the British Union of Fascists,

[30] See footnote 23, p. 35.

but the debate on this proposal was not notably rational. The left wing of the party knew it could overcome the NEC on the question because the amendment was opposed by the overwhelming majority of constituency delegates. Not only did the ambiguity of the proposed amendment make it an easy target for ridicule, but the regard for tolerance inherent in the Labour Party operated against making the change. Constituency party leaders admitted that proscription must sometimes be resorted to, but they wanted no more of it than was necessary, and they wanted the rules under which the NEC functioned to be as well defined as possible. At the conference the issue never actually came to a vote, for after vigorous discussion a motion was made to pass to the next business, with the vote on this motion being carried 3,487,000 for and 2,793,000 against.[31] Some constituency delegates may have opposed the motion in the hope of being able to vote for the amendment, but there was evidence to support the contention that most of the contrary votes came from sources other than CLPs, namely, the trade unions.[32]

TABLE 2.7. *Attitude of all CLP leaders toward amending membership clause of Party Constitution, expressed by percentage of constituency type*

	Opposing amendment	Supporting amendment
All constituencies	81	19
Strong	77	23
Marginal	78	22
Weak	87	13

Four out of five CLP leaders opposed the amendment of Clause II, Section 4. Table 2.7 also indicates that there was no difference between strong and marginal divisions on this question. As might be expected, in view of their reaction in Table 2.4, the weak divisions were noticeably more opposed to the amendment than were the strong and marginal constituencies. No differences of consequence

[31] *Labour Party Annual Conference Report, 1962*, p. 152.

[32] For the importance of non-aligned partisans in the Labour Party, see Richard Rose, "Parties, Factions, and Tendencies in Britain", *Political Studies*, February 1964, p. 42. Their role in this incident was an excellent example of his analysis.

were found among types of leaders on the membership amendment.

There was considerable variation in the response of different age groups to the proposal to amend the membership clause of the Party Constitution. The 26–35 age group was virtually unanimous in its opposition to the membership clause amendment, and the two categories between 36 and 55 also recorded great hostility to the measure.

TABLE 2.8. *Attitude of CLP leaders toward amending membership clause by age-percentage*

	Opposing amendment	Supporting amendment
Under 26	75	25
26–35	96	4
36–45	88	12
46–55	81	19
56–65	64	36
Over 65	80	20

Somewhat less expected was the response of the under 26 age group in regard to amending the membership clause, with three-quarters of these respondents opposing the amendment even though all four of them had supported the proscription policy. The over 65 group exactly reversed its position on this question, surpassing the inconsistency of the youngest age group.

4. *Attitudes of CLP leaders toward five major issues*

As well as exploring attitudes on internal party policy, the study gathered data relating to the response of CLP leaders to five substantive issues: British membership of the European Common Market (EEC); Defence Policy; the Cuba crisis of 1962; the Sino-Indian border war of 1962, and the comparative status of the United States and the Soviet Union among CLP leaders.

i. Attitudes of CLP leaders toward the EEC

Information on the question of Britain's joining EEC was affected by two events which occurred while the study was in progress. After months of non-committal statements on the subject, Hugh Gaitskell delivered a long, impassioned speech at the 1962 Annual Conference objecting to Britain's entry, largely on political grounds. The speech disappointed many of Gaitskell's loyal followers who had supported him in his internal party struggles over Clause IV and unilateral disarmament, but it delighted, though perhaps also confused, many who had been his opponents in these battles.

The other event, mainly because Labour Party attitudes toward EEC had crystallised by late 1962, had a less discernible effect on these attitudes than had Gaitskell's speech, which was to prove his valedictory to the party. This was the occasion of President de Gaulle's press conference which took place within two weeks of Gaitskell's death on January 18, 1963. At this time de Gaulle declared that Britain was not prepared to accept all the implications of membership in EEC. Employing arguments other than Gaitskell's, de Gaulle confirmed the genuine fears held by Labour supporters over the wisdom of joining the Common Market. Although negotiations for admission to it had been conducted by the Conservative Party, de Gaulle was informing all Britons that they were not welcome in the Market, and the national pride of Labour, Conservative and Liberal supporters alike was undoubtedly wounded. Angry letters to newspaper editors and other expressions of annoyance uniformly followed the theme of 'They were happy enough to have us in Europe in 1944 when we had to fight our way in.'

Even without these events, it is probable that the weight of opinion in the constituency parties was not in favour of Britain's becoming a member of the European Economic Community. Table 2.9 shows that more than three out of four respondents were either strongly or moderately opposed to the idea of entry, while less than one respondent in five gave moderate or strong support. Although middle- or right-wing members of the party, such as Denis Healey and Douglas Jay, were among the opposition to EEC, most of it was actuated from the left syndrome rather than the right. The response of the three classes of constituency to this question lent weight to this contention. From strong to marginal to weak divisions there was an increase in opposition uniform with a decrease in support for British involvement in EEC.

With two exceptions the reactions of leadership categories to joining EEC were generally alike. The exceptions were MPs and parliamentary candidates. On this issue the MPs were evenly divided, four strongly and one moderately opposing, four strongly and one moderately supporting. Among the parliamentary candidates none strongly supported and 8 per cent moderately supported entry. In the same group 44 per cent moderately opposed and 48 per cent strongly opposed joining.

These findings were an interesting contrast to a recent study of the European Economic Community, in which it was established that Britons with more international contacts and more extensive travels were more likely to have supported EEC than their countrymen who had fewer contacts and travelled less. The same study also showed that younger, better-educated individuals in higher prestige occupations were more likely to support British entry into EEC than those

TABLE 2.9. *Attitudes of all CLP leaders toward EEC, expressed by percentage of constituency type*

| | Constituencies | | | |
	All	Strong	Marginal	Weak
Strongly opposed	40	33	36	50
Moderately opposed	36	33	39	36
Neutral	4	4	6	2
Moderately favourable	10	12	13	4
Strongly favourable	8	12	6	6
No opinion	2	6	0	2

persons in the population who were older and less advantaged.[33] However, the response of parliamentary candidates who comprised the most privileged leadership category, was not consistent with this evidence. Parliamentary candidates were younger (Table 1.5), more of them were in professional or business occupations (Table 5.6), and they were more highly educated (Table 1.13). Despite these factors, parliamentary candidates evinced no great interest in entering EEC. The anomaly suggested that ideology may be a more potent factor in individual decision-making than other influences frequently deemed to have great impact on political behaviour.

Reasons advanced in support of Common Market attitudes. These covered a wide range, and certain attitudes were expressed in more than one

[33] Robert L. Pfaltzgraff, *Britain Faces Europe, 1956–66*, Chapters 2 and 7 (publication forthcoming).

way. Unfortunately for easy analysis, 44 per cent of all respondents cited a structural or institutional objection to the Treaty of Rome as their reason for opposing British membership in EEC. Included were references to differences between the British people and Europeans, to the fact that certain aspects of British economic policy would be made not by Parliament but by EEC Commission. Furthermore, the Commission would not be subject to political controls. To most respondents, France and Germany were dominating the Market and would continue to do so. De Gaulle and Adenauer were not admired by CLP leaders, who considered them old, inflexible, and very conservative. The Treaty of Rome was, by its own phraseology, a 'capitalist device' since it assumed the existence of competitive economies in the member states. British membership in EEC would make achieving socialism in Britain more difficult, and would prevent a British government from directing industry to areas of persistent unemployment. Although a number of respondents referred to the fact that both de Gaulle and Adenauer were Roman Catholics, and attributed the conservatism of both men to their common religious persuasion, only one, an MP, viewed the whole Common Market proposal as a 'Catholic plot'. He noted that President Kennedy, also a Roman Catholic, was urging British entry into EEC, and concluded his comment by saying meaningfully: 'It is called the Treaty of Rome, you know, and we all know what is in Rome.' The general impression gathered was that Labour Party members in general objected to the ideology of the Treaty of Rome, to its supra-national implications, and to the nations and leaders who had concluded it.

Equal proportions of the respondents, some 12 per cent, opposed British entry into EEC because they feared the move would aggravate East-West tensions, or because they thought Commonwealth nations, particularly the emerging, underdeveloped, non-white members of the Commonwealth, might suffer thereby. Of those who supported to some degree Britain's joining EEC, nearly all advanced the reason that long-run economic advantages would accrue to Britain or that the force of events to come would ultimately impel Britain into EEC. About 7 per cent of the respondents gave the first reason as a basis for their support, while 5 per cent offered the second.

An ancillary conclusion drawn from responses to this question was that CLP leaders were more than passingly familiar with the arguments used by party leaders in the debate over Labour's position *vis-à-vis* the Common Market. No argument advanced by an opponent of EEC had not already been expressed in public remarks or writings of such prominent Labour figures as Ian Mikardo,[34] Barbara Castle,[35] William Pickles,[36] Douglas Jay, Clive Jenkins, John Stonehouse, and R. W. Briginshaw.[37] Similarly, the respondents advocating entry displayed the same familiarity with the views of party leaders with whom they agreed. These respondents cited the promotional activities and quoted the reasons expressed by such Labour MPs as John Diamond, Roy Jenkins, the late John Strachey, and the Labour Common Market Committee. Whatever the stand taken by the respondents, all were able to justify their position in a manner which indicated that considerable thought and study had been expended on the issue.

II. Attitude of CLP leaders toward Parliamentary
Labour Party defence policy

By the autumn of 1962 the controversies over defence policy which had torn the Labour Party during 1960 and 1961 had subsided. Although twenty-seven resolutions and amendments proposed to the 1962 Annual Conference were critical of various aspects of the defence policy of the Parliamentary Labour Party, the conference supported the Arrangements (Programme) Committee in its decision to allow no time for discussion of foreign affairs,[38] and less than an hour for a resolution expressing opposition to the testing of nuclear weapons by any country.[39] Specific points of criticism in most of the

[34] Ian Mikardo, "Common Market", *Tribune*, September 28, 1962, p. 7.

[35] Barbara Castle, "The Anti-Socialist Community", *New Statesman*, March 30, 1962, p. 442.

[36] William Pickles, *Not With Europe: The Political Case for Staying Out*, London 1962.

[37] These persons worked for the Labour Committee on Britain and the Common Market, and the Forward Britain Movement, both organised to oppose the Market. Jay and Stonehouse are MPs. Clive Jenkins is General Secretary of the Association of Supervisory Staffs, Executives, and Technicians; R. W. Briginshaw is General Secretary, National Society of Operative Printers and Assistants.

[38] *Labour Party Annual Conference Report, 1962*, pp. 92–4.

[39] Ibid., pp. 225–33. This resolution, similar to that adopted by the 1961 Annual Conference, was not opposed by the NEC and was carried unanimously.

twenty-seven resolutions and amendments dealt with the rejection of unilateralism by the PLP, continued support of NATO by the PLP, and its failure to take any action on a resolution passed by the 1961 conference condemning the establishment of Polaris bases in Britain.[40]

The authors of these resolutions were correct in their analysis of PLP defence policy, which was based on the presence of the American nuclear deterrent in Europe, on continued British membership in NATO and other regional alliances, and upon a rejection of unilateral disarmament. The PLP believed that the British independent nuclear deterrent was neither independent nor credible, and had the disadvantage of arousing the envy of France and other nations, thus contributing to the ominous spread of nuclear weapons. Because of the lack of credibility of British nuclear arms, their tremendous expense, and their effect on other powers, the PLP proposed to phase out the 'V-Bomber' force and utilise the expenditures saved to raise the British Army of the Rhine to its full NATO commitment and to improve the effectiveness of all British conventional forces. This policy was accepted without reservation by more than half of all CLP leaders. Another fifth of the constituency leaders was willing to accept PLP defence policy with some reservations, but nearly a quarter of them rejected PLP defence policy in its entirety.[41]

TABLE 2.10. *Attitudes of all CLP leaders toward PLP defence policy, expressed by percentage of constituency type*

| | Constituencies | | | |
	All	Strong	Marginal	Weak
Accept policy	56	66	70	33
Accept with reservations	19	14	17	25
Reject policy	23	14	13	40
No opinion	2	6	0	2

On this question there was little difference between the strong and marginal constituencies, where two out of three respondents accepted PLP defence policy without reservation. The weak constituencies

[40] *Agenda, Labour Party Annual Conference, 1962*, pp. 68–75.
[41] See Bealey, Blondel and McCann op. cit., p. 281, for attitudes of constituency party members on this topic.

showed greater differences on this question than on any other. Only a third of the party leaders in weak districts were willing to accept PLP defence policy without reservation. A quarter accepted it with reservation, and two out of five respondents in weak constituencies rejected it out of hand.[42]

By leadership categories, the reaction to this question was not unexpected. Nine out of ten MPs accepted PLP defence policy without reservation. More than half the parliamentary candidates either had reservations or rejected completely Parliamentary Labour Party defence policy. This is less serious than it appears, for as the additional breakdown for parliamentary candidates in Table 2.11 indicates, all party leaders who rejected PLP defence policy and half of those expressing reservations came from weak divisions where Labour ran poorly in the 1964 election.[43] After the MPs, the secretary-agent group was the most loyal to the PLP defence policy. Chairmen and delegates were the most critical, with delegates from the weak divisions again composing more than half the respondents in this category who accepted with reservations or rejected entirely PLP defence policy.

The reasons given for the views of the respondents assumed a distinctive pattern. Those CLP leaders who clearly supported party defence policy, 56 per cent of the total, indicated also general approval for NATO. Conversely, 30 per cent of the sample were critical of NATO. These criticisms included objections to reliance on nuclear as opposed to conventional arms, opposition to military pacts outside the UN, hostility to having nuclear weapons based in Britain, support for pacifism and for unilateral disarmament. Among this group a few thought that Britain should stress the UN rather than NATO, and that Britain's first responsibility was to work for East-West accord, which she could not effectively do as a member of NATO. Unilateral disarmament was favoured by 5 per cent, who felt also that Britain could 'give the lead for peace' by working toward this goal and by assuming the leadership of the neutralist nations. Another 5 per cent thought the expenditures made by Britain for

[42] Cf. Keith Hindell and Philip Williams, "Scarborough and Blackpool: An Analysis of Some Votes at the Labour Party Conferences of 1960 and 1961", *Political Quarterly*, July–September 1962, p. 315.

[43] The twelve weak divisions in this study polled between 18 and 32 per cent of the total votes cast in the 1964 general election.

defence, particularly for nuclear weapons, would more wisely be used for social services such as education, pensions for the aged, and improved medical services. A number of respondents in this group mentioned that reductions in defence spending might permit Britain to afford more extensive foreign aid, especially for underdeveloped nations, and that such aid might be administered through UN auspices.

TABLE 2.11. *Attitudes of CLP leaders toward PLP defence policy, expressed by percentage of leadership category and constituency type*

	Accept	Accept with reservations	Reject
MPs	90	10	0
Parliamentary cands.			
All constituencies	48	32	20
Strong	4	4	0
Marginal	32	12	0
Weak	12	16	20
Chairmen	51	14	35
Secretary-agents	61	21	18
Delegates			
All constituencies	50	19	31
Strong	22	6	6
Marginal	22	3	10
Weak	6	10	15

III. Attitudes of CLP leaders toward United States action in Cuba, October 1962

Many Britons, and not all of them are to be found in the Labour Party, have an ambivalent attitude toward the United States. At no point is this ambivalence more apparent than in the reaction of CLP officials to the conduct of American foreign policy. During the 1964 presidential campaign the British press expressed shock and alarm over some of the more incendiary statements made by Senator Goldwater. Their reaction was surprising, for the popular and left-wing newspapers and journals in Britain have been presenting for the last twenty years an American stereotype not unlike Mr Goldwater in his less restrained moments.

Given the highly critical attitudes toward United States foreign policy in many segments of British society, and the traditional left posture of the Labour Party, particularly in the ideologically oriented left-wing, it followed that there would be a critical reaction to President Kennedy's action following the disclosure of Russian missile bases being constructed in Cuba. Although more than half of all CLP leaders strongly or moderately opposed American action in Cuba, there were about two-fifths supporting it to some degree. Among the different types of constituency there was considerable variation in reactions to this matter. In the strong Labour divisions, a small balance actually supported the action of the United States. Marginal divisions were more critical, and in the weak divisions a high degree of opposition was noted. Even in the weak divisions, however, there was a sizeable minority of almost 30 per cent which gave moderate or strong support to the United States in its action.

TABLE 2.12. *Attitudes of CLP leaders toward American action in Cuba, expressed by percentage of constituency type*

| | Constituencies | | | |
	All	Strong	Marginal	Weak
Strongly opposed	36	25	32	52
Moderately opposed	19	21	22	15
Neutral	1	0	2	0
Moderately favourable	14	11	21	12
Strongly favourable	25	39	23	17
Neutral	5	4	0	4

Among leadership categories, MPs, secretary-agents and chairmen were less likely to oppose and more likely to support United States action in Cuba, while parliamentary candidates and delegates tended to the opposite view. Again it was the parliamentary candidates and the delegates from weak divisions who furnished the bulk of the sentiment against United States action. This was particularly true of the delegates in weak divisions, who composed over half of all delegates strongly opposed to United States action in Cuba as opposed to none who gave strong support to the United States.

A far broader range of reasons was advanced for attitudes on the Cuban question than on those relating either to EEC entry or to defence policy. From those respondents who were in some degree critical of President Kennedy's action, the first six of the following reasons were given. Those respondents who moderately or strongly supported the American action in Cuba cited the last three reasons.

TABLE 2.13. *Attitudes of CLP leaders toward American action in Cuba, expressed by percentage of leadership category and constituency type*

	Strongly opposed	Moderately opposed	Neutral	Moderately favourable	Strongly favourable
MPs	30	30	0	0	40
Parliamentary cands.					
All constituencies	56	12	0	20	12
Strong	0	4		0	4
Marginal	24	0		16	4
Weak	32	8		4	4
Chairmen	40	14	3	12	31
Secretary-agents	32	19	3	14	32
Delegates					
All Constituencies	42	32	0	16	10
Strong	9	13		3	7
Marginal	9	13		10	3
Weak	24	6		3	0

TABLE 2.14. *Reasons given by CLP leaders in support of their attitudes toward American action in Cuba*

	Percentage
1. America deliberately created a dangerous situation	16
2. There was a real danger of nuclear war.	12
3. Russian missiles in Cuba were no different from American missiles in Turkey.	9
4. Unfriendly American action toward Cuba prior to October 1962 was responsible for Russian–Cuban friendship.	5
5. The issue should have been taken to the UN.	5
6. The incident made Khrushchev look good, i.e., reasonable and responsible.	3
7. The United States had to stand up to the USSR on this issue.	14
8. The move was successful—a change from a critical attitude to one less critical or of approval.	12
9. The incident made Kennedy look good, i.e., firm, restrained, courageous.	11

Note: 13 per cent of the respondents gave no reason to support their attitudes on this question.

Respondents seemed to feel no reluctance to stating their opinions on this question in the frankest terms. One critic said that the action was 'definitely a case of American aggression; their piracy [stopping and searching Russian ships] on the high seas was against international law'. Another stated that he could 'appreciate American concern [over Cuba], but could not defend this and at the same time oppose Russian aggression in Hungary and elsewhere'. Still another characterised the American action as 'hysterical foolhardiness'. The most extreme comments came from those respondents who were certain that full scale nuclear war would ensue. One of them noted that schoolgirls and younger teachers broke down during the crisis, and expressed grave concern that Khrushchev's actions and the American response might cause people to have faith in the deterrent.[44]

Most supporters of American action in Cuba thought the United States had no alternative but to oppose forthrightly and directly the installation of Russian missiles on the island. An MP who held this view thought that the United States had erred in not acting sooner, and another respondent thought that American action was not extensive enough. In his opinion, 'America should have invaded Cuba, and not having done so, has made itself vulnerable to possible destruction'. There was a strong personal response to President Kennedy among the CLP leaders who sided with the American action. Whether these persons had always held the late President in high regard was not ascertainable, but it was impressive to hear a pacifist and unilateralist, who admitted he was in the Labour Party only because there was no longer an Independent Labour Party, say that 'Kennedy had acted precipitately, but under the present set-up, everything cannot go through the United Nations. I like Kennedy from a distance.' In another part of Britain a Nonconformist Welshman described Kennedy's performance as 'one of the greatest acts of statesmanship in history'. A councillor of a London borough 'rather admired Kennedy. He chose the right time to make his moves. History will show he affected the safety of the world.'

A most interesting reaction was that of the rather large segment of CLP leaders who were critical of Kennedy's action at the time of the crisis, but who later saw the incident in a different light. For example, a Scottish parliamentary candidate's reaction to the question was: 'Horror! Must admit that hindsight indicates that

[44] The nagging idea suggested itself that this person might have been happier if a nuclear bomb had been dropped because this would then have proved the fallacy of the deterrent.

President Kennedy's action was the right one, but the risk at the time was appalling. Who was to know how far the Russians were prepared to go?' A unilateralist CLP secretary said, 'It was pretty high-handed, but it had its results'. A CLP chairman on the south coast of England replied: 'At first I thought it was a wild escapade, but within three days, and by going to the trouble to get more information, I thought it was a wise move. Kennedy prevented what could have been a disaster.'

IV. Attitudes of CLP leaders toward Chinese action against India, October 1962

Following the question relating to United States action in Cuba, the CLP leaders were asked their reaction to Chinese action in India. During the Cuban episode the period of high tension extended from October 22, 1962, when President Kennedy announced the quarantine on nuclear arms shipped to Cuba, until November 10 when American naval vessels viewed and photographed, without boarding, Russian ships removing missiles from Cuba. The Chinese–Indian border dispute began on October 21 of the same year, when it was announced that Chinese troops had over-run many Indian border positions, until December 4 when the Indian prime minister, Pandit Nehru, confirmed the withdrawal of Chinese troops from their deepest points of penetration into India.

TABLE 2.15. *Attitudes of CLP leaders toward Chinese action against India in 1962, expressed by percentage of constituency type*

	Constituencies			
	All	Strong	Marginal	Weak
Strongly opposed	44	59	30	42
Moderately opposed	31	23	38	31
Neutral	7	0	13	7
Moderately favourable	3	4	0	6
Strongly favourable	0	0	0	0
No opinion	15	14	19	14

Throughout the constituency parties there was general condemnation of China's aggressive action. Three out of four CLP leaders strongly or moderately opposed the attack upon India. Only 3 per cent could be said to have moderately supported it, and no respondent would say that he strongly supported the action. Constituency differences were not great and did not follow the usual pattern, for on this question the weak divisions opposed Chinese action somewhat more strongly than did marginal constituencies. The highly unusual feature of the response to this question was the large proportion of 'neutral' and 'no opinion' answers obtained. On the defence question a 'neutral' response was not appropriate but on the Common Market issue the neutral response was 4 per cent and on Cuba 0.6 per cent as compared with 7 per cent on the question of Chinese action on the Indian border. A 'no opinion' response was available on all four of these questions, with 0.6 per cent choosing this in relation to EEC and defence policy, 3 per cent on Cuba, and 14 per cent on China.

The high incidence of indeterminate answers on the China–India issue was significant, as were the reasons offered by CLP leaders in explanation of their attitudes. A large proportion (28 per cent) of CLP leaders simply considered the Chinese action rank aggression against a peaceful neutralist state. Another 8 per cent was critical of India for not developing its defences. In the words of one MP, this group thought India 'got what it deserved'. Because of the old relationship between Britain and India, 7 per cent of the respondents were sympathetic toward India.

Some respondents tended to apologise for China's actions, or to withdraw in a sense, from the implications of the affair. About 22 per cent of the respondents gave no reason for their attitude on this matter, as opposed to 14 per cent who gave no reasons for their stand on EEC, 8 per cent on defence policy, and 13 per cent on Cuba. To 16 per cent China's action in India was inexplicable, and to another 7 per cent the cause of the dispute lay in the ill-defined border separating the two countries.[45] Some 5 per cent thought China would have acted differently if it had been a member of the United Nations, and blamed the United States for the exclusion of China. A minority of 4 per cent declared that the situation did not achieve visibility as an issue or that there were no reliable sources of information.

[45] Two respondents volunteered that the border had not become ambiguous until China annexed Tibet.

It is relevant to speculate on the high rate of indeterminate answers and the substantial proportion of respondents who withheld the reasons for their attitude toward the Chinese action in India, as well as the 20 per cent who professed not to understand the incident or for whom it did not achieve visibility. By comparison, the response of CLP leaders in regard to the Cuban matter was patent. On this issue almost all respondents were willing to express an opinion, and few of them did not attempt to justify their position. Almost every party official questioned was well informed on the Cuba affair and had no reluctance in determining for themselves the extent of American or of Russian culpability. Admittedly there were differences between the two incidents, the chief of which was that in Cuba two nuclear powers were confronting one another, with Britain's anxieties aroused both as a NATO ally of the United States, and as a nuclear power conscious of the dangers of nuclear escalation. The Cuban crisis was of shorter duration, and caused more suspense because of the speed with which events moved. The sense of emergency was heightened by the swift American intervention which followed the announcement that Russian missiles were being installed in Cuba, and President Kennedy's message on Cuba to the citizens of the United States was carried by the BBC at midnight and heard with great attentiveness.

Although there were valid reasons for the deep imprint left on the minds of the British people by the Cuban crisis, there were others for regarding the Chinese action with equal seriousness. An historical and cultural association of some four centuries still links Britain and India. India has derived its political and governmental institutions from those of England, and the Indian system of public values are part of the heritage of the British Raj. India is a valued member of the British Commonwealth of Nations, and the role played by the Labour Party in the struggle for Indian independence is well known. Beyond this, India has developed a neutralist foreign policy which should have increased the sensitivity of the unilateralist members of the Labour Party to any difficulties suffered by India.

It has been suggested that the Cuban crisis engendered a clear response because this seemed a classic example to men reared in the socialist tradition of how the capitalist world operates. As they saw it, the entire crisis was part of the Cold War, which many members of the Labour left believe was started by Sir Winston Churchill's

'Iron Curtain' speech given at Westminster College in Fulton, Missouri. Some members of the Labour left are not entirely sure that they want to see the balance in the Cold War swing in favour of the United States. In their judgment, American action in Cuba was of an imperialistic nature, as could only be expected from a capitalist country. War, the threat of war, and defence against war were considered by some CLP leaders to be integral parts of the capitalistic, but not necessarily part of the non-capitalistic, world. A parliamentary candidate in one weak division explained these ideas as follows:

> Nuclear weapons should be associated with a capitalistic society. Defence is more important in a capitalistic world. The British people on the whole have an objection to other nations maintaining bases in Britain for the purpose of defence against the USSR. The Soviet Union is not a potential aggressor, and has never been given a fair chance and has been forced by the capitalist states into the position it now holds.

The indistinct reaction of CLP leaders in regard to the Chinese–Indian affair, may be attributable to the fact that the entire episode violated the mythology and rhetoric of socialism. It was one thing for the Soviet Union and Cuba to confront the United States, but an attack on a neutralist 'Social Democracy' by a 'People's Democracy', especially when the victim has previously advocated the admission of the aggressor to the United Nations, is more difficult to explain. Such an event did not easily fit into socialist expectations of abiding peace among non-capitalist nations. China's untoward behaviour placed some respondents under such cross pressures that they took refuge in indeterminate responses or in refusals to answer at all. The confusion among some CLP leaders was expressed by a parliamentary candidate who said: 'I am sad about this, but quite honestly, I have not studied the facts of the case. I am hoping the efforts made by Mme Bandaranaike will bear fruit, and that the affair can be settled fairly and finally.'

v. Attitude of CLP leaders toward the Soviet Union and
the United States as world powers

In the process of testing this questionnaire in the field, a pattern of response developed on party and public policy questions which led to the introduction of another question asking whether the fact that the United States was a capitalist and the Soviet Union a communist nation affected in any way the attitude of the respondent toward these nations.[46] Twenty-three per cent of the respondents expressed a preference for the Soviet Union, while the same proportion favoured the United States, 29 per cent were neutral, 8 per cent were critical of both, and 17 per cent had no opinion. It is worth noting that the proportion having no opinion on this question was practically the same as that expressing no opinion on the Chinese–Indian issue.

TABLE 2.16. *Attitudes of CLP leaders toward USSR and USA, expressed by percentage of constituency type*

| | Constituencies | | | |
	All	Strong	Marginal	Weak
Pro-Soviet	23	13	21	37
Neutral	29	41	23	23
Pro-American	23	24	34	13
Critical of both	8	8	11	6
No opinion	17	14	11	21

As one proceeded from strong to weak divisions, there was a steady increase in pro-Soviet attitudes. Marginal divisions had the greatest amount of pro-American sentiment and weak divisions the least, with feeling in strong divisions midway between. On this particular question a neutral response did not necessarily constitute an evasion. Persons giving a neutral response often elaborated by saying that 'each country should determine its own way of life'; or 'I consider events involving the two countries on their merits'; or 'one cannot help admire Russian achievements but I have never swerved from my hostility to the lack of democracy in the USSR'. A response with some nationalistic overtones was advanced by a Scottish CLP secretary who said: 'I believe nations of different ideology should be able to exist in peace. I feel no more antipathy toward the Russian people than toward the American people. I believe ordinary people everywhere want to live in peace. In America the political structure is such that governments can be changed, but I feel politically she is about a hundred years behind Britain.'

[46] See Bealey, Blondel and McCann, op. cit., p. 282, for attitudes of party members on this topic.

The respondents who were critical of both countries were those who held most strongly to the traditions of social democracy. Many of them were outspoken and candid in their remarks. An MP stated: 'I don't want either system and I don't want to get too close to either.' A conference delegate from a constituency in the Midlands described her attitude in vivid language when she said: 'They are two extremes; where you have capitalism you have poverty and where you have communism you have dictatorship.'

The usual tendency of parliamentary candidates and conference delegates to express a radical or more 'progressive' view was disrupted on this question. In their responses here parliamentary candidates showed almost the same balance as did MPs. Granted that a greater proportion of parliamentary candidates took a pro-Soviet position than did any other leadership category, but this was offset by an almost equal proportion of pro-American responses. The attitudes of chairmen and delegates on this question were quite similar, with the secretary-agents as usual being the least 'progressive'.

TABLE 2.17. *Attitudes of CLP leaders toward USSR and USA, expressed by percentage of leadership category*

	MPs	Parl. cands.	Chairmen	Sec.-agents	Delegates
Pro-Soviet	10	32	29	16	31
Neutral	50	24	31	24	28
Pro-American	10	28	14	40	16
Critical of both	30	12	6	3	9
No opinion	0	4	20	17	16

In the discussion of defence policy and of the Cuban affair it was the parliamentary candidates and delegates in weak divisions who were primarily responsible for the 'progressive' response of weak divisions. This proved true when Russian *versus* American attitudes were explored. The candidates and delegates from strong divisions indicated no great bias towards either the Soviet Union or the United States. Parliamentary candidates from marginal divisions were divided evenly on this question, and delegates from marginal divisions were also evenly balanced in the proportion of pro-Soviet and pro-American predilections. The same could not be said for the candidates and delegates from the weak divisions, as their response was characterised by a clear pro-Soviet bias.

TABLE 2.18. *Attitudes of parliamentary candidates and conference delegates toward the USSR and the USA, expressed by percentage of constituency type*

	Pro-Russian	Neutral	Pro-American	Critical of both	No opinion
Parliamentary cands.	32	24	28	12	4
All constituencies					
Strong	0	4	4	0	0
Marginal	8	12	16	8	0
Weak	24	8	8	4	4
Delegates					
All constituencies	31	28	16	9	16
Strong	0	19	3	3	9.5
Marginal	15.5	3	13	3	0
Weak	15.5	6	0	3	6.5

Summary

The findings presented in this chapter strongly support the contention of those scholars who maintain that the politics of the constituency parties cover the spectrum of Labour Party politics.[47] Sizeable minority opinions were registered on almost every policy question in strong, marginal, and weak divisions. Broad differences on policy matters developed within discrete constituency parties. In fact, there were only eight divisional parties in which all the respondents were uniformly on the right or the left,[48] just as there were very few respondents who gave unwavering loyalty to any identifiable policy line.

While it is true that most individual respondents, constituency parties, and categories of constituency parties held differing policy views, the data suggest that the electoral strength of constituency

[47] Rose, "The Political Ideas of English Party Activists", op. cit., p. 371.
[48] Three strong CLPs had a right-wing bias, while three weak and two strong divisions showed a left-wing orientation.

parties *does* affect the distribution of political attitudes.[49] As Table 2.19 shows, weak divisions were to the left of the strong and marginal divisions on all policy issues with the exception of Chinese action in India, to which question there was a general confused and unclear response.[50]

TABLE 2.19. *Summary of attitudes of CLP leaders toward questions of Labour Party policy, by type of constituency*

	Strong	Marginal	Weak
Acceptance of *status quo in re* general Labour Party policy	54	51	25
Acceptance of Labour Party proscription policy	87	92	57
Opposition to amendment of membership clause	76	77	87
Opposition to joining EEC	65	75	86
Acceptance of PLP defence policy	65	70	33
Opposition to American action in Cuba	43	54	67
Opposition to Chinese action in India	81	68	73
Presumption in favour of the USSR	13	21	37

The complaint registered by Richard Rose during the summer of 1962 regarding the dearth of studies concerning the relationship between the political attitudes of party leaders and voters is still valid.[51] The only substantive issue discussed in the study on which there is any comparative data available is that of Britain joining the EEC. Although 75 per cent of all CLP leaders opposed joining the EEC during the winter of 1962–63, only 56 per cent of those who identified themselves as Labour supporters took the same position in

[49] Rose, "The Political Ideas. . .", op. cit., p. 371. The differences between these findings and those of Rose may stem from differences in the nature and source of the respective data. His three categories of 'Safe', 'Marginal', and 'Hopeless' included all English constituencies, while the three categories in the present study were based on samples from the extreme and middle quintiles of all British constituencies, Northern Ireland excepted. Also, the issues used in this study provide sharper differences in attitudes than could be inferred from an analysis of conference resolutions whose content might be affected by other than purely political factors.

[50] See Austin Ranney, *Pathways to Parliament: Candidate Selection in Britain*, Madison 1965, p. 129, and Samuel H. Beer, *British Politics in the Collectivist Age*, New York 1965, p. 221.

[51] Rose, "The Political Ideas. . . ", op. cit., p. 371.

September 1962.[52] However, even without empirical evidence on
the other issues, it seems unlikely that the Labour electorate in strong,
marginal and weak constituencies in 1959 held the same clear
attitudinal differences on contemporary party and public issues as
did their party leaders. Studies in this area of American politics
suggest that there are substantial differences between the political
attitudes of leaders (represented by national convention delegates)
and of party supporters in the United States. This is not to say that
party activists in America are militant ideologues, but in the context
of American politics, the followers of both parties tend toward a
politics of moderation while the leaders of both parties are inclined
to support stronger liberal or conservative positions.[53] Thus, the
congressional party in the United States may be confronted with the
same dilemma posed by David Butler for parliamentary party
leaders in Britain, that 'their most loyal and devoted followers tend
to have more extreme views than they have themselves, and to be
still further removed from the mass of those who actually provide
the vote'.[54]

Until there are more data available relating to the congruence of
the political attitudes of party leaders and followers in Britain, the
impressionistic judgment must prevail that CLP leaders, like their
equivalents in the United States, do not accurately reflect the political views of the Labour electorate. Harrison states: 'Many local
parties, led by semi-oligarchic cliques, have no better claim that
their decisions are "representative" than some of the unions they
reproach for being out of touch with the rank and file.'[55] Butler and
Rose note that 'only after the 1959 election did [the Labour Party]
show much awareness of what Mr Denis Healey called the "big and
growing gap between the active party workers and the average
voter". A failure to recognise this gap misled many into assuming
that the increased enthusiasm shown by the faithful during the
campaign foreshadowed a higher Labour poll.'[56]

[52] National Opinion Polls, *Bulletin*, September 1962.

[53] Herbert McCloskey, et al., "Issue Conflict and Consensus Among
Party Leaders and Followers", *American Political Science Review*, June 1960,
pp. 411–15.

[54] David Butler, "The Paradox of Party Differences", *American Behavioral
Scientist*, Vol. IV, No. 3, 1960, p. 5.

[55] Harrison, op. cit., p. 111.

[56] Butler and Rose, op. cit., p. 198.

There are a number of reasons for this alleged isolation of CLP leaders from the Labour electorate. The General Management Committee of a constituency party is composed of delegates from organisations affiliated to the constituency party and from subsidiary units within the party, such as women's sections and ward committees. In other words, Labour Party members, who constitute a minority rarely exceeding 10 per cent of the Labour electorate in the division, select a minority of themselves to serve on the General Management Committee. There is no institutionalised arrangement whereby CLP leaders can determine the political views of their traditional supporters, particularly on questions of national policy. The opportunity of CLP leaders for contact with a voter outside their own circle of activists is severely limited, for they must earn a living for their families as well as assume party and local government responsibilities. To all this should be added the well-documented tendency for people to associate with those who share their values and prejudices, which in this situation would probably be other party leaders. It is quite possible that further study will confirm the impressionistic evaluations of the incongruities between the politics of CLP leaders and the Labour electorate.

3

The Labour Campaign in Three Marginal Constituencies, 1964

EXPERIENCED STUDENTS of British politics contend that constituency campaigns are at present less important in the conduct of a British general election than they once were. They attribute the lessened significance of the constituency campaign to the growth of a national press and the development of other national communications media and to the enforcement of party discipline in the House of Commons. The latter has reduced the importance of the individual MP, just as the former has magnified the influence of party leaders who can reach the voters in any constituency by means of the press conference and the political broadcast. Indeed, the constituency voters are often more accessible to the national leaders than to the local candidate who must go to considerable lengths to reach an audience.[1]

Despite the centralisation of politics which has taken place in the last few decades, there can be found in every election a group of marginal divisions in which the constituency campaign can make the difference between victory and defeat. Butler and Rose have indicated that some eighty seats are responsive to the influence of effective divisional campaigning.[2] This number is considerable and constitutes sufficient reason for the national parties to exert them-

[1] Butler and Rose, op. cit., pp. 119–20.

[2] Two points can be made here. Those seats which are marginal differ from one election to the next, depending upon the balance between the Conservatives and Labour, and upon the number and strength of Liberal

selves in the divisions in which the outcome may be decided by the quality of the local campaign. The Labour Party often encounters difficulty in turning out the Labour vote. Moreover, the closeness of the general elections of 1950, 1951 and 1964 provides an additional reason for Labour to exert itself in the constituency campaigns.

It would be difficult to convince candidates and leaders of the three constituency parties studied in the 1964 general election of the inefficacy of campaigning. In Gravesend, Albert Murray won with a majority of 712, and Dennis Hobden won with a majority of seven in the Kemptown division of Brighton. John Lee, the candidate in Reading, lost his division by ten votes.[3]

1. The nature of constituency campaigns

It is undeniable, as Butler and Rose contend, that the campaign activities of the national leaders overshadow those of Labour Party members operating at the constituency level. This is particularly true of the developing of campaign issues, for it is both difficult and hazardous for a candidate to attempt to substitute his own set of issues for those emphasised in the broadcasts and press conferences of the national leaders. It is far easier and more rewarding for the candidate to relate national policies to the conditions existing in his constituency. The local campaign is therefore used to adapt the national campaign to the constituency, and to perform additional functions which are crucial to a parliamentary election and which cannot be easily performed by the national party. It becomes the task of the constituency campaign to seek out and identify Labour supporters, to encourage their voting on election day, and to link the name and goals of the candidate with those of the Labour Party.

The ability of the candidate to build the constituency campaign

[3] In all, there were twenty-three constituencies in which the margin of victory was less than 500 votes in the 1964 general election. There were fifteen additional constituencies in which the majority was between 501 and 1,000 votes. It should be here noted that John Lee won in Reading in the general election of 1966 with a majority of 4,133.

candidates. Seats which were strongly Tory after the 1959 election became marginal after the 1964 election. It is worth noting that eight seats in which Labour won from 35.8 to 40.4 per cent of the vote in 1959 were carried by Labour in 1964. Therefore some unlikely constituencies can be affected by the quality of the campaign which a constituency party develops.

upon the national one varies with his political intuition and experience. In 1964 the strategy of the national Labour campaign was based partly on the opinion of Harold Wilson and market research that stressing foreign policy fails to win elections for Labour and has been known to lose them. During this campaign Labour headquarters suggested to parliamentary candidates that they base their campaigns on domestic issues such as education, housing, pensions and the cost of living. They were advised to avoid the areas of foreign and defence policy unless these issues were brought up during the question period of a public meeting. This predilection for domestic matters proved a hardship for such candidates as John Lee in Reading, who had not been a local government councillor and had never actually participated in the administration of any of the domestic programmes. John Lee's legal training enabled him to master the technical provisions of the relevant legislation and he was entirely familiar with the general aspects of the domestic issues, but his inexperience of local government was a distinct disadvantage. Albert Murray, although he was not a resident of Gravesend, had served for nine years as a borough councillor and was currently serving on the London County Council. When he discussed housing evictions, the problems of pensioners or the virtues of comprehensive schools, his remarks had an authenticity lent by experience. The Kemptown candidate, Dennis Hobden, enjoyed an even greater advantage, for he had been a borough councillor for eight years in the town in which he had been born, educated and was employed. His campaign was convincing and conveyed a strong sense of personal involvement. He was able not only to discuss evictions in the abstract but to say how many had occurred in Brighton during the previous year. When he discussed the effect of land speculation on housing and on municipal recreation costs, he could cite an instance in which the price of a certain acreage had increased from about £9,000 to £125,000 over a four-year period. His familiarity with local problems gave a sense of immediacy to national issues which might otherwise have been difficult to achieve.

The identification of Labour supporters and their participation on election day is a formidable task for the constituency organisation. Labour Party supporters are less inclined to cast their vote than are the voters who favour the Conservative Party, and this tendency is sometimes interpreted as evidence that the Conservative Party organisation is more efficient in this regard. Certainly, the socio-economic composition of traditional Labour Party supporters must also be considered as a contributing factor. Whatever the reasons, a post-election survey in 1955 showed that five non-voters professed a bias toward Labour compared to four non-voters who favoured the Conservative Party. In 1959 Labour's disadvantage was shown to be even greater, with five non-voters expressing a preference for Labour compared to two favouring the Conservatives.[4] After the 1964 election a National Opinion Polls survey found four Labour non-voters for every three Conservatives.[5]

American political custom provides two means of assistance in voter identification that are not available in Britain. Many states of the Union require that a registered voter indicate a party preference, and the registration lists distributed to the political parties prior to each election show this preference. (In jurisdictions where one party is unusually strong, some voters register a preference for the majority party, although they may rarely vote for it. This practice reduces the reliability of registration lists, although the lists are accurate for the majority of voters.) In addition, election returns in every state use the polling district as the reporting unit, and the results are made available to all interested parties.

This is not the case in Britain. There the register[6] carries only the

[4] Butler and Rose, op. cit., p. 238, quoting Gallup Poll results after the 1955 and 1959 elections.

[5] National Opinion Polls, *Bulletin*, October 1964, p. 2.

[6] In October of each year the Electoral Registration Office in each parliamentary constituency distributes forms through the General Post Office to each household in its jurisdiction. These forms are to be completed by a household member and are to list all adults and persons who will reach their twenty-first birthday by the middle of June. The forms are returned postage free to the Electoral Registration Office. If they are not returned by a certain date, a representative of the Electoral Registration Office calls upon the household to ascertain the reason. If no person in the household wishes to vote the matter is ended, for there is no compulsion to have one's name entered on the register. On the basis of the response to the mailed forms and the personal calls, the Electoral Registration Office makes up the Electoral Register for elections to take place during the ensuing year. This procedure is effective enough in that in the 1964 election the Election Registers for the United Kingdom listed 35.4 millions out of adult population of 36.4 million. For Great Britain (excluding Northern Ireland) 35 million out of 35.5 million adults were registered, or 98.6 per cent. See *Gallup News*, No. 6, November 1964, p. 66.

D

name and address of the voter, and it is the responsibility of the constituency organisation of every party to establish through personal contact the political allegiance of the individual voter in order that every person indicating a preference for the particular party is encouraged, and assisted if necessary, to go to the polls. (See Appendix for a current example of the 'Register of Electors' forms.) Since election results in Britain are reported for the constituency as a whole there is no means of corroborating the reports of the canvassers except on a constituency basis, which is virtually useless.[7] Even more serious for the Labour Party is its tendency to overlook what middle-class support it has and to concentrate its efforts in working-class districts where, in 1964, 40 per cent of the voters supported either the Conservatives or the Liberals. Election returns tabulated by polling district might be helpful in discovering those districts in which middle-class Labour supporters reside, and in identifying working-class districts in which there are the greatest number of defectors. However, in light of the high value placed upon personal privacy in Britain by public officials and political workers alike, there is little likelihood that the practices will be altered.

The most important function of the Labour constituency campaign is to associate the name of the local candidate with the Labour Party. That this is necessary may be considered surprising, for an accepted feature of the British political system is that the vast majority of British electors vote for their party rather than the candidate. Nevertheless, the only way in which an elector in Britain can vote for the party of his choice is to learn the name of his local candidate, for neither the name, symbol, nor colours of the parties appear on the ballots used by the voters on election day. The incum-

---

[7] When the polls close, the Polling District Supervisor, who is a local government employee, with police help transports the ballot box from his polling district to the Town Hall or other public building where the count is to be made. The ballot papers are sorted into bundles of fifty, irrespective of candidate, and the number of votes cast in each polling district is verified. Following this, the ballots from all the boxes are combined so that it becomes impossible to identify them by polling district. The ballots are then distributed among tables at which are seated 'counters' and 'scrutineers' who represent the political parties contesting the election. The ballots are assembled in bundles of 500 for each candidate and are placed on separate tables for the final count by the Chief Returning Officer and his assistants.

bent MP, whose name is relatively well-known, has a considerable advantage in this respect. In the three divisions studied, the Labour candidates were the challengers and used every means at their command to identify themselves with their party. Yet the name of the candidate has small intrinsic value, for it is generally used only as the instrument by which the party is identified. Of the three constituency candidates observed, Dennis Hobden was at the least disadvantage because of his life-long association with the division in which he was seeking office.

2. *The length of constituency campaigns*

Officially the general election campaigns in Britain are of three weeks' duration. In many respects this limitation on the length of the campaign is as unrealistic as the three million dollars limit to the expenditure of the National Committees of the Republican and Democratic parties in the United States. Theoretically, an election can be called in Britain at any time the prime minister chooses to do so. In reality no prime minister with a working majority in Commons is likely to call an election before the fourth year of the permissible five-year life of a Parliament.[8] Only in the circumstances of 1950 and 1964 when Labour governments were elected with tiny majorities does the possibility arise that the prime minister will go to the country during the first two years after election. Of the four post-war governments elected with working majorities, the shortest served for three years and seven months, the longest for a few days less than five years. It is no longer possible to generalise that no one can tell when an election will take place in Britain, for political analysts have a very good idea indeed. Given a working majority, a government is unlikely to go to the country until a point during the last eighteen months of its five year term.

Having noted this pattern of elections since the Second World War, political writers began speculating on the date of the new

[8] Crises and wholesale cabinet reshuffling apparently no longer raise the question of the government's resigning. The Suez crisis merely replaced Anthony Eden with Harold Macmillan as prime minister. No one seriously raised the question of Macmillan continuing as prime minister when he dropped one-third of his cabinet in June 1962, nor when twenty-seven Conservative MPs abstained from voting at the end of the debate on the Profumo affair in June 1963.

election as early as 1962. Most observers endeavoured to anticipate some turn of events which would bring the Conservative Party within striking distance of Labour, which had maintained a substantial lead in public opinion polls since the 1959 election. By December 1963, the Conservative Party had not managed to improve its positions and Robert McKenzie wrote ' . . . by 1959 the Conservatives, who alone among the parties had digested the conclusions of the psephologists, began their campaign eighteen months or more before polling day. Now Labour had caught up and both parties had begun their massive election spending by mid-1963. If anything, the run-up to the British election of 1964 is going to prove longer (and perhaps more tedious) than the build-up for the American elections of the same year.'[9] A favourable turn of events had still not taken place by June 1964, at which time the prime minister finally announced that the election would be held in the autumn. Ultimately, the 1964 election was held four years, eleven months and one week after the 1959 election, and was the second consecutive national election for which the pre-campaign period extended well over a year.[10]

The campaign in the constituencies is even longer than the campaign waged at the national level. The local campaign usually begins with the selection of the parliamentary candidate which takes place in the second or third year following a general election.[11] As soon as the candidate is endorsed by the National Executive Committee, he becomes involved in myriad activities known collectively as 'nursing the constituency'. With all the delays in calling the 1964 election, the pre-election campaign which began in mid-1962

[9] R. T. Mackenzie, "Showing Ideology the Door", *Observer*, December 8, 1963.

[10] See Butler and Rose, op. cit., p. 20. If the length of the 1959 campaign were measured by the length of the advertising campaign, then the Conservative campaign exceeded two years and cost nearly £500,000, spent over a twenty-seven month period beginning June 30, 1957.

[11] See Chapter 5, pp. 129–30. The situation in 1965 was complicated by the very narrow majority of the Labour government. In these circumstances, with Wilson under constant pressure to go to the country at a propitious moment in order to increase his majority, the selection of parliamentary candidates began a few weeks after the 1964 election. This rush turned out to be unnecessary as, in June 1965, Mr Wilson announced that he had no intention of calling an election during 1965. The election took place in March 1966. (See Chapter 7.)

extended to nearly two years. When judged in terms of continuous electioneering, the length of campaigning in some constituencies was about two-and-a-half years, and was limited only by the amount of time the candidate could give.

3. Pre-election campaign activities in constituencies

In the constituencies campaign activities revolve around two persons, the candidate and the election agent, the latter exercising general control and supervision of the campaign.[12] Occasionally the candidate and the agent differ on methods, and one agent (at Kemptown) in his election report paid tribute to the candidate for his efforts and for his 'non-interference with organization'.[13] In this division there was potential for disagreement since the candidate had formerly been secretary-agent for the division while the new secretary-agent had been chairman of the General Management Committee. The candidate proved professional enough to recall how he had expected candidates to act, and he followed his agent's direction without question. The agent, on the other hand, gave the candidate every reason to have confidence in him, and the fact that the two men had already worked together for years as leaders of the Kemptown constituency party contributed to the harmonious relationship they enjoyed during the campaign.

In the other two constituencies candidate-agent relations were less satisfactory. The Reading agent had considerable experience in parliamentary by-elections, while the candidate had not previously

[12] An election agent is a professional party organiser responsible for the administration of a constituency party. The agency system in the Conservative Party is better developed than that of the Labour Party, in which the system is likely to be held on an honorary (unsalaried) basis. Reading and Gravesend had full-time agents, but Kemptown did not. In the total sample of thirty-six constituencies there were seven agents, one each in the strong and in the weak divisions, and five in the marginal constituencies. See G. O. Comfort, *Professional Politicians, A Study of British Party Agents*, Washington 1958, and Butler and Rose, op. cit., pp. 119–22. An election agent may be the professional agent, the secretary of the constituency party's General Management Committee, or a member of the GMC appointed to that position.

[13] W. J. Clarke, *General Election Report*, October 15, 1964, Kemptown Constituency Labour Party, p. 4.

run for any public office, much less for Parliament. In Gravesend the situation was reversed, the candidate having run in four local and one parliamentary elections whereas the agent had come to his post only six months earlier after serving as assistant agent in a wealthy but weak Labour constituency. In both constituencies there were subtle signs of tension but no overt notice was taken. If differences arose, they were discussed privately, for the British reputation for restraint and civility is well-merited.

1. The candidate

The principal objective of the pre-election campaign is to have the candidate meet personally with as many voters as possible, and to obtain favourable publicity in the local press. Personal canvassing is the method employed to meet the electorate, and notice from the press is sought by attending every conceivable meeting which the local press might cover.

The amount of house-to-house canvassing performed by the British candidate is sometimes surprising to American and other observers from abroad, but there are cogent reasons for the practice. Such canvassing is relatively easy to organise, requiring only the candidate, a neighbourhood political worker, and the most recent copy of the Electoral Register. It is a form of campaigning which need not be prearranged but can be accomplished at times convenient to the candidate. In divisions where the candidate is not a resident, house-to-house canvassing permits him to establish communication with the voters, to assess his impact, and to reduce his sense of being alien. In a pre-election campaign lasting two years, the candidate who visits fifty homes a week would have reached about 10,000 voters and would give the candidate a familiarity with his constituency impossible to acquire in any other way. Another reason for the prevalence of canvassing is its low cost in every respect except the candidate's time. Although financing the formal election campaign is not a problem in marginal constituencies, any technique which permits the candidate to meet the voters without significant expense to the party is likely to continue. In the 1964 election all three candidates engaged in extensive canvassing, with Dennis Hobden, the resident candidate, doing somewhat less than his non-resident counterparts.[14]

[14] A British candidate who has reached 10,000 voters has met at least

Despite the time involved in canvassing, the candidates must meet groups of residents of the divisions with the hope of obtaining suitable notice in the press. If the candidate is not a resident of the division and is known only to the General Management Committee which helped select him, he must meet the constituency party workers. He must also attend meetings of trade unions and of co-operative societies whose traditional affiliation with the Labour Party renders their support especially important.

In the campaign preceding the 1964 election certain types of public meeting made the attendance of the parliamentary candidate almost mandatory. These included meetings dealing with education, pensions, housing and other domestic problems on which Labour had taken a strong position. At all such meetings the candidate was given an opportunity to express his own and his party's views, but these affairs were regarded less as means of reaching an audience than of obtaining publicity. Eighteen months before the election, John Cartwright, then agent in Gravesend, reported that there had been a weekly story in the local press on the Labour candidate ever since his selection six months earlier. Although Dennis Hobden was a native of Kemptown and a member of the Brighton city council, a series of public meetings was organised on his behalf as soon as he was endorsed. The motive for holding the meetings is suggested by a comment published in the local party's Election Report: 'These meetings proved to be of great value in publicising the name of Dennis Hobden to the electorate.'[15]

The effectiveness of the candidate seemed directly related to his availability for constituency campaigning. Here again, Dennis Hobden had the advantage over the others. Albert Murray, the Gravesend candidate, lived about thirty-five miles from the division and visited it two mornings each week for 'coffee meetings' and Sunday morning for canvassing. Occasionally he was able to visit local plants and factories during the day and to meet with groups informally in the evening. He estimated that he spent on the average twelve hours a week in Gravesend in 1962, fifteen in 1963, and between eighteen and twenty in 1964. The Reading candidate, John

[15] W. J. Clarke, op. cit., p. 2.

one-sixth of his electorate. Congressional candidates in the United States could not match this, since American congressional districts contain two to three times more voters than do parliamentary constituencies.

Lee, was able to give far less time to his constituency. He lived thirty miles away and came each weekend for canvassing, but during the week was almost entirely unavailable.

II. The agent

The task of the candidate, however time-consuming, is simple and direct when compared with the responsibilities discharged by the agent. It is the agent who plans the canvassing, arranges the meetings which the candidate attends, and assures the attendance of press representatives. He must also obtain sufficient funds to finance the election campaign, choose and train an election campaign staff, try to strengthen weak wards in the division, and negotiate with the affiliated organisations such as the trade unions and co-operative societies. These duties are easily summarised, but the time and energy needed to handle them are formidable. Furthermore, parliamentary elections do not take place in a vacuum and it is impossible to separate the campaign activities of a general election and the routine work of the constituency organisation. Electing an MP is probably the paramount achievement of any marginal division, but more mundane tasks must be performed. Appointing and mandating the annual conference delegate, electing representatives to local governing bodies, maintaining a permanent party headquarters— these are functions which claim the attention of the party agent, and at certain seasons even take precedence over the parliamentary campaign.

During the long pre-election campaign the agent must bear the main burden of constituency activities, albeit with some assistance. Once a pattern has been established for the campaign activities of the candidate, the agent tends to spend only minimal time with the candidate, and to devote much of his attention to obtaining funds for the campaign. The financial problems of the Labour Party are less stringent than in times past, but agents are still required to give much time to fund-raising.[16] Of the three agents in the election sample, two gave 20 per cent of their time to fund-raising, while

[16] Secretary-agents in twenty of the thirty-six constituencies in the basic study spent from one-sixth to one-third of their time on money-making schemes of one sort or another. Of these twenty constituencies, ten were marginal divisions. The study also showed that over half the income of the

the third gave 50 per cent of his time. Judging from their total expenditures for the year 1962, Gravesend and Reading were more successful in raising political funds than was Kemptown. (This was not the case regarding campaign funds. All three divisions raised and spent 99 per cent of the legal maximum established by the Representation of the People Act, 1949.)

To avoid being inundated by the work of the election campaign, the agent selects a campaign staff composed of officers for transport, publicity and propaganda, meetings, canvassing and the postal vote. During the pre-election campaign, the Labour Party operates regional schools to train constituency leaders for these specialised jobs. The training classes before the 1964 election were held during the first half of 1963, the only problem being that the election did not take place for another eighteen months, with the result that there was considerable turnover among those who had attended the schools.

Two interesting devices were used by agents to strengthen organisation in sections of the constituency where the Labour Party lacked vigour. One was to send a number of workers into the weak wards to get subscribers to the football pool, lottery, or whatever fund-raising scheme received local support. Party supporters and party workers were discovered in this fashion, in some cases enabling the constituency to organise the ward. The second device was to induce a person to run in a local election even if he had little chance of success, merely to locate and encourage party workers by involving them in his campaign.

One service offered political parties by the state is the free postal distribution of one piece of political propaganda from each political party to each voter on the Electoral Register. Usually the candidate's election address is chosen, and to make the address timely it is not prepared until the campaign is well under way. Envelopes to contain the address may be prepared well in advance, but the voters receive the communication immediately before election day. This project, which would be impossible to attempt in an American congressional district, reaches impressive proportions even in a British constituency, where an average of 56,000 names appear on the Electoral Register.

CLPs came from gambling and social events, with emphasis on the former. About one-sixth of the income came from trade union affiliation fees, and one-twelfth from individual membership dues.

The three divisions studied in 1964 had larger than average electorates, with Kemptown having 61,000 names on the register, Reading 59,000, and Gravesend 63,000.

4. *Election campaign activities in the constituency*

The short time-span of the official election campaign in Britain can lead to an erroneous conception of its character. The election campaign is certainly not three weeks of frenetic activity at the end of which the participants are in a state of physical and emotional collapse. British campaign habits are moderate to a degree which American political workers would find quite tame.

One important reason for the restrained character of the official election campaign is the length of the pre-election campaign. Long before the official campaign begins, much time-consuming work has already been accomplished. The canvassing has been going on for as long as two years and sustained efforts have been made to keep the name of the candidate before the eyes of the electorate. The candidate and agent must continue electioneering so that they are not overshadowed by the opposition, but the basic work has been done —or if it has been neglected, the three weeks of the official campaign are not going to matter much. As a result, British campaign managers, even when their candidate is the challenger rather than the incumbent, do not demand that their man maintain a killing pace up to the eve of the election.

British campaign habits and the British philosophy of living contribute to the relaxed pace of the official election campaign. In the constituencies studied, only one meeting was scheduled each evening.[17] The meetings began promptly, either at 7.30 or 8.0 PM, and lasted less than two hours, adjourning in time for at least a short visit to the local pub before the closing time of 10.30. Saturday being the day on which the British shop or relax, in most constituencies, it

[17] This did not apply to the activities of top leaders of the Labour Party who often made a large number of speeches in an afternoon or evening. For example, George Brown, the Deputy Leader of the Labour Party, spoke in Gravesend early in the campaign. He appeared at 8.30 PM to deliver his eleventh speech of the day in as many constituencies in the south-east London and north Kent region. Again, the compactness of parliamentary constituencies made such a schedule possible.

seems, no effort is made to approach the voters personally at this time, although election meetings may be announced and general 'slogans' delivered by handbills and loudspeakers to shopping or sports ground crowds. The day is often used, however, for motorcades. By custom the Conservatives never campaign on Sunday,[18] but this day is frequently put to good use by the Labour Party. In Brighton and Gravesend Sunday morning and early afternoon were favourite times for staging mass canvassing because more people were thought to be at home.[19]

1. The candidate's campaign

All three of the candidates in the study acknowledged the commencement of the official campaign by taking leave from their work. Albert Murray and John Lee moved with their families to their respective constituencies where they stayed with friends. Their election schedules were quite similar, consisting of an early breakfast, reading campaign news in the morning papers, and hearing briefings from the agent on the activities to follow. Following this, the candidates dealt with correspondence, most of which originated from diverse organised groups which wished to learn or influence the candidate's position on specific issues. Often a short stint of canvassing would complete the morning. After lunch, canvassing would be resumed until 4.0 or 5.0 PM. After meeting with the agent to learn of any events of consequence scheduled for the next day, the candidate would have a leisurely tea and be off to an evening meeting, which would undoubtedly end at a reasonable hour.

Canvassing continued to occupy much of the candidate's time during the official campaign, but the frequency of party meetings showed substantial increase. During the campaign Dennis Hobden spoke at thirteen meetings sponsored by the party and at five factory-gate meetings. He also engaged in debate with the Conservative

---

[18] The second week of the 1964 campaign had gone badly for the Conservatives and they broke precedent on Sunday, October 14, 1964, by holding a press conference at which an effort was made by party leaders to rally the party. This effort to salvage the Conservative campaign was not altogether unsuccessful in view of the election outcome.

[19] See Rose, *Politics in England*, op. cit., p. 24.

opponent on two occasions,[20] the third being cancelled because of
his opponent's laryngitis. It was the consensus of all concerned that
the public meeting sponsored by the party was less effective than it
had once been. Rather modest audiences appeared for the meetings
and it was generally agreed that the culprit was television. Exceptions to this were the meetings which national party leaders addressed,
at which crowds of more than 300 persons gathered.

Much has been said about the fine art of heckling in British
electioneering. In contemporary campaigning, curiously, this is
probably a harassment more likely to be encountered by party
leaders than by local candidates, for little was observed in the constituencies studied. Some Conservatives attending Albert Murray's
meetings asked leading questions during question time, but Murray
seemed to enjoy this and was of the opinion that the participation of
the Conservatives added zest to the meetings. Murray made an
effective response to Conservative taunts when a man who identified
himself as a 'working-class Conservative' asked a lengthy question.
Waiting patiently for the questioner to finish, Murray began his
answer by pointing out that the difference between the two parties
was demonstrated by the fact that Labour had selected Murray, a
printer's assistant, as a parliamentary candidate, while the questioner
was sent out by the Conservatives merely to act as a heckler.

Not many years ago the idea of a constituency Labour organisation staging a motorcade would have been preposterous, simply
because few Labour Party members owned cars. All three constituencies used motorcades in 1964 and were inordinately pleased
with themselves for being able to do so. Gravesend was able to send
two motorcades travelling through the district simultaneously on a
memorable Saturday morning. Like all campaign methods, the
motorcade may or may not be particularly effective in the constituency. At least in Britain the motorcade still has the advantage

[20] These were the only confrontations which took place in the three
constituencies, and may have arisen from an unusual informal political club
in the Kemptown division. The 'Friday Club', consisting of the leaders of
the three parties in Brighton, met each Friday night at a local pub for
uninhibited political discussion. The one concession made by the club to the
campaign was to meet at a pub just outside the constituency, and then
adjourn to the apartment of a member. At least one of these meetings was
attended by Hobden and the Conservative candidate; they seemed on
friendly terms with one another.

of novelty, and British campaign managers, like those in America, are disposed to work with the resources at their command. The fact that the regional office of the party had made available a Land Rover equipped with loudspeakers had much to do with the three motorcades used in Gravesend.[21]

II. The agent's campaign

Judging from the activities of the agents in Gravesend, Kemptown and Reading, the agent is concerned during the campaign with the supervising of last-minute canvassing, the distributing of literature, working on the postal vote, and arranging for transportation and workers on election day. It is his task also to make certain that stories about the candidate and the campaign continue to appear regularly in the local press. The agent had assistance in these activities from various party workers, and it is remarkable how much time the key workers can spend on the campaign even though they do not take a leave of absence from their jobs.

The importance of adequate press coverage is recognised by candidate and agent alike, although the party's relations with the press are more likely to be influenced by the agent than by the candidate. Despite the reputation for partisanship in the national British press,[22] the local press in the divisions studied made at least an effort to be fair. The Kemptown Election Report states that: 'Press publicity was good and the election was kept alive. There was not one issue of the *Argus* ... which did not carry some reference to the contest in Kemptown. Our relations with the press were good at all times, and our appreciation must be expressed to the *Argus* for the assignment to the candidate of its special reporter, Mr Jack

---

[21] The motorcades in Gravesend indicated either an unfamiliarity with their purpose or the restraint of Kentish-men generally. The occupants of the cars did not wave to passers by nor did the drivers use the horn to attract attention. Except for the signs attached to the roofs of the cars and the candidate standing in the back of the Land Rover, it seemed that the object of the motorcade was to move through the countryside as unobtrusively as possible.

[22] The *Daily Express* announced in 1964 that it was taking a poll as it had in past general elections, but that it would not publish the results until it showed the Conservative Party to be in the lead.

Frost, who proved to be most co-operative.'[23] Although the local papers in Reading and Gravesend did not go so far as to assign special reporters to the Labour candidates, the party in both divisions expressed satisfaction with the press treatment they received. In all instances the owners, publishers and editors of the local papers were considered by Labour to have a Conservative bias, but many of the reporters were thought to have strong Labour sympathies.

Despite heroic efforts and good intentions, the best that can be said of the canvassing done during the election campaign was that it was uneven. Some sections of the constituencies which were unpromising for Labour were not invaded, while other areas where Labour was strong received as many as three calls when the first two had elicited no response. The canvassing done just before the election was particularly significant since one objective was to determine how many persons intended to vote on election day, and whether these persons could be expected to support Labour. In some cases the voter would say outright whether he would vote for the Labour candidate, but often the attitude of the voter had to be inferred from his remarks. As might be expected, the wish was sometimes father to the thought. In Kemptown, for example, 27,180 promised commitments to Labour were reported, but Dennis Hobden received only 22,308 votes the following day. Another goal of the election canvass was to distribute political literature and induce party supporters to place in their front window a picture of the candidate or the name of the party. This was particularly stressed in houses located on main streets and bus routes in the constituency.

A most important objective of the general canvass was to locate the Labour supporters on the Electoral Register who were eligible for postal voting.[24] Analyses of the 1959 election agreed that superior Conservative Party organisation caused its candidates to receive a disproportionately large share of the postal vote. In constituencies where the vote was extremely close, it was estimated that this

---

[23] W. J. Clarke, op. cit., p. 3.

[24] Persons eligible for the postal vote include those 'likely to be unable to go in person to the polling station by reason of the general nature of my employment, by reason of blindness, or by reason of physical incapacity, or owing to a change in residence since the Electoral Register was made up'. British law even provides that if the nature of his occupation, service or

advantage may have given the Conservatives from five to fifteen additional seats in the House of Commons.[25] In 1964 Transport House was determined that Labour would not again permit such an advantage to the Conservatives, and throughout the campaign great attention was paid to the postal vote. (It is not only necessary for a party to locate those eligible for the postal vote, but also to ensure that they know the name of its candidate, for they will usually not be subject to the efforts made by the party to make clear the identity of the candidate.) In this regard Reading and Gravesend did a more thorough job than Kemptown, where only 400 postal votes out of 1,446 were processed by the Labour Party. This figure comes to only 28 per cent of the postal vote, and in view of the delicate margin of seven votes by which Dennis Hobden was elected, the postal votes were crucial.[26]

III. Election day activities

Extensive planning and supervision is needed to control party activities on election day. The goal of every party is to get every one of its supporters to the polls, and to do this party workers knock at the doors of tardy voters and provide transportation for those who wish or require it. In the Labour organisations studied, ward headquarters or 'committee rooms' were set up to keep a record of those who had voted, to dispatch workers to knock at doors and drivers to

[25] Butler and Rose, op. cit., p. 143. There was a suggestion after the Leyton by-election that the narrow Conservative margin might well have been the result of superior organisation in regard to postal voting. See *Observer*, January 24, 1965.

[26] Given the differences in class composition of the Conservative and Labour Parties, it is possible that a 75–25 split in favour of the Conservatives would be an accurate representation of the voters eligible for the postal vote in some divisions. Conversely, in a division where a major slum clearance project had been instituted since publication of the register, an accurate ratio might be 75–25 in favour of Labour. See also Butler and King, op. cit., pp. 22–7.

employment is likely to cause a person to be at sea or out of the United Kingdom, the person can apply for a proxy to vote for him. These provisions are quite permissive, but there are limitations. Persons on holiday, or those who move some distance within a big city and have not moved across the city boundary, must vote at their usual or former district of residence or forfeit their vote.

transport. In previous elections tardy voters were not approached until late afternoon, but in 1964 Kemptown began reminding such voters in the late morning of election day. This aggressive effort to turn out the Labour vote may have played a part in the outcome, for in the constituency the Labour vote increased from 19,665 in 1959 to 22,308 in 1964, even though the proportion on the Electoral Register who voted decreased from 75 per cent in 1959 to 72 per cent in 1964. The transport facilities at the disposal of Labour in 1964 may have affected the decision also. The constituency's Election Report records: 'Transportation was handled by Councillor R. M. Millyard, and it turned out to be a much greater and onerous task than was originally anticipated. . . . We reached a peak of well over 300 cars, calling for skill and initiative in their control and allocation. This task was carried out very admirably under the circumstances which were not at all easy due to the fact of the large numbers of offers of cars which came in rapidly at a late stage.'[27]

TABLE 3.1. *Election results 1959 and 1964 in the three constituencies surveyed*

| | 1959 | | 1964 | | |
	Con.	Lab.	Con.	Lab.	Lib.
Gravesend	27,124	24,962	25,362	26,074	6,015
	52.1%	*47.9%*	*44.1%*	*45.4%*	*10.5%*
Reading	26,314	22,372	20,815	20,805	5,759
	54.1%	*45.9%*	*43.93%*	*43.91%*	*12.16%*
Kemptown	25,411	19,665	22,301	22,308	—
	56.4%	*43.6%*	*49.992%*	*50.008%*	—

5. Results and campaign comparisons

Labour's success in winning the Kemptown division of Brighton was striking evidence of the effectiveness of the constituency's campaign efforts. There was no strong Labour tradition in Kemptown, in the rest of Brighton or in the county of Sussex as a whole, and Dennis Hobden was the first Labour MP ever elected in a Sussex seat. The local Labour organisation lacked a full-time salaried agent, and it was in a poor financial condition. In recent years its statements of accounts had ranged from 20 to 25 per cent of those in Reading and Gravesend. During the summer of 1964, with a general election

[27] W. J. Clarke, op. cit., p. 4.

looming in the autumn, the General Management Committee was considering the advisability of discontinuing the telephone service as an economy measure. Since 1959 there had been no noticeable migration in or out of Kemptown. The population had remained almost constant, the Electoral Register showing an increase of 950 names over 1959. The incumbent MP, David James, had held the seat for the Conservatives since 1959. He was an Old Etonian who had gained considerable publicity since 1962 as an investigator into the existence of the Loch Ness monster.[28] During the campaign David James received good coverage in the dailies with a story of his drum playing with a musical group in Brighton,[29] while another paper carried a sketch and a short article depicting his address to his adoption meeting in a room at the Royal Pavilion in Brighton.[30] Very few back-benchers standing for re-election received as much national publicity.

One change in the political climate in Kemptown since the 1959 election of possible benefit to Labour was the establishment of the University of Sussex. When mass canvasses were held, the majority of participants were students from the University, and some faculty members were active in Kemptown CLP. Yet not even the university, or the agent's claim of improved organisation, or the candidate's long association with the division can altogether explain a shift of 6.4 per cent—almost double that of the rest of southern England. The election of the Labour candidate was exceedingly close, and seven recounts were required before the final result gave Hobden a majority of seven votes. Kemptown was the weakest division, measured by the 1959 election results, in which Labour was successful in a straight fight in 1964.

Ian Mikardo had represented Reading in the House of Commons from 1945 until his defeat in 1959. He had barely won in 1955, garnering only 50.2 per cent of the vote cast. In 1959 the swing against Labour was 4.3 per cent—four times the national average.[31]

---

[28] David James, "We Find That There is Some Unidentified Animate Object in Loch Ness", *Observer*, May 17, 1964.

[29] *Daily Mirror*, *Daily Sketch* and *Daily Express*, September 30, 1964.

[30] *Daily Telegraph*, September 30, 1964.

[31] In recognition of his previous contributions to the Labour Party, Mikardo was selected as the 1964 candidate for Poplar, an east London constituency which gave him a majority of more than 14,000.

Reading enjoyed a number of advantages not available to Kemp-town, among them a recent Labour MP and an experienced, full-time, salaried agent. Although the local organisation had been nearly insolvent when the present agent took office, its financial condition was now adequate. The incumbent Conservative, who was elected in 1959, had built no great personal reputation and was considered a personable but undistinguished backbencher. The Labour candi-date had been selected as early as January 1962, and he had been canvassing and 'nursing' the constituency for more than two-and-a-half years. The pre-election campaign was intensive and aggressive, and thoroughly organised. Despite these advantages, the vagaries of politics denied Labour the decision in Reading by ten votes. Reading became an 'if only' division for Labour as Kemptown was for the Conservative Party.

Gravesend was a constituency which the Labour Party was particularly desirous of winning. Because this division was con-sidered a natural Labour seat by the top leaders of the party, it seemed to assume symbolic importance in their eyes. The division had been won by Labour in 1945, but in 1947 the incumbent was expelled from the House of Commons for selling privileged informa-tion to the press. From choosing an MP with too little principle, Gravesend went to the other extreme in the selection of Sir Richard Acland as its member. He won the 1947 by-election and held Gravesend for Labour in 1950 and 1951. In 1955, just before the general election, Sir Richard resigned his seat and in the subsequent election stood as an Independent Labour candidate running on a unilateral disarmament platform. He was defeated, as was the Labour candidate, and Peter Kirk was elected as the first Conserva-tive MP from Gravesend in years. Kirk held the seat in the 1955 and 1959 general elections, the Gravesend Conservative Association wisely permitting him some discretion. He was a mild rebel at the time of the Suez crisis and was one of twenty-seven Conservatives who abstained from voting at the close of the debate on the Profumo affair in June 1963.

The CLP in Gravesend was entirely prepared for the 1964 election. In 1959 Labour had polled 48 per cent of the vote in a straight fight, and 1964 found the division with a full-time salaried agent and a good financial condition. The party had over 2,000 members com-pared with 1,400 in Reading and 1,085 in Kemptown. Peter Kirk had undoubtedly built up a personal following during his ten years as MP, but in Albert Murray the Gravesend CLP had made an astute selection. Murray was chosen and endorsed by June 1962, and came to the constituency an average of three times weekly from that date until September 28, 1964, when he remained permanently. Although there had been a change of agents, the all-important task of administering the postal vote was pursued vigorously, as were other campaign activities. The importance Transport House attached to Gravesend was revealed by the quality of speakers sent into the constituency. George Brown, the Deputy Leader of the Labour Party, spoke in Gravesend on September 28, and Harold Wilson, the Party Leader, spoke on September 29. On October 6, Lord Attlee, frail but determined at the age of eighty-one, arrived to speak on behalf of Albert Murray, who was also supported by Kenneth Robinson, now Minister of Health in the Wilson cabinet, Tom Driberg, MP from Barking and member of the National Executive Committee of the party, and Robert Mellish, MP from Bermondsey. The speakers sent by Transport House to Reading and Kemptown were not undistinguished, but clearly they were less noteworthy than those sent to Gravesend. With all the attention given the constituency, Albert Murray managed to carry Gravesend, but his majority of 712 was not overwhelming.

6. *Importance of CLP campaigns*

The campaigns developed by constituency party organisations are important because of their impact on the outcome of a general election. The general elections of 1950, 1951 and 1955 were so close that the addition of a few Labour seats, perhaps through more effective postal voting activity, might have altered the course of political events which immediately followed. Just as there are general elections with very close margins, so are there close constituency elections. In 1964 the Labour Party won or lost twenty-five seats by less than 500 votes, and in 1966 the same could be said of sixteen seats.

Many more seats are potentially liable to shift from one party to another than actually do so. Thus, in 1966 the Labour Party won seventeen seats in which it had polled from 30.3 to 41.6 per cent of the vote in the 1964 general election. One of these seats was

Hampstead, where Labour had attracted only 28.3 per cent of the vote in a three-way contest in 1959. Without question many elements are involved in a constituency campaign over and above the condition of party organisation. Other factors contributing to the success or failure of the constituency campaign include the calibre of candidate and agent, their skill and experience, population trends in the division, the quality of the national campaign, and, of course, good fortune. Therefore, it is not possible to claim that organisation alone is the deciding factor in close elections; nor is it fair to aver that organisation is a negligible quantity.

Apart from its avowed purpose of influencing election results, the campaign clearly performs additional functions in the British political system. The small constituencies of Britain allow politics to be personalised in a fashion unknown in the United States. It is true that national party leaders can be seen by voters on television, but this is a different experience from having the parliamentary candidate himself stand on the doorstep directly soliciting the support of the voter. The impression of strong voter interest in the campaign was certainly gained in the closely contested campaigns of Reading, Gravesend and Kemptown, where all three communities responded strongly to the efforts of the parties. Perhaps more than his American counterpart, the British voter is sensitive to the fact that, with the exception of the candidate, if he wins, and the agent if he is salaried, political workers donate their time and energy for no remuneration and without personal ulterior motive.

The campaign also serves to unify and strengthen the constituency parties. In the three divisions studied, the agent or candidate could point to instances of party members who ordinarily did not get on well, working together during the campaign without outward sign of tension. In marginal constituency parties all considerations are sublimated to the common wish for victory. Satisfaction is also expressed, particularly by the agents, over the number of new party workers who participate in the campaign. While admitting that local elections lack the excitement of the general election, division officials state that their constituency party is invigorated by the campaign and that the momentum of success, which characterised the efforts of the three divisions under observation, will carry over to subsequent elections.

4

Factionalism in the Labour Party

IN A SELECTIVE bibliography on British political parties Richard Rose comments: 'No one has dealt at any length in print with factionalism as an integral part of the two-party system in Britain.'[1] The scholar who makes such a study will not lack material on the Labour Party, for its literature is permeated with explicit and implicit considerations of factionalism. Indeed, there seems to be no aspect of the Labour Party which has not been subject to factional dispute. Sharp disagreement persists among members over the history of the party, its present status and its future. Controversy accompanies the discussion of such topics as the economic and political philosophy of the party, its response to secular changes in British society and to Britain's altered position in world affairs. The purpose of the Labour Party as a political organisation is disputed, and bitter debate occurs in the consideration of the powers exercised by party institutions. Arguments over specific questions of foreign and defence policies reach a level of virulence and animosity seldom associated with the British temperament.

No basic question relating to the organisation and operation of the Labour Party has been fully resolved by a settlement acceptable to all segments of the party. This was true even in the early days, when the Labour Representation Committee, formed in 1900, chose to reject the ideology and tactics of Marxian socialism in favour of parliamentary democratic socialism. In succeeding generations, new

---

[1] Since compiling his bibliography, Rose has produced a useful analysis on the theme of factionalism entitled "Parties, Factions, and Tendencies in Britain", op. cit.

issues developed and accommodations were made, but in virtually every instance there was a frustrated and dissatisfied minority which, albeit subsiding temporarily, reopened the conflict when an occasion presented itself. Since the end of the Second World War, the party has frequently been rent by dissension, and the contemporary Labour Party, whether in or out of power, creates an impression of turbulence and inability to sustain internal unity. The best that it seems able to achieve is to maintain an uneasy discipline within the Parliamentary Labour Party, and this only in regard to voting in the House of Commons. The extra-parliamentary activities of Labour MPs, and the behaviour of militant party members in trade unions and constituency organisations, are constant reminders of the divisive forces within the Labour movement.

1. *Sources of tension within the Labour Party*

An American observer can find manifold causes for the factionalism which aggravates the problems of the Labour Party. One unfailing source of disagreement within the party is ideological in nature, stemming from the commitment to socialist politics which pervaded the early years of the party. It is written into the Party Constitution, and continues to influence many party members. Controversy is incorporated into the party through its federated structure of trade unions and constituency parties, and by the distribution of power among the Annual Conference, the National Executive Committee and the Parliamentary Labour Party. In addition, the constitution and standing orders provide many opportunities for arguments over interpretation. Ever since 1900, attitudes have evolved which tend to de-emphasise unity as a party value and to foster a political style which engenders contention and acrimony among party members. Then, too, the status of the secondary party in the British party system has led to the introspection and recrimination on which internecine strife flourishes.

i. Ideological basis of Labour factionalism

The struggle over the policy orientation of the Labour Party began with the inception of the party. The meeting in February 1900 of trade unions and socialist societies which established the Labour

Representation Committee (LRC), from which the Labour Party eventually grew, considered two policy proposals. One proposal would have pledged the new LRC to a role similar to that of a political pressure group acting on behalf of the trade unions, while the other would have dedicated the LRC to the doctrine of revolutionary socialism. Neither proposal was acceptable, and the LRC solved the dilemma by adopting a policy so general that all present at the meeting could approve it for the moment.[2]

Some observers of the Labour Party declare that the course of action followed at the first meeting of the LRC has been repeated again and again throughout the party's history, to the disadvantage of the doctrinaire socialists. Miliband writes:

> Revisionist Right and fundamental Left are not the only parties to the debate; there is also the Centre, whose main purpose it is to keep the Labour Party within the bounds of Labourism, and whose main attribute is the invention of formulas that might mean all things to all men. . . . Such appeals overlook the fact that *genuine* compromise between revisionism on the one hand, and socialist purposes on the other, is impossible; and that any verbal compromise which may be reached on the basis of ingenious formulas . . . ensures, in practice, the predominance of policies favoured by a revisionist leadership.[3]

The right, centre, and left groupings seen by Miliband in the Labour Party may be present, but, as he admits, it is a rare situation in which the centre and right fail to control positions of power within the party and to take initiatives which the left can oppose but seldom defeat. Thus the controversies within the Labour Party are appropriately viewed as taking place between broadly based moderate and narrowly based left attitudes.

Miliband's dictum that honest compromise between revisionist and socialist goals is impossible can be taken as an accurate description of the posture of the Labour left. Issues have changed over the years, but the fundamental schism between doctrinaire socialism

[2] Frank Bealey and Henry Pelling, *Labour and Politics 1900–1906*, London 1958, pp. 24–31; Robert E. Dowse, *Left in the Centre*, London and Evanston 1966, pp. 9–10; Philip Poirier, *The Advent of the Labour Party*, London and New York 1958, pp. 82–4; Pelling, op. cit., pp. 119–23.

[3] Miliband, op. cit., pp. 344–5.

and pragmatic reform, between a 'socialist' foreign policy and a British foreign policy, has not narrowed.[4] The struggle is continuous, and not even the responsibilities of power have sufficed to restrain it. There has been opposition within the party to the administration of the National Health Service by the Attlee governments, to such foreign policy proposals as the Marshall Plan and NATO. More recently, Harold Wilson has been the target of harsh criticism from the Labour left because of his government's support of American policy in Vietnam and on his prices and incomes policy. Out of power, the Labour Party was torn by bitterness over the dissipation of its huge majority of 1945, over the question of German rearmament in 1953, and over the decision of the Conservative government to manufacture hydrogen bombs in 1955. After Hugh Gaitskell's proposal in 1959 that Clause IV of the Party Constitution be revised, the debate over the purpose, extent and techniques of nationalisation monopolised the attention of the party. The agony of the unilateral disarmament question, which had been growing since 1957, gripped the Labour Party in 1960 and 1961, and revived the debate over the relationship between the Annual Conference and the Parliamentary Labour Party. Joining EEC might have become a divisive issue in 1962, except that it did not provide a clear choice between the left and moderate wings of the party. Hugh Gaitskell, along with a number of prominent moderates, opposed British entry into EEC, as did almost all members of the Labour left.

The class system in Britain has left a mark on the Labour Party, as it has on every other British political institution. From its beginning, the Labour Party has rejected the Marxian doctrine of class warfare. Nevertheless, the party was formed in response to class divisions in British society and to afford industrial workers a means of political expression. For many years, the special association of the Labour Party with the working class was an accepted norm of British politics, even if many members of this class voted Conservative. Despite some alterations during the first half of the century in the distribution of wealth, the changes were of insufficient magnitude to challenge Keir Hardie's statement in 1910: 'The population of these islands is roughly 43 millions, of whom 1 and ¼ millions are rich, 3 millions are comfortable, and 39 millions are poor, and of

[4] See Beer, op. cit., pp. 217–41, for an extended treatment of recent policy disputes within the Labour Party.

these half are very poor. It is to remedy and redress that condition of things that we exist.'[5]

However static the British economy may have been before 1950, significant changes have occurred during the last fifteen years. Thus, Crosland notes:

> Between 1951 and 1959 the number of middle class workers increased by a million, and the number of manual wage-earners declined by half a million; consequently, the salariat rose from 30 to 34 per cent of the population . . . average consumption per head, which scarcely moved between 1945 and 1951, rose by 20 per cent between 1951 and 1958. . . . The more prosperous half of the working class (which constitutes one third of the electorate) doubled its ownership of most durable consumer goods between 1956 and 1959. By the latter date, 85 per cent of such households owned a TV set, 44 per cent a washing machine, 32 per cent a car, 16 per cent a refrigerator, and 35 per cent owned or were buying a house. . . . Thus a consumption pattern which tends to erase class distinctions has spread most rapidly in a group which was already near a class dividing line.[6]

Crosland goes on to argue the need for Labour to change its image 'in terms of issues, attitudes, and class identification' if it hopes to take advantage of the secular changes taking place in British society.

The Labour left will have none of this opportunism. Some, like Richard Titmuss, do not deny the increased affluence of British society, but dwell instead on the continued concentration of economic power in Britain. Miliband also ignores or considers irrelevant economic and social improvement, and is critical of Labour leaders who wish to modify the class bias of the party in order to appeal to broader segments of the electorate. Commenting on Hugh Gaitskell's statement that 'somehow we let the Tories get away with the monstrous falsehood that *we* are a class party and they are *not*', Miliband writes:

[5] Quoted in Butler and Rose, op. cit., p. 199.

[6] Crosland, *The Conservative Enemy*, op. cit., pp. 151–2. See also Rita Hinden, op. cit., pp. 104–8, and Butler and Rose, op. cit., pp. 9–16. A contrary view is presented in John H. Goldthorpe and David Lockwood, "Affluence and the British Class Structure", *The Sociological Review*, New Series Vol. II, No. 2, July 1963.

In fact, it is not a monstrous falsehood for the Tories to claim that the Labour Party is a class party. . . . But the Labour Party is also a party whose leaders have always sought to escape from the implications of its class character by pursuing what they deem to be 'national' policies: these policies have regularly turned to the detriment of the working classes and to the advantage of Conservatism. Nor can it be otherwise in a society whose essential characteristic remains class division.[7]

The moderate wing of the Labour Party considers class distinctions to be less relevant than was true two decades ago, but the left wing steadfastly affirms that traditional principles of socialism are still germane, and that abandonment of this doctrine is heresy. To Miliband, the basic question is 'whether the Labour Party is to be concerned with attempts at a more efficient and humane administration of a capitalist society; or whether it is to adapt itself to the task of creating a socialist one'.[8] Crosland considers adaptation rather differently when he states: 'If British socialism succeeds in adapting itself and its doctrines to the mid-twentieth century, it will still find plenty of genuine battles left to fight. Besides, it might even get back into power, and have a chance to win them.'[9]

ii. Structural basis of Labour factionalism

The structure of the Labour Party has not served to stifle ideological controversy, but rather to encourage it.[10] The Party Constitution alone is a source of dissension, with its stipulations of conditions of membership, and allocations of power between trade unions and constituency parties, and between the Annual Conference and the National Executive Committee. Undoubtedly the goal of the constitution was the establishment of stability and continuity in party operations, but the constitution assumes a consensus within the party which does not exist, and it is usual that far-reaching amendments

[7] Miliband, op. cit., pp. 343–4. See also Richard M. Titmuss, *Income Distribution and Social Change*, London and Toronto 1962.

[8] Miliband, p. 344.

[9] Crosland, *The Conservative Enemy*, op. cit., p. 126.

[10] Rose, *Politics in England*, Boston op. cit., p. 145: 'The structural complexities of the Labour Party have not been the cause of its difficulties; they only intensify them.'

to the Party Constitution are proposed every three years.[11] In 1962, amendments were introduced that would have limited the independence of the Parliamentary Labour Party, altered the method of choosing the Leader of the Labour Party, limited the powers of the National Executive Committee regarding proscription and endorsement of parliamentary candidates, and radically changed the power relationship between the trade unions and the constituency parties on the National Executive Committee.[12]

The initiative for offering amendments to the Party Constitution comes largely from the Labour left, since the left complains that the present distribution of power within the party works to the advantage of the right and moderate factions. It is a fact that the moderate wing of the party dominates the Annual Conference and the National Executive Committee through the overwhelming numerical strength of the moderate trade unions in conference voting.[13] The moderate faction also dominates the Parliamentary Labour Party because most marginal and strong constituency parties follow a moderate policy line.[14] Its minority position in the party's centres of power does not deter the Labour left from advancing its ideas or seeking to enhance its influence by changes in the Party Constitution. Access to the making of Labour Party policy is permitted by the constitution which recognises three different centres of policy determination, and the Labour left has exploited this.

During the first years of the Labour Party, divisions between the trade unions and other federated organisations were considerable. Not only did the unions have the votes to overcome any opposition from other segments of the party, but until the end of the Second World War the unions consistently adopted a cautious and undogmatic attitude toward questions of party policy. In this regard, the following comment by Beatrice Webb remained relevant for decades after it was written:

[11] *Labour Party Constitution*, Clause xiii, "Alteration to Constitution and Rules".

[12] *Agenda, Labour Party Annual Conference, 1962*, pp. 7–36.

[13] Voting strength at Annual Conference is related to party membership. Direct membership through constituency parties accounted for 15 per cent of the total vote at the 1963 Conference, while indirect membership through trade unions comprised the remaining 85 per cent of a total of 6.5 million votes.

[14] See Chapter 2, esp. pp. 58–61.

The middle and working class socialists are in a quandary. They are hopelessly outnumbered within the Labour Party, and whenever they protest they are voted down. They have pledged themselves to working class representation as part of the process of making the manual labourer conscious of his disinherited condition, and of arousing, in the working class, faith in the class struggle. But they are by their adhesion to the present Parliamentary Party bolstering up a fraud—pretending to the outside world that these respectable but reactionary Trade Union officials are the leaders of the Social Revolution.[15]

The notion of general antagonism between trade unions and constituency party socialists has been assaulted from two directions in the past twenty years. During this period support from the trade unions for National Executive Committee policies has not been monolithic. The highest level of trade union opposition to the NEC was reached on the unilateralist resolutions of the 1960 Annual Conference when the party leadership was twice defeated.[16] There is now an identifiable group of unions which can be linked with the Labour left, although not on every issue. In addition, the radical nature of the constituency parties has come under dispute. It is now claimed that only on rare occasions have a majority of the constituency parties opposed a majority of the trade union vote and that substantial minorities of the constituency parties have supported the party platform on all issues.[17] Careful analysis of the vote on unilateralist resolutions at the 1960 and 1961 Annual Conferences showed that roughly two-thirds of the constituency parties supported the NEC when it was defeated in 1960 and when it won in 1961.[18]

It can be said that, in recent years, a blending of the traditional policy orientations of the unions and the constituency parties has taken place which has reduced but not removed this source of factionalism.

[15] *Beatrice Webb's Diaries, 1919–24*, p. 19, quoted in McKenzie, op. cit., pp. 472–3.
[16] McKenzie, op. cit., pp. 612–17.
[17] Harrison, op. cit., pp. 211–13 and pp. 238–9.
[18] Hindell and Williams, op. cit., pp. 310–11.

III. Traditional basis of Labour factionalism

Empirical data as well as impressionistic evidence point to the relative unimportance of unity as a value within the Labour Party. A recent social survey asked working-class supporters of the party to rank in importance sixteen statements describing British political parties and their policies. The characteristic 'has a united team of top leaders' was placed in eighth position by Labour respondents, with 20 per cent rating this as the most important party characteristic. Working-class respondents who had not supported Labour in the 1959 general election gave this characteristic a rank of fourth, with 29 per cent rating it as the most important.[19]

Unity is important enough to the Labour Party to be a frequent subject of discussion, but with an ambivalency which justifies the lack of unity while appealing for a greater amount of it.[20] This inconsistency can be inferred from C. A. R. Crosland who suggests at one point that there may be a relationship between Labour factionalism and 'the increasingly uncertain image of the Party', yet a few pages later writes: 'Whilst we should . . . conduct our disputes in a more temperate and even comradely tone of voice, we should also seek to bring them to a more definite conclusion so as to let the country know precisely where we stand.'[21] To other Labour members also, conflict within the party may confuse the electorate, but this is equally true of compromises within the party. Even members of the moderate wing seem to hold that unity is a fine thing and that there should be more of it, but only after due allowance is made for the temperament of the party, its democratic organisation, and the need to establish clear policies. The idea of party unity is not considered by the Labour left, since the very subject is foreclosed. As the minority within the party, the left wing must constantly strive to shift the balance of power toward itself and to commit the party to socialist solutions for foreign and domestic problems. Support of unity as a party goal would involve approval of the *status quo* in terms of power and policy. The left wing of the Labour Party must therefore stress the overwhelming importance of socialist principle, the merit of democratic debate, the value of divergent political opinions, and the utility of 'ginger groups' within the party. In

[19] Abrams and Rose, op. cit., pp. 13, 16.
[20] Phillips, op. cit., pp. 19–20.
[21] Crosland, op. cit., pp. 149, 156.

championing these views, the left wing is joined by many moderate party members to whom the Labour Party traditions of freedom and tolerance are particularly meaningful.[22]

The Labour left can accept neither the distribution of power within the party nor its official policies. The party leaders who devise and execute Labour policies are equally unacceptable to the left wing. The Leader of the Labour Party who is elected by a majority vote of the Parliamentary Labour Party and is *ex officio* a member of the National Executive Committee is almost always the object of left-wing rancour. To a very great extent the Labour Party Leader symbolises the power asserted by moderates who control the centres of power within the party. Thus he becomes a logical target for members who oppose party policy. Some Labour Leaders—one thinks particularly of Ramsay MacDonald—were bitterly criticised during their period of leadership.[23] Harold Wilson enjoyed an eighteen-month honeymoon with the left just after his election as Party Leader in February 1963,[24] but he has been under constant criticism by some segments of the left wing since October 1964 when he formed his first administration.[25]

[22] See Chapter 2, pp. 35–41.

[23] Objection to Ramsay MacDonald extended back many years before he left the Labour Party to form a National Government in August 1931. For a left-wing evaluation of the first MacDonald government in 1924, see Miliband, op. cit., pp. 100–13.

[24] Wilson had endeared himself to the left in 1951 when, along with Aneurin Bevan and John Freeman, he resigned from the Attlee government. After Gaitskell's refusal to accept as PLP policy the unilateralist resolution passed by the 1960 Annual Conference, Wilson opposed Gaitskell for the post of Party Leader, and in 1962 he stood against George Brown for the post of Deputy Leader. Whatever Wilson's motives for these actions, espousal of the left was clearly not among them. This alignment with the left was dictated by expedience, with the left needing a candidate and Wilson needing a following. This previous association enhanced Wilson's popularity with the left when he sought the post of Leader in January 1963, after the death of Gaitskell.

[25] The Labour government's domestic policies regarding old age pensions and the budget announced in April 1964 have been assailed by the left, as have foreign policy issues involving Vietnam, Malaysia and the Congo. Leadership in these attacks has been furnished by *Tribune* and a new publication of the left entitled *The Week*. See Ivan Yates, "Thunder From the Left", *Observer*, February 21, 1965. See also Edward Janosik, "Britain's New Labour Leaders", *Orbis*, Vol. III, No. 3, Autumn 1963, pp. 524–5.

The National Executive Committee is also the object of attack by the Labour left. Although it is the Party Leader who is held responsible for presumed shortcomings of the Parliamentary Labour Party, the NEC is required to defend the manner in which it has handled the internal affairs of the party. In recent years controversies have arisen over the responsibility of the NEC to enforce the Party Constitution and to endorse parliamentary candidates.[26] The Labour left has alleged that the NEC has used its powers to discriminate against the left wing, particularly in regard to the Young Socialist organisation and to the endorsing of unilateralists as parliamentary candidates. The NEC has also been attacked by the left wing for its control of the agenda of the Annual Conference in respect to the topics debated and the content of resolutions submitted to the conference.

The style of politics within the Labour Party has been affected by the enduring opposition of the left wing to party leadership. No loss of status within the party is incurred by members who engage in factional dispute, since no reluctance is shown in displaying differences with one another. This statement is as applicable to trade-union leaders and to MPs as it is to the rank-and-file members. Disagreements are openly admitted and paraded before the British public, on television, in the press, and at the Annual Conference. There is such open expectation of controversy within the Labour Party that when peace prevails many members express honest surprise as well as pleasure. The 1962 conference was considered sedate by most delegates because Gaitskell's position on the EEC issue threw the left wing into disarray. When George Brown acknowledged the excellence of Wilson's leadership over the previous six months, the 1963 conference rose with wild applause at this unexampled magnanimity.[27]

[26] Clause VIII 2 (b) requires the NEC: 'To enforce the Constitution, Standing Orders, and Rules of the Party and to take any action it deems necessary for such purposes, whether by way of disaffiliation of an organisation, or expulsion of an individual, or otherwise. Any such action shall be reported to the next Annual Conference of the Party.' Clause IX stipulates: 'The selection of Labour Candidates for Parliamentary Elections shall not be regarded as completed until the name of the person selected has been placed before a meeting of the National Executive Committee, and his or her selection has been duly endorsed.'

[27] Brown, who had been defeated for the post of Leader in February 1963, said: 'Though I had my doubts, perhaps, about the way we reached

IV.   Historical basis of Labour factionalism

The inability of the Labour Party to control the government of Britain for an extended period of time constitutes another cause of faction within the party. Frequent electoral defeats not only deprive the party leadership of the prestige and authority of cabinet office,[28] but cause party members to blame one another for the party's lack of success. Labour's tremendous victory in 1945 was interpreted by left-wing writers as 'a clear mandate for a big leap forward' and a basis for believing that 'now at last was to begin the transformation of Britain into a socialist commonwealth'.[29] Disillusionment swept through the party with the sharp reduction of the Labour majority in 1950 and the Conservative victory in 1951. Further Conservative victories in 1955 and 1959 exacerbated the disillusionment. The 1959 Conservative victory was especially difficult to accept, for there had been indications early in the campaign that the Conservatives were getting the worst of it.[30]

The Conservatives' victory in 1959 increased their absolute majority in the House of Commons to 101 and was the signal for a mood of introspection to pervade the Labour Party. Self-analysis added another dimension to the struggle between the unilateral and multilateral disarmers, for the revisionists unfailingly supported the multilateralists while the fundamentalists were equally committed to the goals of the unilateralists. The revisionist movement received impetus from Hugh Gaitskell's proposal at the 1959 Annual Conference that a section of Clause IV of the Party Constitution dealing with public ownership be modified so as to avoid having Labour's position misrepresented by the Conservative Party.[31] Gaitskell's proposal was the climax of a low-grade argument that had existed

[28] Rose, *Politics in England*, op. cit., pp. 145–6.
[29] See R. H. S. Crossman, op. cit., p. 4; and Miliband, op. cit., p. 285.
[30] Butler and Rose, op. cit., pp. 58–61.
[31] Clause IV Section 4 reads: 'To secure for the workers by hand or brain the full fruits of their industry and the most equitable distribution thereof that may be possible, upon the basis of the common ownership of the means of production, distribution, and exchange, and the best obtainable system of popular administration and control of each industry or service.'

our leadership decision six months ago, I am very glad today, sincerely and honestly, to pay tribute to the way we are being led now'; *Labour Party Annual Conference Report, 1963*, p. 208.

in the party for some years regarding the continued relevance of the socialist dogma that was adopted at the end of the First World War. The Clause IV controversy produced a quantity of literature but little else. Gaitskell's attempt to amend the Party Constitution was not successful, and this issue was replaced as a divisive force by unilateralism. The onset of the 1964 general election imposed some restraints on Labour factionalism, as did the narrow margin of the Labour victory. Ingredients of continuing strife still remain within the party, however, and further defeats will undoubtedly act as a catalytic agent upon them.[32]

2. Factionalism in Constituency Labour Parties

In view of the number and strength of the centrifugal forces within the Labour Party, two hypotheses were proposed for testing by field research. One suggested that factionalism in divisional parties was a major handicap to the local parties in organisation work and in election. The second hypothesis attempted a distinction between different types of factionalism, advancing the proposition that factionalism in strong and in marginal constituencies tended to be personal in nature, while that in weak constituencies tended to be ideological. Both hypotheses were based on the assumption that factionalism was a major characteristic of constituency parties, reflecting disputes between national party leaders at the Annual Conference and within the Parliamentary Labour Party.

i. Incidence of factionalism in Constituency Labour Parties

Interviews with local party leaders proved the first hypothesis to be essentially untrue. In none of the strong or the marginal parties was there a condition of active factionalism in which opposing groups planned their strategy or defined their policy prior to the regular meetings. No instances were noted in these divisions where every contestable issue was debated and brought to a vote. The same absence of organised factionalism was found in nine of the twelve

[32] See Rose, *Politics in England*, p. 155, for the interesting suggestion that factionalism constitutes an important restraint on the concentration of power within parties, particularly the party that is in control of the government.

E

weak constituency parties which were studied. Of the remaining three weak divisions, one was so disorganised that the issue of factionalism could hardly be considered. This constituency party had not functioned for a period of two-and-a-half years between 1960 and 1962. Its General Management Committee did not meet during that interval, funds were not collected, and delegates were not sent to the Annual Conference. In the spring of 1963, when the constituency was visited, there was no chairman of the General Management Committee. The secretary of the GMC had held the position only six months and had had no previous experience as a political organiser. Organisation weakness was being encouraged because the only experienced political worker in the division was a person of moderate policy opinions who refused to participate in the reactivation of a constituency party which would be dominated by left-wing elements and unilateralists. Other party members with moderate views had withdrawn from political work in protest against such actions as censuring Hugh Gaitskell and sponsoring speakers known for the hyperbolic presentation of their extreme views.

In the other two weak parties, there was a direct confrontation of opposing groups. Word had been circulated throughout one of the divisions that the left wing would make a concerted effort to take over the party. The GMC secretary rallied the moderates in an effort to maintain the even balance which existed between the two groups. All important intra-party elections were contested, and considerable controversy developed over the substance of resolutions sent to Transport House for inclusion in the annual conference agenda, and for the purpose of informing party headquarters of the position of the division on current issues. Feeling ran high in the constituency, the left wing looking upon the moderates as unimaginative, uninterested in policy, and too preoccupied with routine party activities. The moderates, while admitting the zeal of the militant groups, objected to the fact that the militants sat together at party meetings, refused to engage in fund raising, and held themselves apart from other members at social affairs sponsored by the party.

In the last weak division, the relationships between the factions were again unique. Ideological differences were, if anything, greater than those which existed in any other division, but here the left wing took the position that the division was so weak that few issues were worth fighting over. Despite an atmosphere of geniality, almost all party elections were contested and there were brisk debates over resolutions sent to Transport House. There was evidence that the left wing was becoming dominant in the GMC, but it was doing so without creating undue ill-will and harming an already weak constituency party.

The thirty-three divisions without a condition of active factionalism were not an undifferentiated group. In six divisions, three marginal and three weak, a condition of latent factionalism existed. Ideological tensions had been sharpened in some divisions by the unilateralist controversy and by the selection of parliamentary candidates. In other divisions personal animosities were the cause of disagreement. Not infrequently a respondent would complete his account of an event with such a comment as, 'I suppose you heard a completely different version of this from ———', although there was seldom a variation in the accounts. Despite the existence of personality conflict among the party leaders and of divergent ideologies, there was no indication that the tension level was rising. However, there was no doubt that in these constituencies a party activist would have no difficulty in recruiting support for a revolt against prevailing leadership.

In fourteen of the constituencies no factional problems were found. In these divisions one faction had such predominance that the opposing group neither contested elections to party office nor advanced policy proposals. In some extreme cases there was not even an identifiable minority group. Those holding minority views were free to express them, but once the democratic forms were observed, the majority quickly prevailed. The over-riding strength of the majority in these divisions was revealed in the answer of a leader from a strong division in the Midlands to a question regarding the substance of resolutions forwarded to Transport House. He chuckled and replied: 'Oh yes, we spend quite a bit of time sometimes arguing over which left-wing resolution we'll adopt.' The constituencies without factional problems included five strong, five weak, and four marginal parties.

Another group of seven constituency parties shared a wide range of opinion without suffering a disruption of their operations. The distinctive characteristic of these two strong and five marginal divisions was that they were the beneficiaries of strong professional leadership. Six of the parties had full-time agents. The seventh constituency had a capable GMC chairman who supplemented the work of a part-time, salaried agent who was preparing to take the agents' examination administered by the National Organiser's office.

The remaining six divisions not confronted by factional problems were notable for their low level of political activity. This category, composed of one weak and five strong constituency parties, was less responsive to requests for interviews than were the other divisional parties. All ultimately participated in the study, but only after considerable negotiation. In some of these divisions the General Management Committee met only quarterly. Some failed to send delegates to the Annual Conference because of insufficient funds; others neglected to choose an alternate if the appointed delegate could not attend. In one district the annual financial report, indicating impending insolvency, was read from a piece of scrap paper without a copy for the GMC secretary. These parties were described by one leader as 'just ticking over'. This was unexceptionably true, and in none of them was there enough energy to generate a factional dispute.

The discovery that a condition of active factionalism existed in only three of thirty-six divisions in the winter of 1962–3 may create a misconception regarding the degree of unity within constituency parties. Nine other divisional parties, two strong, six marginal, and one weak, all experienced intra-party disputes of varying severity during the late 1950s and early 1960s. In each case the difficulties were caused by a resurgence of left-wing opinion which had been activated by the Campaign for Nuclear Disarmament. By the spring of 1963, all but one of these constituency parties had succeeded in reducing the level of dissension and directing their energies toward the general election. The one exception was the weak division whose party was severely damaged by the virulent internal dissension of 1960 and 1961. Until Gaitskell's rejection of the unilateralist resolution passed at Scarborough in 1960, this division had muddled along, experiencing disagreements on the issue of German rearmament and on Clause IV, but managing to survive. Following Scarborough, a meeting of the GMC was called to which were invited expelled members of the constituency party along with certain local members of the Communist Party. A resolution bitterly critical of Gaitskell was introduced, and it became apparent that the GMC chairman intended to permit non-members to vote on the resolution. There was strenuous objection to this, but the chairman was adamant. Four members of the GMC left the meeting in protest. Despite this, the resolution was passed and released to the press in the name of 'members and friends of the ——— CLP'. Because of the withdrawal of moderate party workers, the division fell under the domination of the left wing. Certainly, factionalism is no longer a problem in this constituency, but that is not to say that all problems have been solved. Tension developed between the GMC and the parliamentary candidate in 1963. When asked to attend a special meeting in November with the GMC, he did not appear, and in his absence it was agreed to find a replacement. The candidate thereupon resigned and announced that he had joined the Communist Party. This meant that it was necessary to go through the selection process again, whereby a much more credible candidate was chosen. Thus, as late as the summer of 1964, this constituency party was still struggling with the consequences of its disruption five years earlier.

II. Depressants of CLP factionalism

Considering the number and nature of the divisive forces operating within the Labour Party, the limited importance of factionalism in the constituencies was surprising, particularly since the ideological strife at the national level reflects similar attitudes in the constituencies. The secondary status accorded the Labour Party in British politics causes the same intensive self-analysis in the divisions as it does in Transport House and Westminster. If efforts are made by political pressure groups to infiltrate the Labour Party, the divisions and the trade unions offer the likeliest points of access. There are frequent occasions where controversy could occur as constituency GMCs meet monthly. Nevertheless, there was found only an occasional incidence of constituency factionalism despite the environment which would seem to foster it. One explanation might be the particular period of time during which field research was done; another explanation might lie in the characteristics of political life in the divisional parties.

(a) Special factors discouraging CLP factionalism: 1962–3

One factor which had a depressing effect on factionalism in the interval from 1962 to 1963 was the imminent general election, which most constituency party leaders thought would be held in the autumn of 1963 or the spring of 1964. The impending election tended to focus the attention of all Labour Party members on the Conservatives as opponents and to dissipate rancour within the party. Apart from this, the 1962 Annual Conference had a less divisive effect on the party than had the three previous conferences. In 1959 Gaitskell had urged a revision of Clause IV, and in 1960 and 1961 he had supported a defence policy extremely unpopular with the left wing and with those moderates who responded intuitively to socialist rhetoric. The elements who had opposed Gaitskell in these years were strongly opposed to Britain's joining the European Economic Community, and had Gaitskell supported the proposal, all the old wounds would have been reopened. The opposition of Gaitskell to British entry into EEC blurred the only issue with the potential to disrupt the 1962 conference.

These conditions alone would undoubtedly have reduced intra-party disputes during the period under consideration, but the death of Hugh Gaitskell and the subsequent election of Harold Wilson as Leader were overwhelming influences toward harmony. Gaitskell's untimely death shocked the party, but it removed a man distrusted by the left wing. The depth of feeling against him in many constituencies was demonstrated by an article appearing in a left-wing constituency party journal which ended with the comment: 'We mourn the man, not his policies.' Shortly after Gaitskell's influence was removed at the top level of the party, Harold Wilson was installed as Leader. Many constituency party leaders welcomed the leadership of Wilson whom they assumed to be intellectually committed to the left. The assumption was not correct, but for the moment it had the effect of further reducing tension within the party.

(b)   Personal relationships among CLP leaders

Although delegates at annual conference sessions may take bitter exception to the views of other delegates, in most cases the delegates are not personally acquainted with one another. Members of the National Executive Committee and the Parliamentary Labour Party are in much more sustained contact with one another than are the conference delegates, but even these party leaders are not thrown together as frequently as are CLP members in an active constituency. Personal and intimate relationships characterise active constituency parties where GMC and other members may work side by side, live in the same neighbourhood, patronise the same local stores, visit the same pubs, and be loyal supporters of the same local football team. The small geographical area of British constituencies makes it difficult for party members to restrict their relationships to politics. Even if this were feasible, local party leaders tend to work with one another for years at GMC meetings, selection conferences, local council meetings and at party social affairs. Since it is impossible to work indefinitely in an atmosphere of tension and disagreement and maintain effectiveness, there was a predisposition in all but a few divisions to avoid or to settle internecine disputes.

(c) Predominance of particular policy views

Moderate or left-wing opinion so completely dominated some constituency parties that opposition to the prevailing view was abortive. Even though minority opinions were freely expressed, they were seldom accepted. For this reason such divisions were unlikely to attract workers whose policy positions were basically incompatible with those of the majority. In one constituency arguments developed only over which particular left-wing resolution to adopt. In another division the chairman was not even challenged when he ruled out of order a resolution critical of United States action in Cuba on the grounds that the mover knew nothing about the matter. Certainly, no moderate would feel comfortable in the constituency party whose prospective parliamentary candidate resigned to join the Communist Party, and a left-wing supporter would feel equally out of place in the division whose short list of five names for the selection of parliamentary candidate contained four nominees suggested by the Campaign for Democratic Socialism. Under these circumstances, there is justification for the belief that parties with a narrow range of policy views might unwittingly discourage those with divergent opinions from becoming active in party affairs. That this could be a purposeful action was demonstrated by two constituency parties which made no effort to conceal their uninterest in applicants for membership whose views clashed with those of the majority in the divisional association.

(d) Limits of politics

Politics is not the over-riding factor in all decisions reached by the constituency parties. It is clearly an important influence, perhaps the most important, but other considerations have great significance in the divisions. For example, in one weak division a spirited contest had developed between the right and left wings. The secretary had been selected as the 1962 conference delegate, but upon receiving a scholarship to Ruskin College at Oxford, he had resigned his position and his appointment as delegate. Although an avowed right-winger, he suggested that, instead of holding another election, the division send the runner-up for delegate in his place, even though the replacement was an active left-winger. The same division had two nominees for parliamentary candidate, one from the left and the other a moderate. Although the moderate nominee lived in a ward whose representatives to the GMC were members of the left wing, they proposed to vote for him because they thought their ward party would be heartened if one of its members were the parliamentary candidate.

In a marginal division a local man with CND sympathies was a nominee for parliamentary candidate, but he did not receive the votes of all CND supporters at the selection conference, nor was he selected as the candidate, because his personal life was not highly regarded. In another marginal division the local party re-adopted the candidate chosen for the 1959 election. At the time of his first selection the candidate was a unilateralist, as was the majority of the selection conference. He informed the new selection conference which was considering him that he no longer subscribed to the unilateralist position. Despite the fact that the party was still strongly unilateralist, the candidate was again selected on the first ballot, receiving only a slightly smaller proportion of the vote than in 1959. An important element in this decision was the excellent campaign waged by the candidate who had been chosen on very short notice in 1959. Regardless of his changed position on defence policy, most of the selection conference thought the constituency owed him another opportunity. Thus, values such as civility, loyalty, forbearance and obligation impose substantial limits on the political factor in constituency decision making.

(e) Professional political leadership

Experienced and purposeful political leadership served to overcome the factional tendencies in some constituencies. No effort was made in these parties to avoid policy discussion, nor was there a lack of interest in political questions, for the professional Labour Party agent was as likely as any other constituency leader to hold strong attitudes on questions of party and national policy. However, policy debate did not dominate the political life of these divisions, but had to vie with such time-consuming activities as selecting parliamentary and local candidates, staging local elections, preparing for the general election, raising funds, and participating in local government. All this left little time for the development of fine ideological differences among party activists, and thus distracted attention from potentially disruptive questions.

III Nature of constituency factionalism

The hypothesis relating to the prevalence of personal factionalism in the strong and in the marginal divisions, and of ideological factionalism in weak Labour constituencies was also proved incorrect. Admittedly, ideological factionalism plagued the three weak divisions suffering intra-party strife, but personality conflict never achieved the destructive proportions it sometimes assumes in American local party organisations. At most, personal factionalism in the Labour Party can be described as a cause of low grade tension in a number of constituency parties.

More than two sources of tension were isolated, but by far the most common causes were either personal or ideological in nature. Religion and geography were found to be the source of dissension in a number of local parties. In two strong divisions local leaders stated that there was a large turnout for local selection conferences in wards with predominantly Roman Catholic populations. The point at stake was that in Britain, unlike the United States, the local governing body through its school committee determined the amount of subsidy given to parochial schools from public funds. Therefore, the selection of local Labour candidates who favoured increasing or maintaining the subsidy level for parochial schools was an important decision. In one other strong division there was a link between religious and ideological differences. The leaders of this left-wing constituency party thought that there was a relationship between the moderate politics of one of their wards and the fact that most of its residents were Roman Catholics. The only other reference to religion as a factor in organisational matters was heard in a marginal division. A Roman Catholic had been selected to run for Parliament in a recent by-election and had been successful. In the general election which followed the candidate was defeated. When the time arrived to choose a candidate for the 1964 general election, this person was passed over although still active in the divisional party. The action was not personal but reflected the recognition of local leaders that the electorate of the division included Labour voters who would not accept a Roman Catholic candidate.

Another source of tension revealed by the study linked geographical and occupational factors. Two marginal constituencies and one weak division were involved, with all three sharing the characteristic of being largely agricultural. The leaders of all three divisions came from small towns and villages rather than the surrounding farms, and complained of the 'feudal attitudes which still exist between the agricultural worker and the land owner'. This deferential relationship was described in terms of still seeing the gesture of fingers to the forelock when the agricultural worker greeted or took leave of the 'master', of having to contend with the worker's fear to vote or to become engaged in open political activity, and of overcoming his suspicion of the 'town' leaders of the party.

(a) Factionalism and party strength and weakness

Although all cases of active factionalism occurred in weak divisions, party strength and party weakness alike tended to discourage party dissension. This was due primarily to the unstructured condition of the party organisation in a few weak and in a number of strong divisions. Unlike the situation in professionally led constituencies where activities crowded policy off the agenda, these divisions often had no agenda. It followed that the saliency of policy in these divisions was quite low. Leaders had opinions on policy matters, but these were not discussed with much intensity or frequency.

(b) Marginality and factionalism

The most overt effort to avoid the harmful effects of factionalism was discovered in some of the marginal constituencies. In these divisions the party leaders were eager to win and sensitive to any development which might cause the loss of even a few votes. Their attempts to avoid sources of possible tension extended beyond an arduous schedule of activities designed to strengthen party organisation. One marginal division went so far as to scrutinise applications for party membership to assure that no individual was admitted who might cause disruption to the party. When a number of young members of CND applied for membership, they were interviewed by the GMC chairman and the agent. During the interview the applicants were told that the party was unified and intended to remain so. They were admitted as members with some reluctance and only with the understanding that the Labour Party was to receive their first loyalty and that they would be subject to the discipline of the party.

3. *Effects of factionalism in Constituency Labour Parties*

The effects of constituency factionalism were even less conspicuous than its incidence. With the exception of the two weak divisions in which the party seemed moribund, and the other weak division in which the party was disrupted, the tensions which existed in the winter of 1962–3 and in the few years preceding it, did not limit the ability of the constituency parties to perform their expected functions. Respondents in all divisions agreed that party members, regardless of differences expressed at GMC meetings, approached the constituency electorate as colleagues rather than opponents. This claim was persuasive, since the respondents represented the entire range of policy opinion within the party. There was also complete agreement that neither factionalism nor passing differences of opinion within the constituency parties had an effect on their ability to obtain popular support for their candidates in local and general elections. Internal problems were confined to official, closed meetings of the divisional party and GMC members co-operated to prevent information about controversies from receiving public attention.

Party officials were also asked to evaluate the effect of disputes among national party leaders upon popular support in their constituencies for Labour candidates in local and general elections. There was a consensus that such controversy was impossible to keep within the party because of the interest a generally unfriendly press and other communications media took in strife within the Labour movement. The effect of widely publicised battles within the party varied according to the type of constituency. In strong constituencies, twice as many leaders considered national factionalism to have no effect on party efforts to obtain electoral support as did those who thought it had a deleterious effect. While the leaders from weak divisions were divided equally on this question, twice as many leaders in marginal constituencies thought the party was harmed by national factionalism as thought it was unaffected. The marginal constituency parties seemed sensitive to factors which might cause even a slight loss of votes.[33] Weak divisions which have no chance of victory are less concerned with the loss of a small number of votes, while strong divisions see themselves as unaffected by such losses.

A number of CLP leaders volunteered comments on the harmful effects of national factionalism in their divisions. One stated that dissension among national leaders 'gave the impression of an uncertain, divided party. Political opponents take extreme statements of factional leaders and represent these as being the policy of the party.' Another respondent, a trade union official, noted that 'rank and file voters and trade unionists wondered what kind of Government a disunited party could operate'. A third leader, after pointing out that factionalism gave the Labour Party a bad press, asked: 'How can a party run the country if it can't run itself?'

There is evidence that CLP leaders who feel that factionalism has a negative effect on the image of the Labour Party are not alone in their sentiments. The findings of social surveys indicate that the British electorate associates the characteristic of unity with the Conservative rather than the Labour Party. A survey made between January 12 and February 29, 1960, shortly after the 1959 general election, revealed that non-Labour supporters in the working class overwhelmingly associated 'a united team of top leaders' with the Conservative Party. Even Labour supporters in a 2:1 ratio recognised the greater degree of unity among Conservative leaders.

The British Gallup Poll has produced a similar pattern of response on this topic, although the differences are not as great as those found by Abrams and Rose. The Conservative Party was considered to be

[33] Marginal constituencies are justified in their concern over small numbers of votes. In the 1964 general election, twelve constituencies were won by Labour candidates with a plurality of less than 500 votes. In thirteen constituencies the Labour candidate lost by less than 500 votes. See *Labour Party Annual Conference Report, 1964,* p. 195.

slightly less unified in 1964 than in 1959, and the Labour Party more unified. Even so, unity as a party characteristic was much more likely to be associated with the Conservatives, for when Gallup asked the respondents to rank ten statements as they applied to the major parties, unity was ranked close to the top for the Conservatives and close to the bottom for Labour in both years. Table 4.2 is also interesting in view of events in both parties during the five-year interval from 1959 to 1964. The Labour Party had yet to experience

TABLE 4.1. *Attribution of the statement 'Has a united team of top leaders' to major parties by working-class voters*[34]

	Labour supporters %	Non-Labour supporters %
Labour	18	4
Conservative	38	65
Both	21	11
Neither	12	7
Don't know	11	13

TABLE 4.2. *Attribution of the statement 'Unity and agreement within the party' to major parties by all voters*[35]

	Con.	Rank	Lab.	Rank
	%		%	
1959	11	3	6.3	9
1964	10.6	3	8	8

Note: Ten statements were included in the list shown the respondents. The data for both surveys were gathered about six weeks before the 1959 and 1964 general elections.

the peak of discord caused by unilateralist influence within the party, culminating in the passage of unilateralists' resolutions at the 1960 Scarborough conference and Hugh Gaitskell's rejection of the conference decision. This commitment to unilateral disarmament was

[34] Abrams and Rose, op. cit., pp. 13–16.
[35] *Gallup Political Index*, Report No. 54, Social Surveys (Gallup Poll) Limited, December 1964, p. 127.

reversed in 1961, but it was not until Gaitskell made his Common Market speech at the 1962 conference that, impelled by the pre-election drive toward unity, discord within the party subsided.

Harold Wilson's election as Party Leader and George Brown's generous tribute at the 1963 conference to Wilson's successful leadership added to the impression of unusual unity among Labour's top leaders.

During the period of increasing harmony in the Labour Party, the Conservatives abandoned their old customs of close party loyalty, of settling differences in private, and of presenting a common front to the enemy. Starting with Harold Macmillan's purge of the cabinet in the summer of 1962, one crisis followed another in the Conservative Party. Later in 1962, the Vassall affair broke, indicating a major breach of national security. The Profumo scandal broke in the spring of 1963, culminating in the abstention of twenty-seven Conservative MPs on the vote concluding the debate on the question of how the government had handled the matter. Macmillan's illness in the autumn of 1963 required the party to select a new prime minister, which it did with so little grace that great controversy was created among Conservatives. This was exacerbated by the appearance of a book by Randolph Churchill in December 1963, purporting to explain the selection of Sir Alec Douglas-Home as prime minister: an explanation which Iain Macleod, in a stinging riposte the following month, declared singularly wanting.[36] The spring of 1964 again found the Conservatives wrangling, this time over a series of anonymous articles appearing in *The Times*, and over speeches and articles by Enoch Powell, the Minister of Health in Macmillan's cabinet, who had joined Iain Macleod in refusing to serve under Home. The main thrust of the remarks by the anonymous author and by Powell was that the Conservative Party leaders were sacrificing principle to expediency and were following policies calculated to make the expansion of socialism by a Labour government much easier.[37]

[36] Randolph Churchill, *The Fight for the Tory Leadership*, London 1964; and Iain Macleod, "The Tory Leadership", *Spectator*, January 17, 1964, pp. 65–7.

[37] Powell concluded an article in the *Observer* of March 15, 1964, entitled "Little Trojan Horses", with the following story from the classics: 'Herodotus tells of an Egyptian king who started to dig a canal from the Nile to

The result of this uncharacteristic fratricidal conduct was discussed by Robert McKenzie, who wrote in March 1964: 'In the past
the opinion polls have repeatedly shown that the public saw the
Conservatives as a cohesive and united team which was better qualified to rule than Labour with their perpetual squabbles and feuds.
But during the past two years, the Tories have squandered this asset
with profligate abandon. They have so conducted their affairs . . .
that the electorate is now convinced—the polls report—that it is
Labour rather than the Conservatives who have a united team of
leaders.'[38]

The fact that unity is one of the most clearly perceived differences
between the Labour and Conservative parties has apparently led
many students of British politics to assume that this difference has
some effect on the electoral behaviour of British voters. The evidence
on this point is not clear. The Abrams and Rose study found that 29
per cent of non-Labour working-class voters rated unity as being
important for a good political party and ranked this characteristic
fourth in a list of sixteen. Only 20 per cent of working-class Labour
supporters thought unity was important for a good party and they
ranked this quality in eighth place. Unity as a party virtue was far
less important in the Gallup poll results. In 1959 only 7 per cent of
the respondents referred to unity as an aspect they 'looked for first
of all' and ranked it sixth among ten statements. In 1964 the proportion mentioning this quality dropped to 3.2 per cent and its rank to
eighth. The Gallup findings are the more impressive of the two since
these are based on data gathered just prior to two general elections.
The Abrams and Rose study was made after a general election in
which the Conservatives increased an already wide margin in the
House of Commons, and just after the 1959 Labour conference at
which Gaitskell proposed that the party statement regarding
nationalisation be altered.

If the Gallup findings regarding the importance of party unity to
the British voter are accepted, there is other evidence that suggests

[38] Robert McKenzie, "The Tories in Turmoil", *Observer*, March 15,
1964. See also his *British Political Parties*, op. cit., p. 641.

the Red Sea, a canal which was afterwards finished by the Persians when
they had conquered Egypt. While he was at work, a message came to him
from an oracle to say that he was "working for the barbarian". Herodotus
records that Pharaoh stopped.'

the British voter talks one way and votes another. Increasingly since the end of the Second World War, independent and minor party parliamentary candidates have found it difficult to obtain electoral support. Several instances can be found of incumbent MPs who, failing readoption by their constituency parties, stood for Parliament independently and succeeded only in losing their deposits. Since it is the British voter who enforces party discipline by refusing to vote for parliamentary candidates who do not bear the *congé d'élire* of an established party, it seems reasonable to infer that he does indeed attach a great deal of importance to party unity, and that he is either consciously or intuitively aware of the necessity for a high degree of discipline within the respective parliamentary parties. It may be that he perceives parliamentary discipline differently than he does unity within the party as a whole, but available evidence does not provide the answer to this proposition.

5

Selection of Parliamentary Candidates

Political practices and customs which develop in different countries reflect the basic characteristics of their respective societies. Thus, the egalitarian traditions peculiar to America have resulted in attempts to achieve popular control of the political process by such devices as the direct primary. Britain, perhaps because its society is structured by a class system which has been a dominant feature for many centuries, has never employed such a means. The direct primary and even the political convention have not been considered relevant to a society which gravitates naturally toward the caucus. Selection of parliamentary candidates has been accomplished by the caucus since the inception of Parliament as a governmental institution. There was no reason to expect the Labour Party to forsake this tradition when the party was organised early in the twentieth century. Although the Labour caucus differed in composition from the caucus of other parties, the nature and aims of each were similar. All consisted essentially of a small group of party activists meeting privately to determine party policy, including the selection of parliamentary candidates.[1]

Perhaps the most important activity of the party caucus, as represented by the General Management Committee of the constituency party, was its power to select parliamentary candidates. Butler and Rose have written: 'Constituency parties influence the conduct of British politics more by their choice of candidates than in

[1] See Austin Ranney, *Pathways to Parliament . . .,* op. cit., for a comprehensive treatment of candidate selection in Britain.

113

any other way.'[2] Robert McKenzie has observed: 'It is sometimes argued that they [CLPS] have ultimate control over the parliamentary party since they determine its composition by their choice of candidates.'[3] It must be acknowledged that secular changes in the composition of the Parliamentary Labour Party have been brought about largely by choices made at constituency selection conferences, and that the perpetuation of certain internal tensions within the Labour Party has been aided by the choices of some strong Labour constituencies. However, the socialisation processes of the House of Commons and the Parliamentary Labour Party are strong. Access to more information, frequent contact with party leaders, the impact of the group life of the PLP, the opportunity for wider travel and a broader range of contacts have had an impact on most new MPS, although a few Labour MPS have withstood such influences remarkably well. In view of the willingness with which Labour voters apply sanctions to independent Labour candidates, it is clear that the voters expect the member to follow the lead of the PLP, rather than rely on his independent judgment in public policy matters or on the views of his constituency party. These factors diminish the importance of candidate selection, but they have their limitations. For example, if there occurred a pronounced shift to the right or to the left among Labour candidates in marginal divisions in an election like 1964 when there was an increase of fifty-nine Labour MPS, the political outlook of the PLP could be materially altered.

1. *Preliminaries of the selection process*

The rules of the Labour Party are deceptive in the selection of parliamentary candidates. If read literally, the rules would impose stultifying conditions on constituency parties in performing this function, with the result that the selection process would actually come under the control of Labour Party headquarters in Transport House. It is stipulated in the rules that consultations be held between the constituency party and the National Executive Committee to determine whether the constituency party should contest the next election. If the decision is affirmative, the General Management Committee is asked to give authority to its executive committee to

[2] Butler and Rose, op. cit., p. 122.
[3] McKenzie, *British Political Parties*, op. cit., p. 556.

obtain, in co-operation with the NEC, nominations for parliamentary candidates. Nominations may be made by the constituency executive committee, by one of its constituent elements such as a ward or village party, or by an affiliated organisation such as a trade union or a local co-operative society. The NEC may also propose names on its own initiative.

Nominations, after they have been received by the constituency party, are forwarded to the NEC for 'validation'. The nominations are then returned to the constituency party where the General Management Committee executive prepares a 'short list' of the nominees considered best qualified. After the short list has been prepared, a notice is sent by the constituency party secretary to all members of the General Management Committee to attend a 'selection conference'. On the appointed day, each nominee delivers a ten to fifteen minute speech before the selection conference and answers questions for an additional ten minutes. The balloting is by show of hands, and continues until one nominee has an 'exhaustive' or absolute majority of those in attendance. A representative of Transport House, usually the regional organiser,[4] is present to guarantee that the selection conference has met the procedural requirements of the party rules. The name of the chosen candidate is forwarded to Transport House by the constituency party secretary, and the regional secretary also submits a report. The selection is not considered final until the NEC has endorsed the candidate. This is done only after the NEC is assured that the candidate will present the views and policies of the party during the election campaign and that, if elected, he will support the programme and principles of the party, i.e., the majority decisions of the Parliamentary Labour Party.

1. Decision to contest

The requirement that a constituency party GMC consult with the NEC to determine whether the ensuing election should be contested

---

[4] Britain is divided by the Labour Party into twelve regions, each headed by a regional Organiser. There is also a semi-detached Northern Ireland Labour Party, but still associated with Transport House. In the 1966 general election, Gerard Fitt was elected from Belfast West, having stood as a Republican Labour candidate. Though having no formal connection with the NILP, Fitt supported Labour policies in the House.

in the constituency was not mentioned by any CLP leader interviewed, and it seemed unlikely that the requirement was being
honoured at present. The rule may have been relevant during the
early years of the party when Liberal–Labour pacts were reached in
certain constituencies, or when the resources of the party were so
limited that a candidate could not be supported in every constituency.
Whatever the basis of this provision, it is now largely historical. The
only current adherence relates to the custom that the Speaker's seat
is not contested. The Speaker in 1962–3 was Sir Harry Hylton-
Foster, who represented the Cities of London and Westminster
where the Labour Party normally polls about 25 per cent of the
vote. Not wishing to be deprived of an opportunity to strike a blow
for Labour, the constituency party in this division pressed for the
privilege of fielding a candidate, and in July 1963 the request was
granted by the NEC.[5]

II. Nominations

Although it may have express authority to do so, the NEC does not
secure or submit nominations for parliamentary candidates for
general elections. The NEC does maintain two lists of possible
nominees which it furnishes to the constituency parties on request.
Panel A is composed of party members who belong to trade unions
and whose names have been placed on the parliamentary panels of
their unions, usually by a general ballot of the union membership.[6]
Panel B is made up by constituency parties forwarding to the NEC
the names of those of their members considered to be suitable as
parliamentary candidates. Those individuals are not sponsored by
any organisation affiliated to the party, and if a constituency party
were to choose one of them as its candidate, it would be required to
finance his campaign out of its own resources.[7] Beyond providing
the service of maintaining the two lists, the NEC remains aloof from
this phase of the selection process.

Nominations are submitted by affiliated organisations or by constituent elements of the divisional party. The formal nomination is
made by the submission of a standard nominating form signed by

[5] *Agenda, Labour Party Annual Conference 1962*, p. 37, and *1963*, p. 8.
[6] Cf. Harrison, op. cit., pp. 274–85.
[7] Cf. Austin Ranney, *Pathways to Parliament . . .*, op. cit., pp. 138–40.

the secretary of the nominating organisation and the nominee. The nominations may be from Panel A, or Panel B, or neither, since it is not mandatory that the parliamentary candidate be accepted from either list. Table 5.1 shows that in the strong divisions two-thirds of the candidates were on either Panel A or Panel B, and in the marginal divisions about 85 per cent of the nominees fell into this category. It should further be noted that only the weak divisions had a clear majority of nominees on neither panel.

TABLE 5.1. *Origin and number of nominations of MPs and parliamentary candidates, by type of constituency*

| | Constituencies | | |
	Strong	Marginal	Weak
Panel A	41	18	1
Panel B	43	41	14
Neither	41	10	19
Totals	125	69	34

Note: The data for the strong constituencies are based on only eleven divisions, as one MP refused to participate in the study. The data for these divisions covered a time period extending from the 1935 general election to 1964 when vacancies caused by two resignations were filled.

Some candidates whose names had not appeared on either panel told interesting stories concerning the origin of their candidacies. One had answered an advertisement run by two constituency parties in a journal which usually supports the Labour Party, asking for expressions of interest in their parliamentary nominations. The constituencies were not identified, and at the suggestion of a friend who had parliamentary ambitions, the candidate answered the advertisement, largely on behalf of his friend. In the ensuing correspondence, one of the constituency parties involved developed an interest in him rather than his friend, and he was eventually selected as the candidate. In another division a schoolmaster recalled a former student who had expressed interest in a parliamentary career. This name was mentioned to the secretary-agent of the CLP, and the former grammar-school student was chosen by a one vote margin as the divisional parliamentary candidate. Many nominees were personally solicited by CLP secretary-agents in order to assemble a larger field of nominees from which to choose.

III. Number of nominees

It can be seen from Table 5.1 that the safer the seat, the greater the competition for the candidacy. However, the raw figures conceal as much as they reveal. Among the MPs, those selected after the Second World War had more competition than those chosen before it. The average number of nominees from which selection conferences held in strong divisions before the Second World War had to choose was five; while, in the years after 1945, the average number of nominees in the same type of division was twelve. This last figure would be even larger were it not for an unusual method of candidate selection in a division which had only four nominees, and which for decades has been represented in the Commons by a member of the National Union of Miners.[8]

The dislocations occurring in Britain as a result of the Second World War were responsible for one MP's entering Parliament who, when he was selected, thought he had utterly no chance of election. Shortly after the Conservative victory in 1935, a hopeless Labour constituency in a Midland city held a selection conference with only one nominee. The single nominee, a young man in his middle twenties who had become chairman of his constituency party, was duly chosen as the parliamentary candidate. The war came with its coalition National government and the election truce which immobilised the political situation in Britain from May 1940 until the general election of 1945. When the election was called, this candidate of eight years' standing was serving as an officer in the armed forces. He returned to his constituency to find that the hopeless Labour division had become a safe Labour seat. It has been represented by him in the House of Commons from 1945 until the present, his usual majority being two to one in a straight fight.

Of the two strong divisions selecting candidates for the 1964

[8] In this division only four nominations were received by the GMC, but the miners had held their own selection conference, at which there were actually eight nominees. However, only the name of the successful NUM candidate was forwarded to the GMC. Should all eight of the miners' nominees be counted, this division would have had eleven rather then four nominees.

election, one had nine and the other thirty-two nominees.[9] The marginal divisions—four of which had four nominees, two had five, and three had six nominees—had far less choice in candidates. Of the two remaining marginal divisions, one had seven and the other fourteen nominees. Constituencies in which Labour candidates polled 45 per cent or more in straight fights in the 1959 election received no more than four to six nominations. In one such constituency, all six nominees were produced for selection by the secretary-agent, and there was reason to believe that this was not an uncommon practice among marginal constituency party secretaries.

The problem of finding nominees in the weak constituencies was even more difficult and less productive. Three secretaries told of actively soliciting nominations, one of them writing fifty letters to A and B panelists. This last solicitation produced eight indications of interest, two from persons who were selected by other divisions, the secretary eventually obtaining four nominations for his own division. Two divisions were forced to postpone their selection conference once, while two others postponed their conference twice. In each of these four there were no more than three nominees from which the GMC could choose a short list. One weak division, located in suburban London, where the Labour candidate would compete against an important leader of the Conservative Party, managed to obtain eight nominations, but this was the exception rather than the rule. The remaining eleven weak constituencies shared a total of twenty-eight nominations, ranging from one to four in each division.

IV. Validation

After nominations are received, they are referred by the CLP secretary to the NEC for validation. Robert McKenzie has written that 'this is intended to give the NEC an opportunity to express its views on an individual whose qualifications have not hitherto been reviewed by the NEC; if the NEC indicates at this stage that the individual concerned will not receive their subsequent approval if he is

[9] Vacancies in these divisions were created by the resignation of the sitting member effective at the dissolution of the 1964 Parliament. The resignation is conveyed to the constituency party in a formal letter, usually well in advance of a general election, in order that the constituency can select a candidate in sufficient time to permit him to gain identification as the Labour candidate.

selected by the GMC, then, of course, the [GMC] executive committee
will convey this information to the GMC and under normal circumstances the individual concerned will have no prospect of selection. . . '.[10] The validation phase of the selection process was probably more important in the past than at present, when this step
seems completely *pro forma*. Of the 140 nominations received by the
twenty-five CLPs without sitting members prior to the 1964 election,
not one was refused validation, regardless of whether the NEC had
been given an opportunity to review qualifications. (A nomination
paper from a strong division in a by-election in 1960 was refused
validation on the grounds that if the nominee were selected as
the parliamentary candidate, the candidate quota of thirty allowed
the Co-operative Party would be exceeded.) Neither did the NEC in
1964 seem to interpret validation as an occasion to indicate its future
action when the name of the successful nominee was presented for
endorsement.[11]

v. Short-listing

After the validated nomination papers have been returned to the
constituency party, the GMC executive committee convenes to draw
up a 'short list' of nominees to be submitted to the selection conference.[12] Where there were only a few nominees, it was the practice
to short-list the entire group, with the possible exception of the few

[10] McKenzie, *British Political Parties*, op. cit., p. 550.

[11] A letter dated August 18, 1964 from Reginald Underhill, Assistant
National Agent of the Labour Party, states the following in regard to
validation: 'Validation means that the nominations are checked to determine whether the forms are properly completed with the details of individual
membership and trade union membership, and that the nomination is
submitted by an organisation entitled to nominate and that the form is
signed by the nominee. *It is the form of the nomination that is concerned in the
validation and not the suitability of the individual to be nominated.*' (Italics added).

[12] These decisions are made on the basis of personal knowledge of the
local nominees, and on the basis of the paper qualifications of non-residents.
The occasional practice mentioned by McKenzie of submitting a questionnaire 'to "outsiders" who have not been locally nominated to determine
their views on various matters of party policy' was not encountered, possibly because there were no nominees who were not locally nominated.
Neither was there any differentiation in the composition of the short list
between nominees on the basis of the organisation making the nomination.

nominees clearly unsuited or unqualified. The average number of nominees on short lists from which incumbent MPs were selected was four. The two strong divisions choosing candidates for the 1964 general election had five and seven names, respectively, on their short lists, while the lists of the marginal divisions had a range of three to seven names, with a total of fifty nominees contained on the short lists for eleven selection conferences. In the weak divisions the range was from one to four names, the last figure reached by only two divisions. There were twenty-nine nominees on the short lists of the twelve weak divisions and the average was less than three names per constituency.

A complication occasionally developed between the date of the short list's compilation and the date on which the selection conference was held. During this interval some nominees found themselves on the short list of more than one constituency and were selected by the division holding an earlier conference.[13] More rarely, two conferences were called at the same time and the nominee was required to choose the division where his chances of success were better. For these or other reasons, five nominees in the marginal divisions did not appear before the selection conferences for which they were short-listed. In one case this reduced the number of nominees to two,[14] and in three other divisions to three, four, and five, respectively. Two weak constituencies reported that two nominees on the short lists either withdrew or failed to appear, causing a postponement of the selection conference.

2. *The selection conference*

Depending upon the strength of the constituency party and its affiliated organisations, the size of the General Management Committee

[13] Multiple nominations are not frowned upon or discouraged. Since some 360 constituency parties select candidates within an eighteen-month period, some overlapping of names inevitably occurs.

[14] This was the third strongest of the marginal constituencies and one in which only a modest swing from Conservative to Labour was needed to elect the Labour candidate, who in the 1964 election gained more than 45 per cent of the vote cast in a three-cornered fight.

The short list is made up from all the nominations, and there is not any category of nominations that automatically goes before the selection conference. See McKenzie, *British Political Parties*, op. cit., p. 550.

varies from twenty members to over one hundred. Selection conferences occur so infrequently, about once every five years unless a by-election intervenes, and are invested with such significance that the membership of the GMC turns out in full force for the event. Usually the conference disposes of its business in a single session lasting three or four hours. The nominees gave a ten- to fifteen-minute speech of a general nature, designed primarily to establish areas of agreement between the nominee and the conference, rather than to define the nominee's attitude toward broad aspects of party, domestic and foreign policies. The formal remarks of each nominee are followed by a ten-minute question and answer period. Depending on the length of his answers, each nominee was required to answer at least five questions, but rarely more than eight or nine. The questions posed were not always pertinent or penetrating. At a selection conference in the spring of 1963 each of the five nominees was asked a question about rates.[15] Three of the five were asked their opinions on the late opening of shops, a matter on which the Commons was unlikely to legislate. Two were asked whether their wives were members of the Labour Party and would help in the campaign. The remaining questions were of a more substantial nature, dealing with the Common Market, East–West trade, defence policy and underdeveloped areas, particularly in Africa.

Apart from the brief exposition of the nominee's views elicited at the selection conference, the only other source of information available was a short biography of each nominee that seldom exceeded 300 words in length. For nominees who lived or worked in the constituency, or who represented a segment of it on the local government council, there was no problem. However, 75 per cent of the nominees on the short list of marginal divisions and 60 per cent of those in the weak divisions were relatively unknown to the members of the selection conferences which they faced. Although the American student of British politics is well aware of the custom of choosing

[15] In Britain, taxes are paid to the national government and rates are paid to local government units. Rates are levied by the local government, and the revenue derived is used to provide part or all of the cost of a wide variety of government services, including education. The basis on which rates are levied was changed by the Conservative government in 1963, and as the change resulted in higher rates for many property owners, the issue was particularly sensitive at this time.

non-residents of a division to stand for Parliament, he is nonetheless shocked to observe strangers appearing for twenty minutes before a selection conference and summarily judged as parliamentary candidates. This was the practice not only in weak but also in marginal constituencies where the prospect of victory was favourable. At a by-election in the early 1950s a selection conference in a strong constituency passed over a former Labour minister and one of its own leaders to choose the only stranger among five nominees. This was a division which, even in 1959, gave more than two-thirds of its vote to the Labour candidate. In a rather unpromising marginal constituency, the candidate was completely unknown until he appeared for the selection conference. His name had simply been taken from Panel B and the preliminary formalities had been handled by mail. A far stronger marginal division which had won more than 45 per cent of the votes in a straight fight in 1959, reported that all its nominees were generally unknown to the selection conference. The nominee chosen was a young man who had attended grammar school in the division some twelve years before but had not lived in the constituency in the intervening period. In one of the weak divisions the candidate stated that when he was advised that his name appeared on the short list, he had to obtain a road map to locate the constituency and the town in which the selection conference was held.

Some constituency parties made an effort to learn something about the aspirants for parliamentary candidacy. Two of the weak divisions asked their nominees to meet the GMC executive in one case and the entire GMC in the other prior to the opening of the selection conference. One marginal division had the aspirants meet with CLP and ward party officials before their nominations were submitted, and a second division obtained supplementary information from friends in Transport House and from leaders of the Campaign for Democratic Socialism[16] before the selection conference met. The only organised effort by a constituency party to develop real

[16] The Campaign for Democratic Socialism was a Gaitskellite intra-party group designed to organise moderate elements within the party to revoke the decision taken by the 1960 Labour Party at Scarborough to support unilateral disarmament. Under the direction of William Rodgers, now MP for Stockton-on-Tees, the organisation performed additional services, such as keeping an unofficial list of nominees for parliamentary candidacy. The Campaign for Democratic Socialism tried no more along these lines than

knowledge of its nominees was undertaken by a marginal division which came close to winning in 1959. This division was able to obtain fourteen nominees, all of whom were invited to canvass parts of the constituency for a local election which gave party members an opportunity to observe how the nominees handled themselves with prospective voters. In addition, each nominee appeared at some local party meeting and eventually each was interviewed by the GMC executive. Only then was the short list formulated. Finally, the five short-listed nominees met informally for tea with the GMC before the selection conference commenced.[17]

1. Lobbying before the selection conference

In theory, the selection conference is composed of delegates from various elements of the Labour Party who come to the conference with open minds and a desire to choose the best candidate for their division. Presumably, they are expected to look to the merits of the respective nominees rather than to their group affiliations. It must be admitted that these conditions did prevail at a small minority of the selection conferences, but there were notable instances of submission to group influences. The most obvious example of group pressure on the choice of a parliamentary candidate was that in the division which customarily selected the choice of the miners' group. In approximately half of the divisions visited, some amount of lobbying took place during the selection process. The trade unions were especially active in lobbying in the strong divisions, and in times past the NEC would attempt to aid some defeated ministers to return to the House of Commons by using its influence in constituency

[17] The NEC heard of this reception and raised questions as to its appropriateness. Approval was finally granted provided all nominees be given equal attention by the GMC. This stipulation is difficult to interpret, but there are some persons in Transport House subtle enough to consider it a superb example of British humour. It is difficult to believe that the decision was made with the serious expectation that it would be honoured by the GMC executive.

Victory for Socialism and other left-wing groups operating within the Labour Party had done over the previous fifteen years, but perhaps it accomplished more than Victory for Socialism.

selection conferences.[18] The eighteen months of greatest activity in
selecting parliamentary candidates for the 1964 election coincided
with the period in which the CND was losing influence within the
Labour Party. Even so, the CND was powerful enough to be active on
behalf of nominees in four marginal and three weak divisions. Not
only were well-organised groups attempting to influence the selection of candidates, but many unorganised partisans also made
informal but sometimes effective efforts on behalf of favourite
nominees. One candidate in a strong division stated that he was
assisted by the description in Theodore White's study of the 1960
presidential election[19] of how the supporters of John F. Kennedy
worked to gather enough votes to enable him to win the nomination
on the first ballot of the 1960 Democratic Convention. As the parliamentary candidate expressed it: 'The book was a wonderful manual
for the organisation of support at selection conferences.' The candidate also had considerable aid within his constituency, but he was an
apt pupil of the Kennedy techniques, making a point of communi-
cating with almost half the delegates to the selection conference and
with key members of the important organisations in his district some
time before the selection conference met. In retrospect he was able
to say: 'I knew what shifts would come after the first ballot, for I had
obtained second ballot support of delegates who were initially
voting for my opponents.[20]

II. Balloting procedure at selection conferences

With the speeches and question periods completed, selection conferences proceeded to the voting. This was done by ballot and

[18] See pp. 135–6 below regarding NEC influence in arranging candidacies
for defeated ministers. See also Austin Ranney, "Inter-Constituency Movement of . . . Candidates", op. cit., pp. 38–9. In this regard, Harrison writes:
'Nowadays it [Transport House] will intervene to support a candidate only
in the most pressing circumstances. Transport House helped Ernest Bevin
and Mr Attlee in 1950, but party officials were clearly upset at having to
persuade constituencies to accept Dr Edith Summerskill when she was
crowded out at Fulham, just before the 1955 election'; Harrison op. cit.,
p. 302.
[19] Theodore H. White, *The Making of the President 1960*, New York 1961.
[20] These lobbying activities are quite contrary to the ideas of some
experienced British political writers. See Nora Beloff, "Where Votes Don't
Count", *Observer*, August 16, 1964.

continued until one of the nominees had the support of an absolute
majority of those attending the conference. Because of commitments
made before the conference, or because the brief appearance of
the nominees had established the precedence of one nominee over
the others, or because of a severely restricted field of candidates, the
conference usually reached a decision on the first ballot. This was
particularly true in the weak constituencies and only slightly less so
in the marginal divisions (see Table 5.2). A higher level of competition in the strong divisions was reflected by the smaller proportion of first ballot decisions. There was also a difference among the
strong constituencies relating to the length of service of the MPs.
Those selected before 1950 were much more likely to have been

TABLE 5.2. *Number of ballots required for
selection of parliamentary candidate, by
type of constituency*

	Strong	Marginal	Weak
First	4	7	10
Second	2	3	2
Third	1	1	—
Fourth	1	—	—
Fifth	1	1	—
Sixth	1	—	—

chosen on a single ballot than those selected after 1950. In fact, the
strong divisions that required from three to six ballots to make a
selection all fell into the 1951–63 period.

The most difficult selection of a parliamentary candidate encountered in the study occurred in a strong division preparing for a
by-election. Six ballots and two sessions of the selection conference
were required to resolve a struggle between the constituency agent
and a total stranger who had been nominated, with the decision of
the conferees turning on their personal reaction to the agent, a
capable man with a very strong personality. In the marginal division
that cast five ballots before reaching a decision, it was clear that
none of the nominees applied the techniques described in *The Making
of the President 1960*. The amazingly even distribution of support for
the first three candidates in Table 5.3 suggests an unstructured
selection conference that had a bias toward the better educated

professionally trained type of nominee as opposed to the less well-educated technically employed man.

The name of the successful nominee is then forwarded to Transport House for endorsement. A separate report on the proceedings of the selection conference is made to Transport House by the regional organiser, who is present to assure that all procedural requirements of the selection process are complied with, and who also apprises Transport House of any significant policy differences between the views expressed by the candidate and those of the

TABLE 5.3. *Pattern of voting in a strongly contested selection conference in a marginal constituency*

Candi-date	Age	Occupation	1st	2nd	3rd	4th	5th
A	47	School Teacher	17	18	24	26	—
B	32	General Practitioner	19	20	23	27	47
C	39	Jig Borer-Engineer	21	23	24	27	33
D	41	Railway Engineman	9	9	—	—	—
E	31	College Lecturer	3	—	—	—	—
F	46	School Teacher	10	10	9	—	—
G	50	Railway Inspector	1	—	—	—	—

Labour Party. On rare occasions, the regional organiser's report plays a role in the endorsement phase of the selection process, as the following discussion indicates.

3. *Endorsement by the National Executive Committee*

Of all steps in the selection process, this without doubt was the most controversial. This is the point at which the NEC exercises a modicum of control over the selection of parliamentary candidates, a control based on the Constitution and Standing Orders of the Labour Party, Clause IX, of which three sections are relevant. They are:

Section 3. The selection of Labour Candidates for Parliamentary Elections shall not be regarded as completed until the name of the person selected has been placed before a meeting of the National Executive Committee, and his or her selection has been duly endorsed.

Section 7. No person may be selected as a Parliamentary Labour Candidate by a Constituency Labour Party, and no candidate may be endorsed by the National Executive Committee, if the person concerned . . . (c) does not accept and conform to the Constitution, Programme, Principles, and Policy of the Party or (d) does not undertake to accept and act in harmony with the Standing Orders of the Parliamentary Labour Party.

Section 8. Any candidate who, after election, fails to accept or act in harmony with the Standing Orders of the Parliamentary Labour Party shall be considered to have violated the terms of this Constitution.[21]

Although on paper the NEC does have a fearsome power over the selection of parliamentary candidates, in the selection of candidates for the 1964 election it refused endorsement to only two of the 360-odd names that were submitted for approval, one of which was subsequently approved when forwarded by another constituency.[22] There were also two candidates in the sample on which this study is based who experienced some difficulty in obtaining endorsement.[23] In one marginal division the candidate was a man whom the NEC had refused to place on Panel B because of criticisms of the NEC and Labour Party policy which the candidate had expressed in a published article and in a speech at an annual conference. Endorsement was withheld for three months, but was eventually granted after one meeting between the candidate and NEC representatives. The second incident involved a weak division in which the candidate had been the sole nominee. During the selection conference, which was a formality only, the nominee declared that if elected, he would not

[21] *Labour Party Annual Conference Report, 1963,* pp. 279–80.

[22] Ernest Roberts, Assistant General Secretary of the Amalgamated Engineering Union was refused endorsement for Horsham (West Sussex). Illtyd Harrington, a teacher, was refused endorsement for Dover, but was approved when his name was forwarded by the Wembley North CLP.

[23] There is no means of establishing how many other cases of delayed endorsement there were during 1962 and 1963, if indeed there were any. Had there been additional instances of this nature, it is safe to assume that *Tribune* or the *New Statesman* would have given them full publicity. The *New Statesman* attempted to manufacture an instance of purported NEC tyranny in Ealing North, but a pointed letter from the Chairman of the Ealing North CLP brought this venture to a swift end. See letter from Howard Whitten in the *New Statesman,* June 15, 1962.

support any policy leading to the use of nuclear weapons by a Labour government. This statement was included in the report sent by the regional organiser to Transport House. The candidate was invited to meet with the NEC to discuss foreign and defence policy, following which the NEC decided not to endorse the candidate. Representations on behalf of the candidate were made by his constituency party, and his candidacy was ultimately endorsed after an unusual understanding was reached. The understanding was that if the candidate would explain Labour Party defence policy during his campaign, he might reserve the right to voice his personal disagreement with it.

4. *Relationship of candidate selection to the general election*

Incumbent MPs were readopted by their divisions within a few days after the dissolution of Parliament and the setting of the date of the general election. There was the usual strong presumption in favour of the incumbent's being selected as the candidate. If an incumbent was to be dropped, the decision was made well before the closing of Parliament and the new nominee was chosen by following the customary selection process. Such an incident took place in the Wolverhampton North-East division early in 1963 when steps were taken to replace the incumbent. A similar incident had occurred in 1945 in another strong division in the Midlands where the member who had served since 1935 was found to be unacceptable. Another candidate was chosen for the 1945 election, but the incumbent ran independently and, true to the form of British politics, lost his deposit. In neither of these instances did the GMC feel compelled to make a public explanation of its actions, although they were called upon to justify their actions to the NEC.[24]

The general election of 1964 was delayed so often that excessive newsprint was expended in speculating just when it would take place. Cogent reasons were put forward for holding the election in the spring of 1963, in the autumn of 1963, and later for holding the election in March, June or October of 1964. When the prime minister, Sir Alec Douglas-Home, called the election for October 15,

[24] For a further discussion of this point, see Butler and Rose, op. cit., pp. 123–4, and McKenzie, *British Political Parties*, op. cit., p. 557.

F

1964, the constituency Labour parties had been prepared for an election for eighteen months. Except for a single weak division in which personal and ideological factionalism had caused utter disorganisation, all the parliamentary candidates had been chosen by April 1963. Some divisions had begun much earlier, within eighteen months of the 1959 election, but twenty-two of the twenty-five divisions selecting candidates did so between December 1961 and April 1963.

TABLE 5.4. *Selection dates of parliamentary candidates, by type of constituency*

| | Constituencies | | |
	Strong	Marginal	Weak
1961			
February		1	
April		1	
December		1	
1962			
January		2	
March		1	
May		1	1
June	1	1	
July			1
September			2
October			1
November		1	
December		1	1
1963			
January			1
February		1	2
March			1
April	1		1
July			1

Table 5.4 shows the distribution of dates on which the candidates were endorsed by the NEC. The dates on which the two strong divisions selected candidates were determined by the date on which the incumbent wrote his letter of resignation. Marginal divisions were well ahead of the weak in selecting their candidates and in making preliminary plans for the general election campaign.

5. *Post-dissolution selection*

Although very much of a formality, selection conferences are held in each constituency after the dissolution of Parliament. Technically speaking, incumbent MPs become 'former' Members of Parliament upon dissolution, and must be officially readopted by their constituencies. A candidate in a division not held by his party is technically only a 'prospective parliamentary candidate' until he is adopted following the dissolution of Parliament and upon the opening of the official election campaign.

The tentative nature of a non-incumbent's status is made necessary by the Representation of the People Act of 1949. As it is interpreted, all the campaign expenditures of an official candidate for Parliament are liable for inclusion in his actual election expenses. Since these are rather sharply limited by the Act—ranging from a basic £628 to £1,328, depending on the size of electorate and whether an urban or a widespread rural constituency—a non-incumbent in a campaign with a long preparatory period might exhaust his legal expenses before the election proper got under way. The fiction of being the 'prospective candidate' permits him to start on even terms with his incumbent competitor regarding the legal date his election expenditures commence.

6. *Central control of the selection process*

Despite the fact that the NEC interviewed only a handful of candidates, and denied endorsement to but one, there is a strongly held popular impression that the NEC can control the process of selecting parliamentary candidates at will. This conception of overwhelming and arrogantly used power is fed by writers and newspapers with a broad range of political views. Robert McKenzie quotes from an article by Mark Abrams written in 1951 to the effect that NEC powers over nominations had resulted in ' . . . a state of affairs not unlike the era of rotten boroughs before 1832; but with one difference—where the great Whig and Tory families disposed of dozens of safe constituencies, Transport House now has under its patronage hundreds of safe seats'.[25] This accusation is categorically rejected by

[25] McKenzie, ibid, p. 552, quoting Mark Abrams, *Parliamentary Affairs*, Winter 1951, p. 232.

McKenzie, but by describing in minute detail the powers which the NEC theoretically has over the selection of candidates, he may have inadvertently furnished ammunition for those more inclined to oppose the NEC than to regard the situation realistically.[26]

Another suggestion of covert power wielded by the NEC is made by Nora Beloff, political correspondent for the *Observer*. In commenting on Austin Ranney's study of the parliamentary selection process, she writes: 'A major conclusion of Ranney's inquiry is that the two parties' central organisations have much less power to place candidates than the public supposes. Perhaps if the professor had been tapping telephone wires linking central office, regional agents and the constituency headquarters, he might have been less ready to dismiss the central office influence as "almost nil".'[27] Resisting the temptation to ask whether it is on information obtained in this fashion that Miss Beloff bases her patronising evaluation of Professor Ranney's conclusion, it is relevant to point out that some British political writers approach this topic with the same attitude as those who insist there is an organised and identifiable power structure in every community. No matter how many charges are shown to be without foundation, those who feel that the NEC surely must have control over selection of parliamentary candidates end up insisting that the researcher did not dig deeply enough and that the NEC does indeed have such powers. Thus, when Ranney says that Transport House has much more nominal power to intervene in candidate selection than does the Conservative Central Office, Miss Beloff observes: 'In fact, Labour constituencies recently received a governessy directive from national agent Sara Barker reminding them "that the National Executive Committee must be represented at all meetings concerning the selection by one of its officers".'[28] In effect, it turns out that the NEC officer referred to is the regional organiser for the Labour Party, or if he is busy, some one on the regional organiser's staff. In addition, physical representation at all meetings falls some distance short of control, particularly when the regional organiser or his representative play the discreet role that they do.

Important as these allegations of NEC control of the selection process are, those having even greater effect, particularly on the

[26] McKenzie, idem, pp. 549–53.
[27] Beloff, op. cit.
[28] Ibid.

left-wing of the party, are to be found in *Tribune* and the *New Statesman*. These weekly journals became particularly excited over the Roberts and Harrington cases, carrying long accounts of the incidents over a six-month period.[29] On February 9, 1962, *Tribune* claimed that more than sixty constituency parties had joined the battle to have Roberts reinstated as the Horsham candidate, presumably by forwarding resolutions to that effect to Transport House. Rumours circulated in some constituencies that as many as nine candidates had been refused endorsement by the NEC. The Agenda for the 1962 Annual Conference also gave evidence of the suspicion with which some CLPs viewed NEC endorsement, for no less than five resolutions and one amendment, all critical of the NEC, were presented on this subject.[30]

The allegations by Abrams and Beloff of NEC control over the selection of parliamentary candidates do not involve charges of political bias, but those of the Labour left do accuse the NEC of discriminating against candidates who hold unilateralist or generally left-wing views, particularly on foreign and defence policies. This discrimination is supposedly achieved by Transport House control over admission to Panels A and B and by the endorsement phase of the selection process. While it is true that the NEC has refused to place the names of certain applicants on its lists of candidates, it is not necessary for constituencies to select candidates from the panels. One of the two candidates who had difficulty obtaining endorsement had previously been refused a place on Panel B. He was selected by his CLP nonetheless, and endorsed with some delay but without extraordinary representations on his behalf. Table 5.1 shows that about 15 per cent of the nominees in marginal divisions, about 33 per cent in strong divisions, and over half in weak divisions were on neither panel.

[29] *Tribune*, December 29, 1961; January 5, 1962; January 26, 1962; February 9, 1962; June 1, 1962; June 8, 1962; and June 22, 1962. See also the *New Statesman*, June 1, 1962; June 8, 1962; June 15, 1962 and June 22, 1962. In many ways, in recent years, the overall tone of the *New Statesman*'s socialism has been 'moderate' rather than 'left', but on this issue its reporting was quite as vigorous as that in *Tribune*.

[30] *Agenda, Labour Party Annual Conference, 1962*, p. 36. The resolutions were not debated at the Conference, and a motion to refer back to the NEC a portion of its Annual Report dealing with parliamentary candidates was defeated. Ibid., p. 223.

The charge that the NEC discriminated against those holding left-wing views on foreign and defence policy hardly agrees with the results of this study regarding the political attitudes of parliamentary candidates. Table 2.11 in chapter 2 reveals that 32 per cent of the parliamentary candidates had reservations regarding the Parliamentary Labour Party's defence policy and another 20 per cent rejected it outright. Similarly on questions like response to United States action in Cuba in the autumn of 1962 (Table 2.13) or general attitudes toward the Soviet Union and the United States (Table 2.17), parliamentary candidates, particularly those in the weak constituencies, exhibited strong left attitudes. While it is true that most of the candidates holding these views were running in hopelessly weak constituencies, the charge was not that the NEC endorsed left-wing candidates only when they had no chance of winning, but that it was reluctant to endorse them under any circumstances.

Since the criticisms of the NEC now are based on an alleged power over the selection of parliamentary candidates that it uses to discriminate against left-wing candidates, it would perhaps be more appropriate to raise some doubt concerning how effectively the NEC accomplished its duties. It is interesting to note that, with all its purported power and bias, the NEC endorsed some unusual candidates for the 1964 election. One of these, selected by a marginal division with excellent prospects of victory, privately expressed the idea that if Labour were to lose the 1964 election, he would be inclined to question seriously whether it should not forsake the parliamentary path to political power and use industrial action instead—presumably something along the line of a general strike. A weak constituency chose a candidate whose name was approved by the NEC only to have the man resign his candidacy not long before the 1964 election to join the Communist Party, from which he soon moved on to another political group. It would seem that the endorsement activities of the NEC are not as rigorous as the Labour left suggests, nor as extensive as other British political observers have described.

Among CLP secretary-agents there was unanimity of opinion that Transport House was powerless to influence the selection of parliamentary candidates for general elections. In response to a question about how Transport House would go about such an effort, the answers were: 'I don't know'; 'Never heard of it being done';

'Nothing they could do'; 'I really have no idea'; 'Never encountered it in sixteen years as an agent' and 'They simply can't'. One party veteran disposed of the question by suggesting that Transport House should endorse all nominees except the one they wanted chosen. A few respondents thought that Transport House might be able, very indirectly and diplomatically, to get a person nominated, but they were agreed that little could be done to make certain this person was short-listed. Influencing the selection conference itself was completely beyond the powers of Transport House. Regional organisers who read this may be assured that, if this description does not accord with the facts in their regions, the security system in the Labour Party regarding the selection of candidates easily surpasses that of the Admiralty. It should be emphasised that the opinion of the constituency secretary-agents on this matter is probably the best evidence that can be produced. These officials have no reason to dissimulate for the benefit of Transport House. A number of them are well to the left in the Labour Party. When one man who says that he is in the Labour Party only because there is no Independent Labour Party which he can join, and another who says that the only newspapers he trusts are *Tribune* and the *Daily Worker*, together insist that their constituency parties are completely independent of Transport House influence in the selection of candidates, these opinions are not to be taken lightly. In addition, the complete agreement within a widely separated and varied group of constituency party leaders must be emphasised. There was no other item in an extensive questionnaire that resulted in such a broad consensus.

7. *Influence of the NEC in by-elections*

When a sitting member is removed by death or resignation and a by-election is required, the regular rules of procedure governing the selection of parliamentary candidates are suspended. Party regulations provide that 'the National Executive Committee shall co-operate with the Executive Committee of the [Constituency] Party in the nomination of a candidate. The National Executive Committee may, if it deems it necessary in the interests of the Labour Party, advise the Executive Committee of the [Constituency] Party to select a nomination it may submit to it.'[31] Again there is a difference

[31] *Model Rules*, Set A, Clause XII, Section (5).

between the appearance and the reality of power wielded by the NEC over the divisional party. It is undeniable that a few young and talented men close to the late Hugh Gaitskell were selected as candidates in by-elections in the early 1960s, and there may have been pressure from Transport House in their favour. In light of other information gathered in the constituencies, such pressure was not likely to have been very effective, and it is likely that these men were selected simply because they were the superior nominees, or because they were backed by the Campaign for Democratic Socialism, rather than because Transport House submitted their names.

Transport House has not always distinguished itself in the past when it has made an effort to influence by-election selection conferences in favour of men it very much wanted in the House of Commons. Three of the strong divisions in the sample had engaged in by-elections over the years, and in two of them the NEC attempted to find a safe seat for ministers defeated in the previous general election. Both attempts failed, the NEC nominees being among the first to be dropped as successive ballots were taken. The NEC had gone to great lengths to arrange one of these by-elections. The sitting member had been given a peerage in order to create the vacancy, but the NEC was still unable to place its nominee in candidacy.[32] In the third by-election an MP was retiring and a short list of five nominees was submitted to Transport House, which added the name of a nominee who had been passed over when the CLP executive made up the list. This action, which was legally permissible, was apparently taken because of the pressure from one of the important trade unions in the division. It is difficult to assess the actual interest of Transport House in this man, but he was the second of six nominees on the short list to be dropped.

8. *Influence of trade unions in candidate selection*

Some party members fulminated against the NEC for possessing too much power, but others felt the NEC lacked sufficient influence.

[32] Harrison, op. cit., p. 302, states that 'after the St Helens selection conference in 1958, the NEC decided that it would make no more nominations for selection at by-elections'. The NEC made an exception to this

Disenchantment of the trade unions with certain CLP selection conference results extended back to the early 1950s. Their dissatisfaction was neatly encapsulated in a resolution tabled by the National Union of Furniture Trade Operatives at the 1955 Labour Party Conference, and quoted by Martin Harrison:

> This Conference, while recognising that the selection of a Parliamentary candidate must rest with the Constituency Party, notes with concern the diminishing number of Trade Union sponsored candidates at succeeding General Elections, and accordingly requests the National Executive Committee to consider this matter with the object of strengthening the Trades Union group of Labour Party Members of Parliament.[33]

There was little that the NEC could do to remedy this situation. This had already been recognised by union leaders, one of whom had said two years earlier: 'The bald fact is this, that the autonomy in the selection of a candidate is with the local CLP concerned. . . . whether he be a man sponsored by a trade union or any other political organisation.'[34]

The 1964 election did not reassure the trade union leaders concerned for their waning role in the Parliamentary Labour Party. Of the MPS and parliamentary candidates in the strong divisions, six were sponsored by trade unions, one by the Co-operative Party, and five by the constituency parties. Only two candidates in the marginal districts were sponsored by unions, one of whom won. Of the candidates sponsored by their constituency parties, five were successful. In the weak divisions none of the candidates was sponsored by a trade union.

[33] A. G. Tomkins, quoted in Harrison, op. cit., p. 300.
[34] Percy Knight, quoted in Harrison, op. cit., p. 302.

---

decision in 1965 when vacancies were created in Leyton and Nuneaton *via* the peerage route so that Patrick Gordon Walker, defeated at Smethwick, and Frank Cousins, appointed from outside the House of Commons to Harold Wilson's cabinet, could be elected to Parliament. The NEC was successful in getting Gordon Walker and Cousins adopted by the constituencies, but Gordon Walker was defeated in Leyton and Cousins' majority in Nuneaton was halved.

9. Personal characteristics of parliamentary candidates[35]

I. Age

Leaders of the Labour Party have for some time been concerned with the ageing of the party, particularly within the PLP.[36] Because of the unstructured character of the selection process, any policy

TABLE 5.5 *Age distribution of Labour candidates in the 1964 general election*

	Strong	Margi- nal	Weak	All Cands.	MPS	MPS and cands.	Age[37] distribution of 1959 cands. %
21–25	0	1	1	2	0	2 ⎫ 17%	5
26–30	0	0	4	4	0	4 ⎭	
31–35	0	5	2	7	0	7 ⎫ 26%	24
36–40	0	1	1	2	0	2 ⎭	
41–45	2	2	1	5	1	6 ⎫ 31%	27
46–50	0	1	2	3	2	5 ⎭	
51–55	0	1	0	1	2	3 ⎫ 20%	28
56–60	0	0	1	1	3	4 ⎭	
61–65	0	0	0	0	1	1 ⎫ 3%	12
66–70	0	0	0	0	0	0 ⎭	
Over 70	0	0	0	0	1	1 3%	4

decision made by the NEC would be made operational only with some difficulty. However, as far as the age of candidates was concerned, the NEC seemed able to make its wishes known. True, it made little difference what the ages of Labour parliamentary candidates were

[35] See Butler and King, op. cit., pp. 232–40, and *The British General Election of 1966*, London 1966, pp. 207–12, for comparative data on personal characteristics of Labour candidates.

[36] Phillips, op. cit., pp. 15–17.

[37] Butler and Rose, op. cit., p. 125.

if they were not elected. In four successive general elections the presumption was against younger candidates from the marginal divisions winning, for the CLPs in safe Labour seats tended not to select younger men as candidates. When Morgan Phillips noted that 'the average age of Labour MPs has gone up at every election since 1945, and today [1960] the average Labour MP is, at 55, seven years older than his opponent', he was merely recognising the impact on the Labour Party of the heavy losses sustained in four successive elections, beginning when it had come out of the 1950 election with a majority its leaders found unworkable.

Table 5.5 shows that the median age of all 1964 parliamentary candidates was about 34 years. There were no differences by type of constituency, although there were only two candidates in the strong divisions. The only difference, so small as to be negligible, between the weak and the marginal divisions was that the latter had no candidates in the 26–30 age category and only five in the 31–35 age group. The weak divisions had four candidates in the 26–30 age group, and two in the 31–35 group. The comparison between the age distribution of Labour candidates in the 1959 general election and the 1964 election was striking. Only 29 per cent of the candidates in 1959 were under the age of 40, while 43 per cent of the 1964 group were in this age group. At the other end of the scale, 44 per cent of the 1959 Labour candidates were over 50 years of age, as compared with 26 per cent in 1964.

II. Occupation

Not only the age structure of candidates in the 1964 election changed markedly from that of 1959, but their occupational background also. Following closely the occupational classifications used by Butler and Rose, Table 5.6 suggests that the proportion of skilled and semi-skilled workers was reduced considerably, with the reduction distributed rather evenly among the other three occupation categories. In light of the sharp drop in the proportion of workers standing for Parliament, the 'cloth cap' tradition of the Labour Party has been modified, and certain groups in British society without historic support for Labour have begun to furnish increasing numbers of parliamentary candidates.

TABLE 5.6. *Occupational distribution of Labour candidates in 1964 general election*

	Strong	Margi-nal	Weak	All cands.	MPS	MPS and cands.		Occu-[38] pational distri-bution of 1959 cands. %
Professional	0	8	2	10	5	15	43%	40
Business	0	0	3	3	1	4	20%	15
White collar	0	1	1	2	1	3		
Skilled	0	1	2	3	1	4	17%	28
Semi-skilled	0	1	1	2	0	2		
Party or union employee	1	0	1	2	2	4	20%	17
Housewife	0	0	1	1	0	1		
Journalist	1	0	1	2	0	2		

III. Religion

Of the twenty-five parliamentary candidates, eighteen of them claimed no religious affiliation. Three of the remaining seven were Methodists, two were Roman Catholics, one was a Jew, and one a member of the Church of England. Seventy-two per cent of the candidates subscribed to no organised religious group as compared with 60 per cent of all CLP leaders who made the same claim. Among the various types of constituencies, there were no differences on this point.

IV. Education

Clear differences were indicated between the educational backgrounds of candidates in the weak and in the marginal divisions in respect to the school-leaving age. Eight of the eleven candidates in the marginal divisions attended school after the age of eighteen, while nine of the twelve candidates in weak divisions had completed

[38] Butler and Rose, op. cit., pp. 126–7.

their formal education by the age of eighteen. Sitting members fell into the extremes, either having ceased formal education by the age of fourteen, or else having pursued it past the age of eighteen. One-fourth of the MPs and candidates as a group had finished school at fourteen years, another quarter had finished at eighteen years, while half had continued formal education after the age of eighteen.

It was noteworthy that candidates in weak divisions had a wider range of distribution in type of education, school-leaving age, occupation, and age than did the candidates for the marginal constituencies, where the candidates invariably clustered in one very

TABLE 5.7. *School-leaving age of Labour candidates in 1964 general election*

	Before 14	15–18	After 18
Constituencies			
Strong	0	2	0
Marginal	3	0	8
Weak	2	7	3
All	5	9	11
MPS	4	0	6
MPS and candidates	9	9	17

large cell with the others virtually non-existent. This pattern in marginal divisions may have reflected an unspoken consensus on the kind of candidate likely to win in a marginal division. Whatever the cause, marginal candidates as a group had more in common with one another than did candidates in the weak divisions. It was also indicated that there was some similarity between candidates in the marginal divisions and MPs.

Limitations imposed by the lesser size of the sample made comparison with data presented by Butler and Rose on education of parliamentary candidates somewhat difficult. Three of the educational categories shown in Table 5.8 showed considerable congruency, but the other three showed far less. The first three categories, which represented less formal education, comprised 51 per cent of the 1959 and 46 per cent of the 1964 candidates. The last three categories represented 49 per cent of the 1959 candidates and

54 per cent of the 1964 candidates.[39] Therefore, there was a 10 per cent shift toward a higher level of formal educational attainment among the 1964 candidates, which was a change of some magnitude.

TABLE 5.8. *Type of education received by Labour candidates in 1964 general election*

(*El.*=*Elementary; Gr.*=*Grammar; P.S.*=*Public School*)

	El.	El.–Other	El.–Gr.	El.–Gr.–Other	El.–Gr.–Univ.	P.S.–Univ.
Constituencies						
Strong	0	1	0	0	1	0
Marginal	1	3	0	0	5	2
Weak	2	2	3	1	3	1
All	3	6	3	1	9	3
MPS	0	4	0	2	4	0
MPS and Cands.; %	3; 9%	10; 28%	3; 9%	3; 9%	13; 36%	3; 9%
Educ. distribution of 1959 Cands.[40]	11%	16%	22%	10%	27%	12%

10. *Candidate-constituency ties*

The freedom of British parliamentary candidates from legal or customary residence requirements has long intrigued American political observers.[41] The residence requirement has been applied with vigour in the United States, particularly at the congressional level, although it has not been unknown for members of Congress to maintain a voting address in their constituency while actually residing outside it.

The data assembled for this study did not bear solely on the point of residence, but also on whether there was some family connection between the candidate and his constituency. When presented in these terms, two out of three marginal and strong division candidates had either residential or family ties with their constituencies. In the weak divisions, two out of three candidates had neither family nor residen-

[39] Two per cent of the 1959 candidates had attended public school and no other, but no candidate with this educational background appeared in the sample.

[40] Butler and Rose, op. cit., p. 128.

[41] For an excellent recent treatment of this topic, see Ranney, op. cit., pp. 39–40.

tial ties with the divisions adopting them. Constituency ties were noticeably strongest among incumbent members and candidates having the best apparent chance of election. This does not imply that the residential or family ties had a basic effect on the candidate's chance of electoral success, but merely that residential or family connections constituted an advantage in the selection process.[42]

i. Past candidatures and short-listings of 1964 parliamentary candidates

In his article on British parliamentary candidates, Ranney pointed out that 51 per cent of those Labour candidates who ran for the first time in 1951 and 1955 did not obtain a second candidacy.[43] According to Ranney, 19 per cent of first time candidates in 1951 and 1955 were readopted by the division which had given them their first opportunity. Of those given a second chance, 24 per cent stood for election in a constituency more favourable to a Labour candidate than the first division in which they ran. The findings presented by Ranney confirmed those of this study, although the data collected here dealt only with candidates selected for the 1964 election. In this sample more than three-fifths of the divisions chose candidates who had never before stood in a general election. One-fifth of the divisions selected persons who had one previous candidature, and one-eighth chose candidates who had been selected twice before. A 1964 candidate who had been chosen four times before was a special case. Each time he had been a candidate in the same division, one adjacent to the constituency where he was born, resided and worked, and which had been a sure Labour seat until 1959. The Labour incumbent was defeated in 1959, but in 1964 there was no doubt that the Labour candidate would be elected in a division where only the slightest swing to Labour was needed. In Ranney's study 24 per cent of the candidates selected a second time were chosen by constituencies in which their chances of winning were improved, and in the sample this occurred with 28 per cent of such candidates.[44] However,

[42] Ibid., pp. 40–1.
[43] Ibid., Table III, p. 39.
[44] A candidate in one weak division was the only one of eight experienced candidates who had not bettered his position. In 1955 he received 30 per cent of the vote in his first division; in 1959 he received 21 per cent of the

only one constituency in the sample readopted its 1959 candidate (4 per cent) as opposed to 19 per cent in Ranney's study. The prospective parliamentary candidates as a group not only lacked experience in a general election prior to 1964, but also had seldom sought selection as a nominee. Of the 1964 candidates, 44 per cent had never been short-listed in a division other than the one in which they were then standing, 28 per cent had been short-listed once before, 16 per cent twice before, and 12 per cent three or four times.

Studying the competition for selection as Labour candidate for Parliament had some interesting aspects. Apparently those in the Labour Party who entertained hopes for a parliamentary career persisted for only a limited period of time, if their hopes were unrealised. Furthermore, most constituency selection conferences did not place high value on experience, or, stated conversely, they did not consider inexperience a handicap. The result was an extensive turnover of candidates in divisions which had been unsuccessful in electing their candidates in the previous election. Most of the individuals who remained in the competition for selection as parliamentary candidate endeavoured to better their chances by being adopted in a stronger constituency. Failing this, they tended to withdraw entirely from the contest.

The statement that most constituency parties placed a low value on electoral experience may require explanation. The statement is essentially accurate, but the stronger divisions certainly gave more attention to campaign experience. The five marginal divisions which chose candidates who had never before stood for Parliament were the less promising marginal constituencies. With one exception, the six more promising marginal divisions selected candidates who had already stood in from one to four general elections. The number of candidates in strong divisions was too small to permit generalisation, but of the two strong divisions, one chose a man who had not been short-listed or selected up to that time, while the other chose a man who had been short-listed four times before and was a candidate in the 1955 general election.

Five of the ten MPS had been neither candidates nor nominees on short lists before their selection in divisions where the lowest Labour

---

vote in his second division; in 1964 he was adopted by a division in which only 20 per cent of the voters supported the Labour Party in 1959.

vote was habitually about 60 per cent in general elections. The remaining MPs in the strong divisions shared six short listings and five candidatures.

II. Present public and party offices of parliamentary candidates

One of the qualifications for being a Labour parliamentary candidate is that the individual be a member of the Labour Party. Since the only way of becoming a Labour Party member is to join a constituency party, every candidate has had the opportunity to hold office in a divisional party and in some local government capacity. Generally, parliamentary candidates had not availed themselves of these opportunities to a discernible extent. Five of the entire group of parliamentary candidates held no party or public office, and ten held only one. Six candidates held two offices each, and four held three or more. On this point there were no differences between the marginal and weak constituencies, with each group holding a total of sixteen public and party offices.

III. Political relationship between constituencies and MPs or prospective parliamentary candidates

A majority of 72 per cent of all respondents thought that their MPs or prospective parliamentary candidates reflected the political attitudes of their respective constituency parties. Their present or potential parliamentary representative was considered by 19 per cent to be to the left of the local constituency party, while 9 per cent thought their representative was to the right. In the field of foreign policy deviations were more conspicuous and were mentioned by twenty-five respondents. Domestic policy deviations were mentioned by eleven respondents. The nature and extent of deviations varied little between strong and marginal divisions, nor was there much variation in the relative importance of foreign policy as compared with domestic issues. In both strong and marginal divisions foreign policy was mentioned four times as often as domestic policy.

In the weak divisions 68 per cent of the respondents thought that their candidates reflected constituency political attitudes. Three times as many respondents in the weak divisions stated that their candidates were to the left of the division as believed that their candidates were inclined to the right. It was pertinent that the three respondents who placed their candidate to the right were all in the same division, but the nine respondents who placed their candidates to the left were divided among six constituencies. There was no distinction made in the weak divisions as to the relative importance of foreign and domestic issues, each field being referred to by seven respondents.

In five of the weak and three of the marginal divisions there were no policy differences between the CLP and the candidate, yet some respondents attributed some policy deviation to their particular candidate. When questioned on the subject, the respondents answered in terms of temperament, attitude and style, giving rise to the supposition that the responses to this question were probably of a personal nature.

IV. Incongruous relationships between CLPs and prospective parliamentary candidates

Evidence that the selection process did not produce distorted knowledge about the nominees is based on the finding that only three marginal and one weak divisions were found where the selection resulted in candidates whose politics were appreciably different from those of the CLP.

The weak division was confronted with a choice between only two nominees. One of these was a local man with strong unilateralist sympathies, and the other a complete stranger who had never had any past connection with the division and whose policy views in all areas were quite moderate. The latter nominee was selected, even though there was unanimous agreement among all the respondents that he was to the right of the constituency party on all major issues. The reasons given for his choice in preference to a man whose policy views were much more in accord with those of the CLP were that he was clearly the better candidate of the two, and that there would probably be more agreement between the views of the successful nominee and those of the electorate in the division.

The selection in one of the marginal divisions resulted from a series of fortuitous circumstances. One of these was the recollection of a schoolteacher in the constituency that about fifteen years ago he had a student who expressed a strong desire for a parliamentary career. Another was the decision of the secretary-agent to begin the selection process just prior to the election of a new General Management Committee in which unilateralist sentiment would probably have been less strong than in the GMC that made the selection. A third was the personal connection the candidate had with the constituency, which had the dual advantage of giving him the aura of a home-town boy without the members of the selection conference knowing very much about him. To these was added the characteristic that selection conferences usually have of not providing an opportunity to look into the policy views of the nominees, and a situation out of which an inappropriate selection could develop was created. There was general agreement among the respondents in the division that the candidate was perceptibly to the left of prevailing political attitudes within the CLP. The candidate thought the differences were not enough to cause disharmony, and the agent thought the strong left views the candidate voiced at the selection conference were not an accurate reflection of his political opinions. As measured by the response to the series of questions on policy matters, the candidate took a strong left position on all questions but one, that relating to Chinese action in India.

A similar situation developed in another marginal constituency, but with more serious consequences. Here the basic problems were limited competition of indifferent quality and a genuine misunderstanding concerning the candidate's views on defence policy. One respondent felt the candidate had concealed his unilateralist views, while another noted that the selection conference had been told the candidate was not in favour of atomic weapons when actually he was strongly opposed to them.[45] The candidate thought he had been selected primarily because he was young and had professional training, and that the party leaders in his constituency were not strongly

[45] This is more than a semantic difference. A member of the Labour Party who was not in favour of atomic weapons, to which almost everyone is unfavourable, could support the Parliamentary Labour Party's defence policy with no reservations, while a person who was strongly opposed to atomic weapons could be a member of the Campaign for Nuclear Disarmament and in favour of British withdrawal from NATO as well as of removal of all American military bases from Britain. While not accepting the total unilateralist position, the candidate admitted strong tendencies in that direction.

oriented politically. This may have been true at the time he was
selected, but his choice had the effect of sharpening the political
perceptions of the CLP leaders. Apparently the questioning had been
of such a general nature that the views of the three nominees on
political matters were not established, and some members of the
conference had wished to forego selection and begin the process
anew by soliciting new nominees. With some reluctance the candidate was finally chosen, whereupon tension soon developed between
him and the party leaders because of the discrepancy between his
views on defence policy and those of most of the local leaders. The
rift, which was recognised by the candidate and the constituency leaders, nullified any prospect of an enthusiastic campaign in that division.

Divergence over policy which existed in the remaining marginal
division was neither a real nor a potential hazard. This division, alone
among the twenty-four weak and marginal parties, readopted the
candidate it had chosen for the 1959 election. In that contest his
selection had been made the day the campaign opened, just twenty-
one days before the election. This unusual circumstance was caused
by the failure, due to illness, of the first candidate selected to
participate in political work, with the result that the GMC withdrew
his name. The new candidate did so well on such short notice that
he was chosen again early in 1961, even though his ideas on defence
policy had changed appreciably since 1959. When first chosen, the
candidate had pronounced unilateralist views, but by 1961 he had
accepted a multilateralist position on defence policy and had
moderated his ideas on domestic issues as well. The candidate
informed the selection conference of his altered views, even though
an opposing nominee was chairman of the GMC and a unilateralist,
and was given a clear majority on the first ballot.[46] Because there
were no evasions, and because the division was well led and strongly
motivated to win the coming election, the presence of a moderate
candidate in a constituency with a strong left bias created no
problems in the 1964 general election.

[46] The result became more significant when the date of the selection was
considered. February 1961 was only a few months after the Scarborough
Conference which adopted a unilateralist resolution, and well before the
Blackpool Conference which overturned the resolution. Unilateralism,
which has since become an increasingly irrelevant issue, was at its peak in
the winter of 1961, and especially strong in this division.

There were no differences of consequence between each of the nine strong constituency parties and its member. Two of the members from strong divisions had indicated to their parties a decision not to stand for re-election in 1964. One incumbent member refused to answer any communication, whether by letter, telephone, or personal message. Of the nine MPs interviewed, four perceived differences between their own policy position and that of their constituency party, although all four construed the differences as minimal. No pattern developed in the deviations. One member placed himself to the left of his division on both foreign and domestic issues, complaining also of the lack of policy discussion there. Another put himself on the right in foreign policy. The other two members thought they reflected constituency opinion on all issues except British entry into EEC, which both of them strongly supported. No member raised a question regarding his freedom of action *vis-à-vis* the divisional party. Differences were openly admitted to exist, but were accepted with equanimity by all concerned.

In a division in which the MP had chosen not to seek re-election, a degree of estrangement had arisen between him and his constituency party on the issue of foreign and defence policy. Whereas the member had followed the lead of the Parliamentary Labour Party, his constituency party leaders were opposed to continued British membership in NATO, preferring to rely entirely on the United Nations. In this division comments were heard to the effect that 'NATO as a power bloc will bring on World War III', and 'NATO is the prime cause of tension between East and West'. The estrangement had little to do with the member's impending retirement since he was of an advanced age and in poor health. Significantly, the parliamentary candidate chosen by this division a few days before he was interviewed stated that his view on foreign policy might be to the left of his constituency, but this was debatable. The candidate's position on NATO was that the European political situation did not require the presence of three divisions in the British Army of the Rhine (BAOR). He advocated staying in NATO, but thought that certain British goals should be pursued regardless of the effect on NATO. There were other positions on substantive questions which he held in common with his divisional party leaders, and there was little reason to suppose a serious divergence on policy would ensue.

The MP who refused to permit an interview was one of five Labour members from whom the whip was removed for almost two years during 1961 and 1963. His divisional party leaders were not critical of his defiance of the PLP, although one constituency leader suggested that the member's permanent left-wing posture had been assumed in part to attract the attention which his service in Parliament had failed to bring. When this constituency was visited in the late spring of 1963, the rapport between the member and his constituency was showing signs of strain. At that time most Britons assumed the general election would take place long before the autumn of 1964. There was talk that an election might be held in the autumn of 1963, and certainly in the early part of 1964. An MP who has had the party whip withdrawn is no longer considered a member of the PLP, and therefore could not be endorsed by Labour leaders in Transport House. In constituencies which have incumbent MPs, no action is taken to adopt a candidate until Parliament is dissolved, at which time the GMC calls a meeting at which the incumbent member is given a *pro forma* selection.[47] As the time grew near when the constituency might have to select a candidate, the permissiveness of the CLP leaders toward their MP fast drew to a close. Fortunately, the whip was restored to the recalcitrant member in the spring of 1963, and the constituency was spared a troublesome decision. If the matter had come to a choice between the MP and the national Labour Party, all respondents in the division agreed that the constituency would follow the lead of the national party, drop the incumbent and adopt another candidate. Considering the strength of the Labour Party in this division, finding another candidate would present no problem. As it was, the member was advised by his CLP to take the initiative in reconciling his difficulties with the PLP, and that if this could not be done on his terms, it must be accomplished on the terms of the PLP. Every intention was evidenced on the part of the CLP leaders not to permit a deadlock to develop between the division and Transport House. As one constituency leader phrased it: 'The MP can be as independent as he wants—within the Labour Party.

[47] Infrequently, a constituency does not select a sitting MP. One such instance occurred in Wolverhampton where the late John Baird was not readopted in 1964. When this happens the CLP has to explain its action to the National Organiser in Transport House. If the office of the National Organiser accepts the reasons advanced, the selection process is begun by the CLP as if the member had announced his decision to retire.

If it comes to choosing between friendship for him and the Movement, the Movement comes first.'

11. Evaluation of the selection process of parliamentary candidates

The process by which parliamentary candidates are chosen by the Labour Party is remarkably unstructured. Labour leaders wrote into the Model Rules of the party the extensive power granted the National Executive Committee over the selection process, but these powers are largely inoperative. There are reasons for believing that the influence the NEC enjoyed before the end of the Second World War has now disappeared. Although the NEC is serious about its endorsement responsibility, it exercises its power with notable restraint. A small segment of the party habitually carps on the manner in which the NEC discharges its responsibilities in the selection process, but it is difficult to see how the NEC could play a lesser role unless it automatically endorsed all names submitted by constituency Labour parties.[48] The influence of the trade unions on candidate selection has also declined in recent years, and with constituency parties sharing in the growing affluence of British society, it is likely that the trade unions will experience even more difficulty in finding divisions willing to accept union-sponsored candidates in return for union contributions to the constituency party treasury.

Observers of British politics and the CLP leaders are in common agreement that most divisional parties give high priority to the selection of parliamentary candidates. This being true, it is surprising that the selection conferences are not more meaningful. If the number of nominations received by the GMC were increased substantially, competition would certainly be keener. It is hard to understand why marginal divisions in which the Labour candidate

---

[48] There were twenty-seven amendments to the Labour Party Constitution proposed in 1962 which would have limited in one way or another the power of the NEC to endorse parliamentary candidates. Significantly, there was not a single resolution that advocated this power be taken away completely. An analysis of these resolutions suggests that their movers want all the authority in the selection of candidates but prefer to have the NEC retain all the responsibility in the matter.

received 45 per cent or more of the vote in a straight fight in 1959 received so few nominations that no screening was possible at the short-listing phase of the process, all nominees going on the short list. One of the difficulties here is that there is no generally recognised means by which potential nominees could learn when various constituencies were beginning their selection process. Great reliance was placed on word of mouth communication, on the secretary-agent's happening to know of the existence of suitable nominees, and other fortuitous circumstances.

If marginal divisions whose candidates had good chances of winning experienced difficulty in finding more than a minimum number of candidates, the weak divisions were in a position even less enviable. Most of them preferred to maintain independence from the NEC to having a meaningful number of qualified nominees. Only one weak division had a large enough group of qualified nominees to afford its selection conference a valid option. The candidates found by the weak divisions were not necessarily unqualified, for with the limited choice at their disposal most of the divisions were able to find candidates of surprisingly high calibre.

The problem of last-minute withdrawals or the failure of nominees to appear before the selection conference plagued the weak and the marginal divisions. No particular difficulties resulted when the short list contained as many as six names, but the inconvenience was great when the lists contained three to five nominees. This happened in some of the competitive marginal districts, and the conference was forced either to delay its selection, or to offer a promising candidacy to an individual chosen from as few as two nominees.

The procedures of the selection conferences left much to be desired. That conferees thought the conference important was confirmed by the statement of every CLP secretary-agent that a parliamentary selection conference attracted almost the full membership of the GMC. Many agents even complained with bitterness that the only time certain representatives of affiliated organisations made an appearance was at the selection conference held about every five years. Theoretically, the selection conference was supposed to be composed of delegates from various elements of the CLP, whose function it was to listen to and question the nominees, and on the basis of available information to select, on merit, the nominee best suited to represent the division. Doubtless, some selection conferences adhered closely to the theory, but there were others which made no pretence of this, perhaps because few conferees could make such an important decision on the basis of the limited information provided in their brief encounter with the nominees. After the nominees appeared before the conference, it proceeded immediately to the balloting, without a recess for caucusing or an opportunity for discussion. Unless they were willing to vote in the dark, most conferees obtained additional information on the nominees in advance of the meeting or accepted cues from a fellow member whose judgment they trusted.

More written biographical information on each nominee would have been helpful to members of the selection conferences. After interviewing some 140 CLP leaders and meeting many more, one gained the impression that these dedicated individuals with their drive to advance the interests of Labour would have welcomed additional information on the nominees they evaluated. There is no other way to obtain it, since introductions at selection conferences are models of brevity and circumspection in order for the chairman to avoid the charge of partisanship; lengthening the written biographies would tend to preclude this charge. In composing the biographies, the common denominator seemed to be the length of the material given for the least impressive nominee. The others, perhaps in order not to appear immodest, chose to say little about themselves even if they possessed worthwhile qualifications that could be listed at length.

Another factor limiting the effectiveness of the selection conference was the custom of reaching a decision in no more than a few hours. With such a consequential decision being made, why could not the conferees have given additional time to the task of choosing their candidate? This quinquennial privilege is both an honour and an obligation, and increasing the dignity and attention given the process might have the happy result of inducing more nominees to participate. It is likely that the procedures of the selection conference were defined half-a-century ago when Labour Party members worked twelve hours a day, six days a week, and had to walk several miles to the site of the conference. If it is possible to assemble the thousands who attend the Labour Party Annual Conference which lasts almost a week, it is certainly possible to extend the CLP selection conference so that each nominee is allowed at least thirty to forty-five minutes to express his views and to permit those attending the conference to probe his political values and attitudes.

During the interviewing accompanying this study, it was sometimes revealed that the CLP leaders knew very little of the ideas held by the candidates they had helped choose. In one division the CLP chairman was present while the candidate was questioned. Afterward the chairman remarked that the interview had been quite illuminating and that he now knew far more of the candidate's opinions than he had at the time of the selection process—not that the newly acquired information was adverse in any way. The incongruities described earlier are inevitable in a selection process which in some ways seems designed to conceal rather than reveal the basic political attitudes of the nominee. One reason given for the absence of a valid confrontation between nominees and those selecting a candidate was that this might encourage the formation of cliques and factions within the party. Assuming that Labour supporters know their own party, and that this argument is true it may be better to continue current practices. If it is not true, the need for some alteration of the selection procedure is indicated.

If the selection process is to be more than an empty ritual, some time should be provided for the delegates to absorb and discuss information given them before deciding on a candidate. With the British proclivity for talk and tea, no great effort would be needed to arrange a recess at which the delegates could engage in mutual discussion and persuasion. Political give and take is conspicuously absent from selection conferences, and the dispatch with which proceedings are conducted give them a hurried quality that detracts from their importance and dignity.

Selection conferences in CLPs have the reputation of being lotteries, with pure chance playing a greater role in their outcome than any other factor. This evaluation overstates the case for in many constituencies it was clear that the prospective parliamentary candidate was a popular choice with wide support within the constituency party. There were, however, a number of candidates who were chosen by small majorities in closely contested selection conferences and whose views differed substantially from those of their constituency party leaders. This unpredictable nature of selection conferences and their independence from central control maintains a degree of flexibility and responsiveness to popular feeling within the party. These are extremely valuable qualities well worth maintaining in a party system whose distinguishing characteristics are central control and discipline. A restricted choice of nominees and insufficient time for obtaining information and for decision making detract from the utility of a political device that has many virtues.

6

The Annual Conference Delegate

THE LABOUR PARTY Annual Conference is the most interesting yearly political event in Britain. Random incidents, such as a general election or the selection of a party leader, may exceed the Annual Conference in significance, but seldom surpass it in drama, displays of forensic skill, or the fascination of a public struggle for power.[1] In its conference the Labour Party has long been accustomed to expose the strife and internal divisions which threaten its unity and its very existence.[2] Representatives of opposing factions follow one another to the rostrum and attempt to sway the disposition of the conference. This spectacle of internecine conflict is often awesome in its fierceness, and occasionally creates the impression that the destruction of the party is imminent.

The sessions of the conference are usually characterised by a high degree of freedom of expression, with supporters and opponents of

[1] The selection of Sir Alec Douglas-Home as Conservative Party Leader and prime minister had most of these characteristics, but was essentially a private affair. Only a few leaders at the very core of the party were involved in the discussions leading to Sir Alec's designation and in the delicate negotiations that preceded the announcement of his cabinet. On the other hand, the entire nation saw Hugh Gaitskell defy the majority at Labour's 1960 Annual Conference when he opposed the imminent decision to pass a resolution favouring unilateral disarmament.

[2] The last occasion when this question arose was in relation to the unilateralist issue. Had the 1961 Labour conference not rejected unilateral disarmament as an element of its defence policy, the viability of a political party whose mass membership and parliamentary party were unalterably opposed on an important issue would certainly have been brought into question.

the substantive issues on the agenda allowed to be heard. It must be granted that not every topic which every group of delegates wished to discuss is given time, and it is also true that speakers representing the official party position receive more speaking time than do their opponents. Even with these imposed limitations, the range of topics considered and the mix of the argument is impressive. The significance of the conference proceedings is enhanced by the presence of the top leaders of the party, all of whom remain on the platform throughout every session, even those in which they do not participate.[3]

1. Characteristics of the Annual Conference

i. Composition

Delegates from the Constituency Labour Parties constitute over half the numerical size of the conference, but cast only about one-sixth the total conference vote. The remaining five-sixths of the conference vote is cast by delegates elected by the trade unions affiliated with the Labour Party.[4] Members of Parliament are present as *ex officio* conference members with speaking privileges but no voting rights, unless, as occurs infrequently, they have been chosen as delegate by their constituency. As a member of the Socialist International, the Labour Party has a global reach, and there are usually in attendance visitors from numerous foreign countries. A sizeable contingent of communications personnel is present, as well as thousands of visitors in the galleries.

[3] For a detailed description of the Annual Labour Conference, see McKenzie, *British Political Parties*, op. cit., pp. 485–517 and 607–26. See also Malcolm Shaw, "An American Looks at the Party Conferences", *Parliamentary Affairs*, Vol. xv, No. 2, Spring 1962.

[4] The number of votes represented at the Annual Conference is related to current party membership. For every unit of 1,000 members, or part thereof, a CLP or trade union is given one voting card representing 1,000 votes. Disparity between the two elements of the party becomes apparent when the membership of South Lewisham (the largest constituency party)—6,014— was compared with that of the Transport and General Workers Union— 1,000,000. See Standing Order 3, Voting, *Labour Party: List of Affiliated Organisations, Membership . . . and Delegates Appointed to the Blackpool Conference, 1961.*

II. Organisation of the proceedings

The evolution of the conference agenda begins some months before the conference meets. In the initial phases, the National Executive Committee performs no more than a secretarial function. Its influence increases when crucial decisions are made just prior to the opening of conference regarding the wording of resolutions to be discussed and the time that is to be allotted to each. According to party rules,[5] each affiliated organisation, whether trade union or constituency party, is permitted to submit a single resolution on one topic to the NEC at least twelve weeks before the conference, which is usually held in early October. All the resolutions submitted are printed and copies distributed among the affiliated organisations. Each affiliate is then permitted to forward one amendment to one of the proposed resolutions, the amendment to reach the NEC at least six weeks before the opening of the conference. These resolutions and amendments compose the agenda of the conference, and are distributed to each delegate well in advance of the conference. Advance circulation of the agenda is necessary because of a pre-conference activity known as compositing (pronounced com'po zī ting). In order to reduce the number of resolutions on popular issues to manageable proportions, compositing meetings are held the Saturday before the opening of the conference. It is at this point that the NEC drops its secretarial role and through its Conference Arrangements Committee begins to exert some influence over the substantive content of the conference. To recognise how formidable is the task of co-ordinating the resolutions, one has only to scan the agenda for the 1962 conference. It contained forty-six resolutions and eleven amendments on the subject of housing, fifty resolutions and five amendments on the EEC, and thirty-four resolutions and three amendments on foreign policy.

Although compositing has become an integral part of conference activity, it is not provided for in the rules of the party. Delegates from all the trade unions and constituency parties which have tabled resolutions or amendments on a particular topic are permitted to attend the meeting dealing with that issue. A member of the NEC is also present who advances the views of that group. With the help of a secretary from Transport House, the compositing meetings usually

---

[5] *Labour Party Annual Conference Report, 1962*, p. 269, Standing Order 2, Agenda.

succeed in reducing the great number of resolutions on the issue to one resolution. Sometimes this goal is not accomplished. At the 1962 conference, compositing meetings reduced multiple resolutions to one resolution in twenty-three out of twenty-five issues. The fifty-five resolutions dealing with the EEC were reduced to two, and the compositing meeting dealing with housing could only replace fifty-six resolutions with four composite resolutions. The fact that no compositing meeting was held on foreign policy was significant, as it indicated the low priority already placed by the NEC on this issue in 1962. The results of all compositing meetings are presented in printed form to the opening session of the conference on Monday morning.

Along with the pamphlet entitled *Composite Resolutions and Amendments*, each delegate, guest and visitor receives an outsized sheet called *Report of Conference Arrangements Committee*. The Arrangements Committee, which meets after the compositing sessions have ended, decides which of the composited resolutions and which of the resolutions on the agenda are to be brought before the conference for full discussion. The committee also decides generally how much time should be allocated each issue by determining the number of resolutions scheduled for debate.

At one session of the 1962 conference five resolutions on various topics were debated, but the Common Market was given all of one session and part of the following. When the chairman of the 1962 Arrangements Committee moved for the acceptance of his report, there were objections from those who thought foreign policy should be debated and from those who thought other important topics had been overlooked, but the conference sustained the Arrangements Committee, as it always does, and the NEC succeeded in limiting debate to those issues it considered of over-riding importance.

III. Conduct of the conference

Labour conferences follow formal parliamentary procedure. Each resolution is formally moved and seconded. General debate follows with the conference chairman making judicious choices between advocates and critics of the resolution under debate. The chairman is expected to maintain a balance between trade unionists, constituency delegates and MPs wishing to speak on the issue. When the time available for debate has elapsed, a member of NEC or the shadow cabinet (or the administration, if Labour is in office), summarises the debate as appropriate and presents a closing statement indicating the position of NEC on the motion at hand, after which the vote is taken.

Most of the persons engaging in conference debate share the national forensic skill, and have refined this by years of party experience in which strong convictions and skilful presentations were indispensable. There are usually many members requesting recognition from the chairman who fail to receive it, and there is always a general sentiment among delegates at the completion of debate that additional time could have been used to advantage.

There are three methods of voting at a Labour conference, but all important decisions are made by a card vote. Voice-voting and voting by a show of hands are generally unacceptable to the trade-union delegates, who equal in number but greatly exceed in voting power the constituency delegates. Some idea of the disparity between the voting power of the two groups of delegates is suggested by the following figures. In 1964, there were 6,353,000 members of the Labour Party, 5,502,000 of whom had indirect membership through trade unions; the remaining 851,000 were members of constituency or borough parties, or of Socialist or Co-operative societies. There were 1,222 delegates at the Labour conference in 1965; of this number, 562 were trade-union delegates and 660 were delegates from other sections of the party. The former cast card votes on the average of 9,790 votes per delegate, while the latter, all told, represented only 1,138 votes. The discrepancy between a vote by a show of hands—which is done on a one delegate, one vote basis, and by card vote, where there is a rough 9 : 1 ratio in favour of the trade-union delegates—frequently provokes cries of 'block vote' from the other delegates, unless the trade-union vote is fairly evenly split, as it often is.

At the opening of the conference, each delegate is given a book of numbered cards, with a *Yes* and *No* card for each number. When a card vote is called, the chairman of the conference announces which number-card is to be used, and the delegate tears out the corresponding *Yes* or *No* card and deposits it in one of the ballot boxes circulated on the floor of the conference. The Arrangements Committee has already appointed thirty tellers and 'scrutineers', and these tally the vote. This is always done with the utmost care, for momentous conference decisions have been made by a majority of as small as 43,000 votes out of 6.5 million cast.[6] Unlike the voting at American national conventions, card-vote balloting at the Labour conference is anonymous, and there is no method of ascertaining how individual conference delegates vote on any motion if they do not choose to say how they voted. This makes it quite difficult to establish how groups of delegates, such as those from constituency parties, have voted.[7]

iv. The unofficial Labour Party conference[8]

Rivalling the regular conference sessions in interest and excitement are the unofficial meetings of the Labour conference. Besides the four-and-a-half days of official debate on internal party management and on party policy, related topics are discussed informally at meetings sponsored by a number of organisations linked with the Labour Party. In 1962 these included not only groups like the Fabian Society with its historic ties to Labour, but also an *ad hoc* group, founded to oppose British entry into EEC, which called itself the Labour Committee on Britain and the Common Market. The ideological range exhibited at these unofficial meetings is a broad one, but their bias is generally to the left.

The unofficial conference in 1962 had two sessions, lasting about one-and-a-half hours each at 5.00 and 7.30 PM. No attempt was made to co-ordinate these sessions, and on occasion meetings that would appeal to the same audience were scheduled at the same time, with some of the speakers appearing on both programmes.[9] This did not create a serious problem as the unofficial conference is dominated by the Labour left almost to the same extent that the formal

[6] *Labour Party Annual Conference Report, 1960*, p. 202. This was the margin on one of the resolutions committing the party to unilateral nuclear disarmament.

[7] See pp. 174–9.

[8] These impressions were derived from attendance at the 1962 conference in Brighton.

[9] The Labour Peace Fellowship and the Brighton Central Labour Party sponsored a meeting entitled 'Make Labour the Peace Party', while the Christian Socialist Movement's session was described as 'The Christian Need for Socialism'. Both meetings were scheduled at 7.30 PM, October 1, 1962, with Anthony Greenwood, MP, on the programme of each.

G

conference is influenced by moderate elements of the party. Apart from meetings sponsored by the Fabian Society and its publication, *Socialist Commentary*, and the meetings sponsored by the Socialist Medical Association on the future of Britain's hospitals, the issues discussed at the unofficial conference were those which the left wing of the party deemed crucial.[10] Peculiar to the 1962 conference was the Common Market issue, which transcended the ideological lines of the party. Because of this, some right-wing members appeared at the unofficial meetings to present their case in opposition to the Common Market, there were far fewer left-wing members who supported EEC than there were right-wing members opposing it.

Ideology aside, the unofficial meetings attracted capacity crowds at each session. The speakers were usually talented and convincing propagandists for their respective causes. Their presentations were forceful and unrestrained, and were invariably followed by equally arresting question and answer periods. There was no reluctance on the part of well-known trade unionists and parliamentary back-benchers to appear, as did Hugh Gaitskell at a *Socialist Commentary* meeting. The rank-and-file members who attended the meetings were able to support favourite causes, see and hear the performances of party luminaries, and obtain information on a variety of issues to use later in intra-party debate and for propaganda purposes in their constituencies.

2. *Appointing the CLP delegate*

i. Selection procedure

Clause VII of the Party Constitution and the Model Rules deal with qualifications and conditions for appointing conference delegates, but the procedures followed by the constituencies in the sample tended to be based upon custom rather than rule. In two divisions

[10] The speakers, many of whom appeared at several meetings, included Barbara Castle, John Stonehouse, Anthony Greenwood, Fenner Brockway, Harold Davies, Emrys Hughes, Frank Allaun, Tom Driberg, Sydney Silverman, Stephen Swingler, William Warbey, Konni Zilliacus, Michael Foot, and Judith Hart—all MPs with leftist inclinations. Also speaking were Clive Jenkins, General Secretary of ASSET, Ian Mikardo, defeated in 1959 and returned in 1964 as the MP from Poplar, and John Horner, Secretary of the Fire Brigades Union and now an MP, representing Oldbury and Halesowen in the industrial area of northern Worcestershire. See *Tribune*, September 28, 1962, p. 2.

no information on delegate selection was available, and in only four divisions did the by-laws include procedures to deal with the appointing of delegates. The remaining thirty divisions relied on practices which permitted flexibility of procedure, and there was little uniformity in the customs.

There seemed to be no favoured method of making nominations for appointment as conference delegate. In thirteen divisions nominations were accepted from the floor only, and fifteen required the more formal method of submitting written nominations in advance of the selection meeting. The other six divisions were willing to accept nominations from either source.

Almost half the divisions called a special meeting to select their delegate. In thirteen divisions the delegate was chosen at the annual general meeting of the General Management Committee. By scheduling their delegate selection for this meeting, the divisions were assured satisfactory attendance, for the AGM attracted a larger audience than any other meeting except for a parliamentary selection conference. Two divisions attached such importance to choosing a delegate that special meetings were held. Thus, only fifteen divisions gave more than passing attention to the selection of the delegate. In nineteen of the divisions the choice was made at the regular monthly GMC meeting. This practice probably reflected the status of the delegate post in some of the divisions, but by no means in all. Some secretary-agents resented those GMC members who were inclined to appear only when an extraordinary decision was to be made, and arranged to have faithful GMC members who attended every monthly meeting select the delegate without interference from members who attended only sporadically. Some secretaries felt so strongly on this matter that they did not put the selection of the delegate on the agenda of the monthly meeting.

Most of the constituencies did not use a method of voting nor did they require the kind of a majority to add prestige to the office of delegate. Twelve used a written ballot and four required an absolute majority of those voting. Twenty-two divisions were satisfied with a show of hands, and twenty-nine with a simple majority of those present. Among the three types of constituencies, there were very slight differences in delegate selection practices. Marginal divisions were somewhat more formal than the strong and weak constituencies but not significantly so.

Much of the informality surrounding the appointment of delegates may stem from the fact that competition for the post was negligible. Nineteen divisions had only one candidate, and seven had only two contenders. In the remaining eight divisions, five of them had three candidates, and three had four or over. All the divisions which had more than two candidates were either strong or marginal constituencies. With aspirants for the appointment so few, the manner of voting and the majority required became academic, as did the question of the number of ballots needed to select the delegate. A vote was not even taken in nineteen of the divisions visited. Twelve constituencies required only one ballot, and the other three divisions took two, three and four ballots, respectively.

Explanations of the lack of competition for the position of constituency delegate included financial and organisational considerations. These considerations were important enough in some divisions to preclude the representation of five divisions at the 1962 conference. (These five unrepresented divisions included one strong, one marginal, and three weak constituencies.) Three of them cited financial problems as the cause. An additional three constituencies which had just resumed sending a delegate after a lapse of some years also stated that lack of money had been the cause. Money was a prime consideration even in those constituencies which had always sent a delegate to the conference. Since an important item in the total expense of a delegate was remuneration for a week of lost wages, some constituencies tended to seek out retired persons, housewives, and even their MP, in order to avoid this particular claim. This restriction curtailed the number of aspirants for the post, since it eliminated the weekly wage earners who compose the greatest segment of CLP membership.

Much of the political work in the constituency parties was done on an honorary basis, and this too affected competition for the delegateship. Some divisions had established a tradition which sought to reward those performing the task of directing CLP activities. Five of the divisions in the sample (one strong, one weak, and three marginal divisions) had made the post of conference delegate a perquisite of the CLP chairman or secretary. When a CLP leader became the delegate on an *ex officio* basis, the question of nomination and balloting was irrelevant.

Two other divisions in the sample failed to send a delegate to the

1962 conference for organisational reasons. One of these constituency parties was disorganised to the extent that it had not met any of its obligations to the national party and was therefore ineligible to send a delegate. The other division represented the nadir of interest in choosing a conference delegate. For eight of the past ten years the secretary had been chosen delegate, but had actually attended the conference only four times. When the secretary was unable to attend in 1962, he could not find a substitute, and this in a division which paid travel, food and lodging, and compensated for lost earnings and out-of-pocket expenses. This was more a reflection on the constituency party than on the post of conference delegate. Nothing was very important in this division.

ii. Informal qualifications of conference delegates

The formal requirements for conference delegates have been specified in the Party Constitution and in the Model Rules, but certain informal qualifications have also evolved. These qualifications fall into two general categories, namely, party service and party loyalty, and the ability to perform the duties of a delegate. Respondents in twenty-three divisions thought current party service a requirement for selection as delegate. Only a few less, nineteen, felt that past service was an equally important expectation. It was interesting to observe that past service was given greater weight in strong divisions, while current service was mentioned more often in marginal and weak constituencies. This may have been a reflection of the advanced age structure in strong as opposed to weak and marginal divisions.

After stressing the importance of party service, both past and present, CLP leaders were concerned with the ability of the delegate to perform the task expected of him. Nineteen CLP leaders thought a proposed delegate should be able to follow the conference debate intelligently, to report to the constituency party upon his return, and to answer relevant questions pertaining to conference proceedings. Eleven CLP leaders thought the delegate should be able to make an effective exposition of the resolution forwarded by the division to the conference, provided he was given an opportunity to do so.

When seeking an appointment as conference delegate, experience was not necessarily advantageous. Fourteen of the 1962 delegates had not served before in that capacity, thirteen had been appointed once before, and only eight had represented their division two or more times. With the exception of the five divisions in which the secretary or chairman served as delegate *ex officio,* it was accepted that the post be shared as much as possible among constituency party members. Four divisions had gone so far as to establish a rotation system based on territorial subdivisions within the constituency, and one of these also alternated the position between men and women.

Another unwritten requirement for an aspirant to the position was the ability to take time off the job at a season long past the usual vacation period. Although more constituency parties were now in a position to pay for lost wages than was formerly the case, many still did not do so, which gave an advantage to those party members who had some control over their work schedule.

3. *Importance of the Annual Conference delegate*

In light of the factionalism which has characterised most Labour conferences, and the possibility that the delegate may be called upon to participate in the conference debate, there is a basis for the conclusion that his office would be prominent in CLP operations. Other factors, however, tend to compromise the significance of the conference delegate and, by derivation, the process by which he is selected. Reference has been made to the fact that trade union delegates cast five-sixths of the total conference vote. This was discouraging to left-wing delegates in the days when the trade union vote was controlled by a few leaders who were unventuresome on both foreign and domestic questions. The pattern of trade-union voting changed in the mid-1950s following the death in 1955 of both Arthur Deakin and Arthur Tiffin, his successor as head of the giant Transport and General Workers' Union. Deakin, who was of the right-wing tradition in the party, regularly excoriated the Bevanite minority, and the very sight of him at conference was enough to send the left wing into paroxysms of anger. It is one of the ironies of Labour politics that Tiffin, surviving Deakin by only a few months, should have been succeeded by a militant leftist. The internal distribution of power within the T & GWU is such that when Frank Cousins became its General Secretary, some 1,000,000 votes assumed a left-wing bias and could no longer be taken for granted by the NEC, particularly in respect to resolutions on foreign and defence policy.[11] The pre-1956 situation no longer prevailed, but the old feeling of futility was hard to erase. Although constituency votes frequently exceed the margin by which conference resolutions pass or fail, the unpalatable truth remains that whatever the vote for or against a resolution, the constituency vote always comprises a minority of it.

The argument that has taken place since 1907 concerning the efficacy of the conference in policy-determination will probably never be resolved.[12] A very small number of respondents advanced participation in policy-making as a reason for attending the conference, thus obliquely supporting McKenzie's contention that the right of the Parliamentary Labour Party to set policy has never been challenged.[13] It is possible that if the constituency parties expected their delegates to be involved in formulating authoritative party pronouncements, the attention given the selecting and mandating of the conference delegate would be much increased. While conference decisions are not binding on the Parliamentary Party, fighting for their passage is of extreme importance to those who conceive the Labour Party less as a means of altering the nature of British society through political action than as a forum for ideological debate. This was seen by Ralph Miliband who wrote that a compromise reached in 1907

. . . greatly enhanced the activists' faith in the efficacy of Conference resolutions and their ineradicable conviction that the passage of resolutions at annual conferences must automatically entail important consequences in regard to Party policy. In fact, the whole history of the Labour Party has been punctuated by

[11] Harrison, op. cit., pp. 130–7.

[12] McKenzie, *British Polical Parties*, pp. 505–16; 613–28 (see footnote 2, p. 626).

[13] Ibid., p. 627. McKenzie quotes two separate statements by Keir Hardie, both of which are most clear in the assumption that to allow an extra-Parliamentary group to control the policies of the Parliamentary Labour Party would be a violation of the British Constitution. 'In the House of Commons the membership of the party decide their own policy without interference from the Executive or any outside authority. This is the right which the Parliamentary Party has always claimed and which has never been seriously challenged.'

verbal victories of the Labour Left which, with some few exceptions have had little influence on the Labour Party's conduct
inside or outside the House of Commons, but which have always
been of great importance in keeping up the hopes and the morale
of the activists.[14]

Despite cogent reasons for regarding as limited the importance of
the office of delegate, the possibility of attending a conference was
alluring to many Labour activists. There was not a great deal of
competition for the position, but constituencies always found someone willing to attend. Very often the attraction of the annual conference was greater among newly recruited CLP members than among
those who had been involved in the work for years and who had
already attended several conferences. In three constituencies the
interviews of secretary and delegate revealed qualitatively different
conceptions of the importance of the conference delegate. The outstanding example was in a West Country marginal division where
the delegate thought the selecting and mandating of the conference
representative ranked just below choosing a parliamentary candidate. In the same division the secretary considered the choice of
delegate to be of minor consequence. At the same time, the secretary-
agent reported that no person had ever been appointed twice as
conference delegate, that there were five candidates for the office in
1962, that four ballots were required to make a choice, and that the
post-conference report of the delegate was given considerable
attention by the constituency party.

No differences were revealed among the three types of constituency in regard to the importance attached to selecting and
instructing the delegate. Table 6.1 suggests that there was a slight
tendency to attach more rather than less significance to the activity,
and no inclination to disregard it completely.

Another indication of the significance placed by the constituencies
on the Annual Conference is based on an analysis of the resolutions
and amendments which composed the agenda of the annual con-

[14] Miliband, op. cit., pp. 26–7. The compromise (quoted from the Annual
Conference Report 1907) stated that 'resolutions instructing the Parliamentary Party as to their action in the House of Commons be taken as the
opinions of the Conference, on the understanding that the time and methods
of giving effect to these instructions be left to the Party in the House, in
conjunction with the National Executive'.

ference. It was generally found that the stronger the division, the less likely it was to regard substantive conference activities very seriously, and differences of some magnitude appeared between strong and weak divisions. It may be argued that this criterion was applicable only to the value attached to the annual conference, and not to the importance of selecting a delegate. This objection created

TABLE 6.1. *Importance attached to selecting and mandating Annual Conference delegates, by type of constituency*

	Constituencies		
	Strong	Marginal	Weak[15]
Great importance	1	3	2
Considerable importance	7	4	4
Little importance	5	5	5
No importance	0	0	0

TABLE 6.2. *CLP activity in tabling resolutions and amendments for Annual Conference agenda, by type of constituency*

	Constituencies		
	Strong	Marginal	Weak
1962			
Resolutions	5	8	13
Amendments	1	3	2
1963			
Resolutions	7	5	9
Amendments	0	1	2
Totals			
Resolutions	12	13	22
Amendments	1	4	4

too nice a distinction, for the tabling of a resolution could be closely linked to the ability of the delegate to offer a convincing case, should he be afforded the opportunity.

Reasons advanced by delegates for wishing to attend the conference were revealing. The conference was not regarded as an opportunity for political advancement, for only 3 per cent of the

[15] Only eleven weak constituencies are recorded, one constituency in the sample being ineligible to send a delegate to the Annual Conference.

responses referred to the possibility that a secretary-agent might make useful contacts or that a delegate might utilise the debate on an issue to establish himself as a potential parliamentary candidate. Eight per cent of the responses indicated that participation in forming policy was a basis for attracting delegates to the conference, whereas 14 per cent considered the conference as an important source of political information.

The great majority of the responses were quite personalised. Thirty per cent of the reasons for wishing to go to conference alluded to selection as a delegate in terms of a personal honour that reflected the confidence of the CLP in the ability of the individual chosen.

TABLE 6.3. *Reasons mentioned by CLP activists for interest in attending the Annual Party Conference*

	Number of mentions	% of total responses
Honorific	18	30
'Busman's Holiday'	10	17
Inspirational and symbolic	9	16
Informational	8	14
Social	7	12
Policy making	5	8
Professional	2	3

Seventeen per cent referred to the fact that the conference furnished the delegate a week free of distractions during which he could engage in political conversations with his peers and with party leaders, many of whom make themselves surprisingly available. A cluster of responses almost as large mentioned the inspirational and symbolic functions of the conference, that attendance at the conference gave the delegate a sense of belonging to a great party, capable of exerting influence on national and international problems. This attitude was especially conspicuous in weak constituencies whose leaders were frustrated by their local minority status. Some of the responses, about 12 per cent, indicated that the social aspects of the conference were not without importance. A number of dances and entertainments were held after the political sessions, and since the conference habitually meets at a seaside resort, places of rest and relaxation are available. Because of the working-class composition of many divisions and their provincial locations, many delegates found the conference setting itself very attractive.

4. Mandating the Annual Conference delegate

Considering the ideological origins of the Labour Party, the custom of mandating conference delegates by constituency parties was logical. A party with no constitution and possessing the flexibility of the Conservative Party could afford permissiveness here,[16] but given the composition of the Labour Party and the manner in which its conference was conducted, there was no incongruity in the wish of constituency parties to give their delegates specific instructions on some issues and general instructions on others.

Investigation during the study indicated that the formal mandating of delegates was more prevalent than had been assumed, even by Labour Party members themselves.[17] Of the thirty-four constituencies that gave information on this subject, twenty-seven customarily mandated their delegate while seven did not. (These seven constituencies included four strong, two marginal and one weak.) Half of the constituencies which gave instructions to their delegate did so at a meeting called specifically for that purpose, and half included this activity in the agenda of a regular meeting of the General Management Committee. Somewhat paradoxically, 75 per cent of the divisional parties mandated their delegate but 75 per cent of the delegates thought they had complete or substantial discretion in their voting activities at the conference. Only 25 per cent of the delegates thought they had little or no freedom of action.

This contradiction stemmed from the fact that the constituency parties were able to give their delegate clear and unequivocal instructions on only one conference voting action. This pertained to the election of seven representatives of the constituency parties to the National Executive Committee, in which only constituency delegates voted, and the election of the five representatives of the Women's Section of the NEC, in which the entire conference

[16] McKenzie, *British Political Parties*, op. cit., pp. 195–6.

[17] Ibid., pp. 493–4. A number of knowledgeable Labour Party leaders, including one member of NEC, expressed surprise at the widespread mandating of conference delegates.

membership voted. Nominations for these positions were circulated far enough in advance for the constituencies to be informed, and in some divisions this was the only matter on which the delegate was mandated. On almost all other specific questions presumed to come before the conference, the divisional party could give only a general mandate to its delegate. Many issues on which popular interest was high had drawn dozens of resolutions and amendments, and it was impossible for the constituency party to give a realistic appraisal of each. The constituency could advocate more money for education, limitations on land speculation, or not joining the EEC, but since the delegate was going to be faced by a composited resolution on these matters rather than a specific one which appeared in the agenda well before the conference, detailed mandating was impossible. The normal practice was to give the delegate instructions on a few points of particular importance in the constituency and then to instruct him to vote on other matters as he felt the division's sympathies lay. As this meant that the delegate's initiative was restricted on very few questions, it was easy to understand why a preponderant majority of delegates concluded that they were allowed great discretion in voting.

A good example of the futility of precise mandating by the constituency party was presented by the 1962 Annual Conference, at which 3 per cent of the divisional delegates were mandated to support entry into EEC, 65 per cent were mandated to oppose it, and 32 per cent had a free vote. A total of fifty-one resolutions and five amendments on EEC had been forwarded for inclusion in the agenda, only two of which voiced support for the proposal in unequivocal terms. All the statements opposing entry were composited into two resolutions. Only one of these was debated by the conference, and it would have placed 'the question of Britain's entry into the European Economic Community . . . before the British people at a General election',[18] on the assumption that, if Labour adopted a position of opposition to EEC, the result would be a resounding victory for the party. However, the National Executive Committee opposed the two composited resolutions opposing entry and asked instead that a statement by the NEC dated September 29, 1962, entitled *Labour and the Common Market*, be adopted by the conference. The crux of this document of almost 4,000 words was contained in five broad condi-

[18] *Annual Labour Party Conference Report, 1962*, p. 169.

tions for entry which the Labour Party considered essential.[19] The document was subject to legitimate difference of interpretation of its language. The question could be asked whether the broad conditions of entry were subject to negotiation or whether they were minimal conditions for entry which Britain would seek to make more rather than less specific during the course of negotiations. Many delegates who voted for the NEC statement did so in the belief that they were voting for unconditional opposition to entry because the conditions mentioned in the document would never be met by EEC. Other delegates voted for the document because they did not think that it committed the Labour Party to a position of inflexible opposition to the Market, but allowed the party certain manoeuverability should conditions for joining become more favourable. Therefore, delegates who had been instructed to oppose British entry into EEC and delegates who had been instructed to support this action deemed themselves equally free to vote for the document.

Whether a delegate was instructed by his division at a special meeting called for the purpose or whether the item was one of several on the agenda of a regular meeting was of no consequence in solving the problem of giving specific instructions on a wide range of issues. In neither case was there likely to be time for a detailed discussion of the resolutions on the conference agenda. The usual procedure seemed to be to explore rather fully the two or three topics of particular importance to the division and then to pass a motion instructing the delegate to exercise his judgment on other questions while bearing in mind prevailing attitudes of his constituency. The problem of wholly inadequate time for exhaustive discussion of the issues prevailed even in divisions where an earnest attempt was made to be thorough. The special mandating meeting in a Norfolk division was presented with a list of thirteen issues which included such pressing issues as housing, the Common Market, public ownership, nuclear weapons, and party organisation and administration.

Most of the delegates to the 1962 Annual Conference were mandated on the election of representatives from the constituency parties

[19] Ibid., p. 246. These conditions were: '1 Strong and binding safeguards for the trade and other interests of our friends and partners in the Commonwealth; 2 Freedom as at present to pursue our own foreign policy; 3 Fulfilment of the Government's pledge to our associates in the European Free Trade Area; 4 The right to plan our own economy; 5 Guarantees to safeguard the position of British agriculture.'

and the Women's Section of the NEC. Only two of the thirty-one delegates had free choice on this matter. Two-thirds of the delegates were given guidance in voting for the NEC amendment to the membership clause of the Party Constitution[20] and to resolutions providing for a ban on nuclear testing.[21]

5. *Voting patterns of Annual Conference delegates*

The voting behaviour of delegates to an annual conference of the Labour Party does not lend itself to exact analysis. This reason is that no one can say precisely how constituency delegates as a group vote, far less how any individual constituency delegate votes on any one resolution or conference action.[22] It is possible to identify much of the trade-union vote because the political positions of many trade unions are publicised at the time of their yearly meetings which take place during the summer, before the Labour Party's Annual Conference in the autumn. The viewpoints of the small unions on various issues can be ascertained by speaking with a relatively small number of union administrators. Moreover, speeches made during conference debate, in which many union leaders take part, indicate the position of delegates from a particular union, at least in regard to a specific question. Having determined the general trend of the union voting, one can inferentially estimate the voting of the constituency parties, as was done by Martin Harrison on a number of issues current in the 1950s.[23]

Harrison's efforts were useful in correcting some false impressions of the respective roles played by trade union and constituency delegates in annual conference voting.[24] Referring to the undifferentiated constituency party vote cast at annual conferences, Harrison writes: 'Support for left-wing candidates in elections to the Party

[20] See Chapter 2, pp. 39–41.

[21] *Annual Labour Parties Conference Report, 1962*, pp. 225–33.

[22] See Chapter 3, p. 66, fn. 7, for a similar instance of secretiveness in voting procedures in British politics.

[23] Harrison, op. cit., pp. 214–38.

[24] Ibid., p. 238: 'The unions have never been as thoroughly unprogressive—nor the local parties as fanatically left-wing—as popular legend decreed. Obviously, the constituencies are on balance to the left of the unions, but the overlap is considerable.'

Executive [NEC] cannot be safely used to "prove" the constituencies views on policy.' This statement is unexceptionable, but the mandates for NEC elections reported by the different types of constituencies in this study were suggestive of their views on policy matters.

TABLE 6.4. *Mandates regarding NEC elections 1962, by type of constituency*

| | Constituencies | | | |
	Strong	Marginal	Weak	Total
Moderate candidates constituency and women's sections	4	4	0	8
Left-wing candidates constituency and women's sections	3	2	9	14
Left-wing candidates for constituency section, moderate cands. for women's section	3	4	0	7

Note: Only twenty-nine constituencies figure in this Table. Five constituencies in the survey sent no delegate, and two others gave their delegates no mandate on NEC elections.

Although there was a very slight inclination to the moderate position among the strong and marginal constituencies, the weak constituencies were consistent in their bias to the left in this instance.[25] This response may have tended to overstate the political attitudes of the weak divisions, but it did correspond to the pattern which was revealed in the analysis of CLP political attitudes discussed in Chapter 2 (esp. pp. 58–6). In almost every respect, the leaders of the weak constituency parties favoured an aggressive policy line, both in the submitting of resolutions for inclusion in the conference agenda and in their tendency to oppose decisions of NEC.

Table 6.2 reveals that the weak divisions were the most prone to engage in the activity of submitting resolutions and amendments for

[25] In addition to the nine weak constituencies reporting a left-wing mandate for both sections, one of the three weak CLPs not sending delegates reported that it usually endorsed left-wing candidates to the NEC.

inclusion in the conference agenda. Table 6.5 suggests that there were qualitative variations in the substance of the resolutions and amendments submitted by the three types of constituencies. In categorising the proposals submitted, any which attacked a course of action or stated policy of the NEC was labelled 'anti-NEC'. Any proposal which supported an action or policy of NEC was considered 'pro-NEC'. Statements bearing on accepted and therefore uncontroversial party policies, as well as statements on issues on which the party had not yet taken a stand, were placed in a common category.

TABLE 6.5. *CLP political attitudes as reflected in resolutions and amendments submitted for inclusion in the 1962 conference agenda, by type of constituency*

	Constituencies		
	Strong	Marginal	Weak
Pro-NEC	0	2	0
Anti-NEC	2	1	7
Statements on accepted or non-declared policy	4	5 (3 EEC)	5 (3 EEC)
Total proposals	6	11	15

From the strong constituencies came two anti-NEC resolutions, one of which was a gentle comment on the manner in which the NEC exercised its power to endorse parliamentary candidates. The second critical resolution originated in a constituency from whose MP the Parliamentary Labour Party had withdrawn the whip, and the resolution was little more than a pro-forma declaration on his behalf. The two pro-NEC resolutions from marginal divisions supported the NEC and the way in which it had dealt with some of the Young Socialists, whose actions it considered inimical to the interests of the party. The lone anti-NEC resolution from the marginal constituencies struck at the basic power balance within the party, for it proposed a change in the Party Constitution which would have permitted all duly endorsed prospective parliamentary candidates to join with members of the Parliamentary Labour Party in the election of the Party Leader.

Nearly half the resolutions from the weak constituencies fell into the anti-NEC group, and none was in the pro-NEC category. Two dealt with foreign and defence policy and were strongly unilateralist in tone. NEC enforcement of proscription policies attracted two critical resolutions, as did the power of the NEC to endorse parliamentary candidates. The last resolution from the weak divisions was submitted by a CLP which, within a few months of the 1964 election, gained the distinction of having its prospective parliamentary candidate resign to join the Communist Party. The resolution of this division was ostensibly concerned with world hunger, but by implication the NEC and the Parliamentary Labour Party were contributing to the problem by doing little to alleviate it.

Certain considerations should be borne in mind when analysing conference resolutions as indicators of the political climate to be found in the divisions which proposed the resolutions. It is possible, but not likely, that a moderate or right-wing division, may in an aberrant moment pass an immoderate resolution. It is much more likely, for a host of reasons, that a radical division will endeavour to pass a resolution at least superficially decorous and reasonable. Certainly, in the constituencies surveyed, there were many indications of left-wing sentiment which did not necessarily appear in the resolutions submitted by the same divisions. One of the most accommodating party officials met during the course of investigations said that his reading of newspapers was confined to the *Daily Worker* and *Tribune*. In this same division the chairman of the GMC was a former member of the Communist Party, while the prospective parliamentary candidate had obtained NEC endorsement with some difficulty because of his opinions on foreign policy and defence matters. Yet in a recent year this division submitted to the conference a resolution on education, moderate in tone and couched in terms of more adequate buildings, smaller classes and better pay for teachers.

The weak constituencies in the sample were not alone in submitting anti-NEC resolutions in 1962. Every third year the Labour conference entertains amendments to the Party Constitution, Standing Orders and rules regarding party administration. Since 1962 was such a year, an opportunity was furnished to observe the extent of anti-leadership sentiment in the party. About 110 resolutions and amendments were forwarded on topics bearing on the CLP–NEC conflict. Of these resolutions, seventy-one were sharply critical of the NEC. Constituencies which had polled 50 per cent or more of the vote in the 1959 general election submitted 22 per cent of the anti-leadership proposals. Another 18 per cent were forwarded by divisions which had won from 40 to 49 per cent of the 1959 vote, and 60 per cent of the critical statements were provided by constituency parties whose parliamentary candidates had received less than 39 per cent of the 1959 vote.[26]

Analysts of delegate voting behaviour cannot learn how each delegate has voted on an issue before the conference, but the constituency parties could establish how their delegate has voted on questions which came to a card vote. If the division were so inclined, this could be done by asking the delegate to show his book of ballots which he has used in card voting. By reviewing the sequence in which the issues were put to a vote and noting what ballots had been used, it would be possible to determine the voting record of the delegate. After the 1962 conference, however, not a single constituency party endeavoured to discover the congruity between the mandate it had issued and the conference votes cast by its delegate. This characteristic trust in the political integrity of the delegates was corroborated by the fact that willingness to accept the mandate of the constituency was never mentioned as a qualification for a delegate. The constituency parties accepted as natural the influence of discussion of issues at the conference itself, and recognised that the final decision of the delegate would probably be affected. To this should be added the statement that there was usually support in the constituency for virtually any stand the delegate might take. As chapter 2 showed, policy differences existed in all three types of divisions and these differences were but the result of individual disagreements within the constituency.

Delegates were rarely appointed more than twice, and then not for successive conferences. If it were customary for one individual to attend a number of conferences, the delegate might develop a better conception of his obligations as an interpreter of constituency political attitudes. On one occasion this was realised by an experienced delegate who was also GMC secretary in a marginal division. Before the 1960 conference, unilateralists had achieved a majority on the GMC Executive Committee with the result that the delegate had been instructed to support a resolution advocating unilateral disarmament. The delegate did not believe his instructions reflected the majority

[26] Cf. Richard Rose, "Political Ideas of English Party Activists", op. cit., p. 368.

opinion of the constituency on this point. He requested and was granted Executive Committee approval to circulate a questionnaire among ward and branch parties to elicit popular reaction to unilateralism. The questionnaire showed a slight majority in the constituency to be opposed to unilateralism, and the delegate chose to vote accordingly at the conference. During the delegate's report to the constituency following the conference, it became evident that the unilateralist victory at Scarborough had been effected without his vote, and he explained the reason for his action. The GMC chairman, a confirmed unilateralist, resigned immediately, but his resignation was not accepted. Subsequently, he refused to stand for re-election and by 1962 had become politically inactive. Although the delegate in question won vindication for his action, the struggle might have been less successful for a delegate without the status of a GMC secretary and with less experience as a conference delegate.

6. Reporting by the Annual Conference delegate

In all constituencies the delegate was expected to make his report to the GMC at its first meeting following the conference. In two-thirds of the constituencies, the report from the delegate was the principal item of business. In the remaining constituencies, one-sixth of the divisions disposed of the delegate's report at the end of the business of a regular GMC meeting, and one-sixth considered the report important enough to call a special meeting for the purpose of hearing it.

Even with the coverage given the Annual Conference by the communications media, two-thirds of the divisions considered the report of conference proceedings by the delegate to be as much of consequence as it was a decade ago. This reaction was especially pronounced in the strong and in the weak constituencies. Only the marginal divisions took an indifferent point of view. A number of party officials thought the television coverage had influenced the type of report the GMC wished to hear from its delegate. What was now desired was essentially an impressionistic account, particularly of the executive sessions where party organisation and administration were discussed. The constituencies also relied on the delegate for a description of the general climate of the conference which, despite the encroachment of mass media coverage, was still essentially a gathering called to transact party business. However, representatives of television, radio and press were not able to cover all interesting incidents that occurred on the conference floor, and sometimes a constituency's delegate could provide local party members with information they were not likely to obtain from any other source. This was especially true of the meetings that comprised the informal section of the Labour conference.

7. *Appointment of an 'alternate' delegate*

Because most delegates are chosen at least six months before early October when the conference is traditionally held, events can occur that preclude the attendance of some delegates. Of the five divisions not having delegates at the 1962 Annual Conference, two were placed in this predicament for lack of an 'alternate' delegate. Only five constituency parties prepared for this contingency by selecting an alternative or allowing the person with the second highest number of votes to become automatically the alternate delegate. The other divisions reported that, if the chosen delegate withdrew, they would send no replacement, or that they would try to find someone at the last minute who could attend, or that one of the CLP officers would represent the division. The relative indifference with which the possibility of having to find an emergency replacement was treated could be laid to two factors. Perhaps the task of finding even one person to attend the conference had been so formidable that the constituency parties were reluctant to embark on the search for an alternate. On the other hand, the failure to select an alternate may have been due to the low significance of the position in the total activity of the CLP.

8. *Expenses of the Annual Conference delegate*

Although not every constituency had a delegate at the 1962 conference, all had a policy of payment of expenses for their delegate. A CLP which lacked the money for at least the transportation, food and lodging of its delegate chose, as a matter of policy, not to select a delegate. Every constituency party claimed to pay the costs of its delegate at the conference. There was no evidence which would support Martin Harrison's contention that 'although some CLPs carefully select their delegate, many are only too pleased to send someone who can pay his own fare, or who has the leisure to go without looking too closely at his political views'.[27]

Of the divisions studied, 40 per cent paid only for the travel, food and lodging of their delegate; 22 per cent paid lost wages in addition to basic expenses; basic costs plus an allowance for out-of-pocket expenses were defrayed by 5 per cent; and 33 per cent paid for all expenses. There was a considerable range in the expenditures of the CLPs for this purpose. An outlay of £10 to £15 was reported by 36 per cent of the divisions, while 31 per cent spent between £16 and £20. Two groups comprising 14 per cent each of the sample gave their delegate amounts from £21 to £25, and from £26 to £30. Two constituencies allowed their delegates over £30 for the week-long conference, which by English standards was munificent. One rather affluent marginal division not only gave its delegate £20, but sent its agent and prospective parliamentary candidate to conference as well, incurring a total bill of about £65. Naturally, not all constituencies could afford such an expenditure, but the impression was gained that the constituencies felt genuine responsibility to defray the conference expenses of their selected delegate, and that the trend of constituency party finances was in the direction of affluence rather than poverty.

[27] Harrison, op. cit., p. 179. Neither is this statement appropriate regarding the political views of delegates. In the first place, it is not necessary for the CLP to examine closely a delegate's political views. Given the size and intimacy of the GMC, they are already well known. The suggestion that a delegate would be chosen whose views differed substantially from those of the GMC merely to obtain a solvent delegate, is not borne out by the responses of CLP leaders.

7

Constituency Parties, the Labour Party and the British Party System

Wﾘﾪﾴ ﾴﾪﾪ ﾪﾸﾪﾪﾪﾴﾪﾸﾸ of the 1945–50 Labour government, British politics from the end of the First World War to the mid-1960s was dominated by the Conservative Party. During this period the Conservatives, as the majority party, were in government for twenty-six years and were the chief party in coalition governments for an additional thirteen years. (The Labour Party formed majority governments for six years and was the governing party during three years of minority government.)[1] The resiliency of the Conservative Party was demonstrated by its recovery following the crushing defeat of 1945. At the previous election in 1935, it had won 387 seats, which, along with thirty-three seats carried by the National Liberals, made a total of 420 seats against 154 for the Labour Party. Ten years later, in 1945, Labour had a 180-seat margin over the Conservatives. The subsequent Conservative renascence, under the organisational leadership of Lord Woolton and the intellectual leadership of R. A. Butler, reduced this impressive margin to seventeen in the 1950 election and led to a Conservative majority of twenty-five in the election held in the following year. Two further electoral successes followed for the Conservatives, their majority over Labour reaching sixty-seven in 1955 and 107 in 1959.

In the 1955–59 Parliament they [the Conservatives] had come through much rougher political weather than in 1951–55 and [in

---

[1] See Rose, *Politics in England*, op. cit., p. 260.

1959] they faced an opposition that was in better heart. Yet they continued to gain seats. For the first time in a century, the longer a government has stayed in office the more established it has become. It is more than ever possible to speak of the Conservatives as the country's 'normal' majority party.[2]

In most stable party systems, either individual parties or coalitions of parties are dominant for extended periods of time, while other parties or coalitions play a secondary role. The latter may control the government in their countries on occasion, but usually infrequently and for short periods of time. Thus, the Democratic Party dominated American politics from 1800 to 1860, and the Republican Party from 1860 to 1932; thereafter since when the Democratic predominance has been so strong as to seem likely to endure for many years to come.

If the Conservative Party has been the sun in Britain's party system, the Labour Party has been its moon. In its very early years, Labour made informal arrangements with the Liberal Party in general elections, enabling Labour to build up strength in the House of Commons. In less than two decades from its establishment, Labour had replaced the Liberals as the second party in British politics.

1. The Labour Party in power

Labour has never formed a government under auspicious circumstances. Its first opportunity came after the general election of December 1923, when 191 Labour members composed the second largest party in the House of Commons. Although 159 Liberals had also been elected, the Labour Party unassisted formed a government which lasted from January to October 1924. It did not establish a distinguished record during that time. During their period in office, the members of the cabinet were limited by their minority status and by their reputation for radicalism. Some members of the cabinet who had risen from the ranks of industrial workers were almost immobilised by the knowledge that they were finally responsible for governmental policy, and in both domestic and foreign policy an exaggerated form of orthodoxy developed. One of the few independent ventures of the first Labour government was to grant diplomatic

[2] Butler and Rose, op. cit., p. 197.

recognition to the Soviet Union and to conclude general and commercial treaties with it, neither of which was ratified because of the dissolution of Parliament and the holding of a general election.

The Labour Party's second opportunity to form an administration occurred on its becoming the largest party in the Commons after the 1929 elections, when 287 Labour members were elected, compared with 260 for the Conservatives and 59 for the Liberals. Again, the party was given complete responsibility with incomplete authority to act, since Labour lacked by a good number an absolute majority in the Commons. Furthermore, the severe economic crisis of the late 1920s and early 1930s had begun. A high level of unemployment in Britain was the most serious domestic problem faced by the new Labour government. The domestic situation continued to deteriorate. Ramsay MacDonald and Philip Snowden, his chancellor of the Exchequer, finally recommended a series of government economies which included a 10 per cent reduction in the unemployment benefit rates. This proposal caused a revolt in the Parliamentary Labour Party and in the cabinet which brought the second Labour government to an inglorious end. In August 1931, MacDonald consented to organise a 'National Government' which passed all the economies previously recommended, and still more, while the Conservatives and Liberals had the satisfaction of seeing these unpopular measures carried out by men identified in the nation as leaders of the Labour Party. The charade came to an end with the general election of October 1931, in which the Conservatives and their associated parties swept to a landslide victory.

Although Labour was elected to office in 1945 with an over-all majority of 146 seats in the House of Commons, and thereby escaped the awkward minority status of the first two Labour governments, the times were such that the lot of the party was not enviable. Rebuilding and rationalising of the British economy in 1945 was a task of awesome proportions, not made easier by the abrupt withdrawal of American help which had been arriving through the Lend-Lease programme. (Many members of the Labour Party will go to their graves believing that this action was taken solely because Britain had a Socialist government.) Economic dislocations consequent to the liquidation of the British Empire added to the troubles of the Attlee governments of 1945–50 and 1950–51. During the winter of 1946–47, even the weather seemed to be against the Labour Party.[3] Until 1964, many British voters seemed inclined to forget the enormous burdens and accomplishments of the post-war Labour governments, remembering only the austerity programmes and the economic chaos of those days.[4]

The Labour government which assumed office in October 1964 did so under conditions that were hardly ideal. Deficits in Britain's balance of payments had risen prior to the 1955 and 1959 general elections, and delaying the 1964 election until the last possible moment had extended the time far beyond the point needed to re-establish the deflationary policies that Conservative chancellors of the Exchequer were accustomed to put into effect just after election victories. When Harold Wilson became prime minister, he was confronted with a balance of payments deficit of £800 million— almost twice the size of the largest previous deficit of 1960.

2. *The Labour Party out of power, 1951–64*

It is possible that future historians of the Labour Party may refer to the decade from 1951 to 1961 as the period of maximum tension within its ranks. Controversy within the Parliamentary Labour Party over the rearmament programme began in 1952. This issue was enlarged in 1953 and 1954 to include the question of German

[3] British weather problems are in part based on the myth that it never really gets cold in Britain. Since it never gets cold, preventive measures are unnecessary. In the winter of 1962–63, fuel in the British Railway diesel engines turned into sludge with the result that in freezing weather the only BR engines in operation were steam engines, many of which were then still in service. Presumably American diesel engines operating in subzero temperatures in the Great Plains and Rocky Mountain areas had conquered this problem; but, because it 'never gets cold' in Britain, the national railway system has not turned its attention to it.

[4] Some voters contend that they minded the austerity programmes less than Sir Stafford Cripps' attitude that austerity should be considered a normal, even a preferred, way of life. This contention receives some confirmation from A. Bullock's biography, *The Life and Times of Ernest Bevin* London 1960. Miliband, op. cit., p. 225, quotes Bullock as follows: 'The contrast between the two men could hardly have been more strongly marked, Cripps slender and ascetic, the passionate doctrinaire to whom ideas were more real than human beings, Bevin thick set and earthy with a critical power of judgment tempered by long experience of men.'

rearmament, and created bitter controversy at the Annual Conference of 1954. In 1955, friction within the Parliamentary Labour Party again appeared over the decision of the Conservative Government to make the hydrogen bomb. At the 1957 conference, nationalisation and unilateral disarmament began to draw the attention of the party. Unilateral disarmament played only a minor role at the 1958 conference but monopolised attention at both the 1960 and 1961 conferences, the unilateralists winning in 1960 and their opponents prevailing in 1961. The chief reason that the 1962 conference was not the occasion of a protracted battle over Labour's response to the Common Market issue was that Hugh Gaitskell came out so strongly against joining the EEC that he threw into disarray his traditional opponents within the party. Disconcerted as they were by Gaitskell's unexpected action, most of them eventually voted for an NEC statement on the issue which was given overwhelming support by the conference.

During this decade of extended controversy, Labour conducted its debate over national and party policy by means of books, pamphlets and articles, as well as through its Annual Conferences. Exchanges were made under the most public conditions, with the press and eventually television cameras usually at hand to transmit the spirited and sometimes foolish arguments made by the participants. Although some members of the Labour Party were convinced that many voters are attracted to a party in which issues are openly fought, the acrimony and disunity displayed by many party members must have alienated some others. The son of a Labour MP, now an MP himself, has aptly described the behaviour of the party during this ten-year period:

> For most of the last ten years, the Labour Party has behaved in a fashion perfectly calculated to destroy its chances of power. The arthritic rigidity of the Old Right has alienated the idealists; the empty intransigence of the Old Left has alienated the uncommitted voter; the most unbelievable personal virulence of both wings of the party has alienated those who dislike the use of character assassination as an instrument of politics.[5]

[5] David Marquand, "The Liberal Revival", *Encounter*, July 1962, p. 66. Depressing as the reading of these Annual Conference debates may prove, they remain an improvement over those of the 1930s when the Labour left, despite its hatred of fascism, refused to support the rearmament proposals of

3. *Labour's return to power, 1964, 1966*

i. The 1964 general election

The course of events which had so frequently favoured the Conservatives during the 1950s began to turn against them shortly after the 1959 election. The domestic economy required extensive deflationary measures during 1961; the implementation of these produced severe political consequences. Among these were a decided drop in the standing of the Conservatives as shown in the opinion polls, and lessened support for Conservative candidates in a number of by-elections during the first half of 1962. The response of the prime minister, Harold Macmillan, to this decline was to decimate his cabinet in the summer of 1962. During the winter of 1962–63, unemployment rose sharply to almost 4 per cent of the national labour force, and to 6 per cent in both Scotland and Wales. Unemployment was reduced during the year but it was replaced as an issue by the Profumo scandal, which was revealed in the spring and summer of 1963. While the reverberations of that incident, which shocked the nation and created a lack of public confidence in the government, were still felt, Macmillan in October 1963 announced that he was forced to retire because of ill health. No pre-eminent choice was immediately found among the aspirants, and the strife within the Conservative Party did not subside with the eventual selection of Sir Alec Douglas-Home (formerly the Earl of Home: a title which he gave up, enabled to do so by recent legislation, in order to maintain the now accepted custom that the prime minister should always be a Commons man). Dissension continued well into 1964, and subsided only with the April announcement that the general election would be held in the autumn, thereby permitting the Conservatives to remain in power until the very end of their five-year term of office.

Meanwhile, fortune favoured Labour despite the occurrence of unexpected tragedy. Gaitksell's speech at the 1962 Labour

---

the government on the grounds that it 'would misuse the military power that was granted to it for its own imperialist purposes'. Sir Stafford Cripps, quoted in Miliband, op. cit., p. 225. Many more such sentiments are quoted in Miliband between pages 220 and 254.

conference opposing British entry into the Common Market had disappointed his friends in the party and confounded his enemies, but it had the virtue of avoiding another annual bloodletting on the conference rostrum. Labour managed to appear more unified, although the semblance of unity was superficial and fortuitous. Slightly more than three months after his personal triumph at the 1962 conference, Hugh Gaitskell died, to be succeeded as leader of the party by his erstwhile opponent, Harold Wilson. Long the darling of the Labour left in both the Parliamentary Labour Party and in the constituencies, Wilson soon disillusioned this section of the party. His pragmatic approach to the development of party policy was the antithesis of doctrinaire ideology. In the twenty-two months that elapsed between his election as Party Leader and the general election in October 1964, Harold Wilson was compelled by the logic of internal Labour Party politics to seek support from the moderate and right wings of the party, and with few exceptions his policies have merited their continued support. Although some members of the Labour left entertained suspicions concerning Wilson's programme after the party won the election, they had little reason to predict that Wilson's goals would be genuinely objectionable.

The 1964 general election was held on October 15 after a campaign which never raised the temperature of British politics to a high point. The Conservatives tried without success to make the retention of the independent nuclear deterrent an issue, while Labour avoided foreign and defence policy, attracting moderate attention near the end of the campaign by criticising the state of the economy. A 3.1 per cent national swing to Labour in the election concealed constituency swings of much larger magnitude, such as the 7.2 per cent shift to the Conservatives in Smethwick and the 6.4 per cent shift to Labour in Brighton Kemptown. Labour won the narrowest of margins in the House of Commons, holding thirteen more seats than the Conservatives and an over-all majority of only four seats. In the immediate post-election period, there was a temptation to speculate on the possible effects of two incidents in international affairs had their timing been only slightly different. If Khrushchev's fall from power had come one day earlier, or the Chinese had exploded their first atomic bomb two days sooner, the admitted tendency of the electorate to vote for incumbents in the face of sudden changes in international affairs might have brought the Conservatives their fourth consecutive victory. They might well have won, however, with as small a margin as Labour obtained, and the 1966 election probably would have occurred when it did with a similar result.

II. The 1966 general election

In retrospect, the eighteen months that elapsed between the 1964 and 1966 general elections clearly favoured Labour. After their defeat in 1964, the Conservatives again replaced their leader, and although the election of Edward Heath by the Parliamentary Conservative Party was accomplished with relative ease compared to the 'evolvement' of Sir Alec, this had only a fleeting effect on the welfare of the party. Heath had not much more effect than his predecessor in opposing Harold Wilson, and he was also unable to prevent the Parliamentary Conservative Party from splitting badly on the Rhodesian issue.

Labour's record during this short Parliament is subject to varying interpretations. There are those who suggest that 'to govern' in the British constitutional sense implies not only remaining in power but also presenting a full array of legislative proposals to the House of Commons. The Labour government did not fall entirely short of this requirement. By the end of 1965, Wilson's administration had passed a rent bill and certain laws relating to trade unions and workers. Bills were pending in Commons at the time of its dissolution which related to rates, the acquisition of land for development purposes, housing and social insurance. Decisions had been made by the government during this period to abandon the TSR-2, to impose new and higher taxes, to establish a prices and incomes policy, and to adopt a group of orthodox economic measures designed to support the stability of the pound. The government refused to advance the effective date of increases in old age pensions and persisted in a plan to increase the salaries of MPs and ministers; it supported American policy in Vietnam and adopted severe restrictions in immigration into the United Kingdom—much to the distress of the Labour left, which also found objectionable the government policies on the Rhodesian situation and its adherence to traditional British defence policy east of Suez. On this latter point, the left was joined by right-wing elements of the Labour Party.

For a government with a working majority in Commons, this record of accomplishment would not be impressive, but it can be counted remarkable for one with an over-all majority varying between five and one. Its mere remaining in power can be considered an achievement of some consequence. The fact that unpopular decisions or controversial policies were adopted might fairly be construed as a successful effort on Labour's part to govern in the full sense of the term. While many difficulties plagued Harold Wilson and the Labour Party, neither the party nor its leader was apparently held responsible by the electorate. The pound was constantly threatened by a lack of confidence among foreign investors, but Labour took care to keep alive the notion that the financial crises Britain faced were the result of Conservative refusal to deal with fiscal policy for two years prior to the 1964 election. Labour's success in getting substantial segments of the British electorate to blame the Conservatives for the £800 million trade deficit at the end of 1964 was attested by the polls taken between the two elections.

The short Parliament of 1964–66 was sufficient to provide Labour with the opportunity to diminish three handicaps which had been faced in 1964. Eighteen months later, the front bench of the party could boast some governing experience. Labour had shown itself not only capable of governing but of doing so under extremely difficult conditions; and the traditional sectarianism of Labour had been restrained. All these accomplishments were attributable largely to Harold Wilson who, moving into the vacuum caused by the death of Hugh Gaitskell and the retirement of Harold Macmillan, soon established himself as the dominant personality on the British political scene. As leader of his party and later as prime minister, Wilson earned the reputation of knowledgeability in public affairs, particularly in economic matters. He became recognised as a skilled political tactician and a formidable speaker within and outside the House of Commons. Partisans and his detractors alike admitted that Wilson was without fear in attacking critics in his own or in the opposing party. The reputation for opportunism persisted, and his aloofness suggested that he was more interested in gaining people's respect than their affection. However, his willingness to cope with the difficulties of governing while holding a preposterously small majority found heartening response in a nation where courage and dogged perseverance are highly regarded. Despite his apparent lack of emotion, he was counted sufficiently human to be charged by some with admiring his own virtuosity excessively and with relishing unduly his expertise in bringing off one of the outstanding feats in British politics. Criticism of Wilson was confined largely to Conservatives in Parliament and to a few lobby correspondents; except for a few months in the summer of 1965, the British public responded strongly to his leadership.

A number of factors other than Harold Wilson's leadership contributed to the ability of the 1964 Labour administration to govern in the full sense of the term. Save for a short time during the summer of 1965, the polls consistently showed that Labour had a comfortable lead over the Conservatives in questions revealing the voting intentions of the electorate. Even if the Conservatives had defeated the government on any important issue arising between May and August of 1965, the timing would have prevented the Conservatives from exploiting the issue, for they were in the throes of a change in leadership from Home to Heath. Thus, during the eighteen-month Parliament, the Conservatives were not eager to force the issue in Commons on any matter significant enough to cause the government to resign if it were defeated. The lack of a working majority proved to be an important advantage for the first Wilson administration. This apparent liability tended to place unusual pressure on all segments of the Parliamentary Labour Party to support the leadership. Only on the White Paper on steel nationalisation did Labour MPs act in a fashion to embarrass party leaders and endanger the government. Equally helpful to Labour from October 1964 to March 1966 was a prevailing sporting attitude among the electorate that Labour should be given a fair chance. Not only did this attitude serve to restrain Conservatives in their attacks on Wilson and his colleagues, but it also undoubtedly contributed to the high level of support given to Harold Wilson and the Labour Party during the life of the Parliament.

In any event, the general election held on March 31, 1966, seemed to be a postscript to the 1964 election, except that few issues of 1964 were revived and new ones were not found to replace them. The principal development in 1966 was that the Labour Party was empowered with a working majority. A shift in all sections of the United Kingdom in Labour's favour gave the party a majority of 110 over the Conservatives and an over-all majority of 97.

4. Current position of the Labour Party

While impressive in its own right, the huge Labour majority in Commons was far from the most significant aspect of the 1966 election, particularly when compared with Labour's over-all majority of 146 in 1945. The real importance of the last election was that the 1945–50 election pattern was reversed. Rather than falling from a position of huge majority to one of political immobility, Labour moved from an unworkable majority of eighteen months' duration to a dominant political position. The 1966 election marked the first time in the history of the Labour Party that it formed two successive governments in which the second had a stronger political base than the first. Labour now seems assured of remaining in power at least until the early 1970s.

From all available evidence, Harold Wilson will continue as leader of the Labour Party for the indefinite future. With Wilson—a vigorous man of fifty years of age on the formation of his second administration, and in full command of his party—it seems inappropriate even to speculate on the matter of a successor.[6] There is no indication that Wilson shrinks from the criticism of his own left-wing—as witness his support of American operations in Vietnam— or of those representing a broader spectrum of opinion within his party, as was evidenced in the Common Market issue.

In addition to concomitant effects—such as lowering the median age of the PLP and increasing the proportion of university-educated members—the successive victories of 1964 and 1966 gave Labour the prize of extended possession of office. It was inevitable that some initial cabinet appointments made by Harold Wilson should have been as much a recognition of past services to the party as of individual ability to contribute effectively in one of the ministries. The naming of two cabinets, accompanied by a number of reshufflings, has permitted the component of merit as the basis of appointment to be expanded, with the result that a younger and increasingly experienced front bench now gives the lead for the Parliamentary Labour Party. Possession of office allows the Labour Party an opportunity to build a record which the electorate can identify,

[6] By December 1967, however, devaluation of the pound and a series of by-election defeats had damaged Wilson's standing.

merely by putting its stated policies into effect. Even more important, having the responsibilities of office permits the Labour Party to confront problems and to develop responses which ameliorate them. It is the good fortune of the majority party always to be associated in the public mind with action and with the actual business of governing. It is the misfortune of the minority party to be confined to talk; as long as it remains a party in opposition, its ideas will not be tested by application. Furthermore, there is a danger that a party which remains too long in opposition will turn inward and engage in self-destructive introspection during which the intra-party battle assumes more significance for some party members than does the struggle between the parties.[7] It goes without saying that the sectarian proclivities of the Labour Party are more easily controlled when the party is in power than when it is not.[8] Presumably Harold Wilson had this in mind when, shortly after becoming prime minister in 1964, he was quoted as saying:

> This party is a bit like an old stagecoach. If you drive it rapidly, everyone aboard is either so exhilarated or so seasick that you don't have a lot of difficulty. If you keep stopping, however, then everyone gets out and starts arguing about which way to go.[9]

Even though the magnitude of Labour's victory in 1966 should not be depreciated, as it was in at least one British newspaper,[10] it would

[7] ' . . . the tendency for the minority major party is to narrow self-destructively its appeal to fit only those adherents who are left within its ranks. The "party principles" of such a . . . party tend to become narrower and narrower. The remaining leaders may even seek to dam up potential tributary sources of strength in order to better control the organisation and to have freedom to expound the ever-contracting party doctrine.' Ivan Hinderaker, *Party Politics*, New York 1956, p. 635. See also Julius Turner, "Responsible Parties: A Dissent From the Floor", *American Political Science Review*, March 1951, pp. 151–2.

[8] See Rose, *Politics in England*, op. cit., p. 146. Douglas Cater has commented on 'the law of inevitable anarchy that seizes a party when it loses control of the White House. Contrary to Lord Acton's axiom, power may corrupt, but being out of power tends to corrupt the American political party more absolutely.' See Cater's *Power in Washington*, New York 1965, p. 185.

[9] Sydney Gruson, "Wilson Stirs Up a Whirlwind", *New York Times Sunday Magazine*, December 6, 1964.

[10] On April 2, 1966, the Political Correspondent for the *Financial Times* wrote: 'Labour's victory is certainly not of landslide proportions, being in

H

be premature at this point to conclude that Labour has become the permanent majority party in the British party system, or even that this system has become a fully-fledged two-party system with frequent alternations of the parties in power. Less than two years before the 1966 election, a foreign correspondent in London observed, with good historical support: 'The British consider themselves conservative and Labour at best is the relief team. Its chance comes when voters want a change from what is still looked upon as the normal governing party.'[11] In 1966, only six-and-a-half years had elapsed since the Conservatives had been given an equally large Commons majority. The volatility of the British electorate which favoured Labour in the last two elections may just as easily take the same Conservative bias it did in the early 1950s, for there are some aspects of British politics which give the Conservatives a long-range advantage.

The disarray of the Conservatives, up to the time of preparing this study for the press, April 1967,[12] cannot be taken as a permanent condition. Although the party did not face a leadership problem after its defeat in 1945, in the immediate post-war period its programmatic reorientation and its organisational rebuilding were accomplished swiftly and with style. While it is possible that the party has lost its capacity to recover from adversity, it is not unreasonable to assume that some of the traditional resiliency still remains. The present leaders of the Conservative Party must pay the price of wretched luck and of dubious political actions by Harold Macmillan during his last two years as prime minister, as well as for the postponement of the 1964 election to the last possible moment.

[11] Sydney Gruson, "Anatomy of Britain's Labour Party", *New York Times Sunday Magazine*, April 19, 1964, p. 106.

[12] This comment does not take cognisance of the widespread success of the Conservatives in local elections in May 1967. Such success has certainly given them heart at a time when their morale was low; but it is premature yet to seek to draw firm conclusions about the effect of Labour's reverse in county and municipal politics in 1967 on its long-term fortunes as the governing party of the late 1960s.

---

fact a few seats smaller than the Conservatives' win in 1959.' This comment was carping or inaccurate, or possibly both. Labour's majority over the Conservatives in 1966 was 110, that of the Conservatives over Labour in 1959 was 107. The Conservative over-all majority in 1959 was 100, that of Labour in 1966 was 97.

The argument that things would have worked out differently had the Conservatives been returned to office is difficult to sustain, and may remind the American reader of the contention still heard in some circles in the United States that prosperity perhaps *was* just around the corner in 1932. It may have been, but none will ever know.

Evidence that the Conservatives have not lost their broad basis of support with the British electorate is found in the group basis of their support in the general election of 1966. One-third of the skilled workers and one-quarter of the unskilled voted Conservative in 1966, these two classes comprising two-thirds of the total electorate. Conversely, Labour was able to obtain the support of 30 per cent of the lower-middle class, the middle and upper classes as a whole composing only one-third of the electorate. Whether this pattern of voting behaviour can be attributed to Conservative skill in consensus politics, or to the opposites of deferential or individualistic attitudes among British industrial workers,[13] is difficult to say, but a political party with an upper-class reputation which draws half its vote from among skilled and unskilled workers remains a formidable political instrument.

Not all the potential problems Labour faces are to be found in the traditions and the historical success of the Conservatives, but rather are contained within the Labour Party itself. The complexity of the inner life of Labour is suggested by Ralph Miliband's brilliant re-statement of the position of the Labour left in his *Parliamentary Socialism*. He uses the terms 'revisionist Right' and 'fundamentalist Left' to describe the adversaries in the permanent struggle within the Labour Party, adding as a third group 'the Centre . . . whose main attribute is the invention of "formulas" that might be all things to all men'. His attitude toward the utility of the moderating function of the Centre is indicated by the following comment:

> Such appeals [for unity] overlook the fact that *genuine* compromise between revisionism on the one hand, and socialist purposes on the other, is impossible; and that any verbal compromise which may be reached on the basis of ingenious formulas . . . ensures, in

[13] R. T. McKenzie and Allan Silver, "Conservatism, Industrialism and the Working-Class Tory in England", in *Studies in British Politics*, Richard Rose (ed.), London 1966.

practice, the predominance of the policies favoured by a revisionist leadership.

And further, in relation to the agreement on Labour nationalisation policy reached by the 1960 conference, Miliband writes:

> It is surely naive to think that these formulations provide the basis of genuine compromise between people who fundamentally disagree on the purpose, nature and extent of common ownership. All that such a compromise can do is to prove a temporary lull in a battle to be resumed so soon as actual programmes and policies come to be discussed.[14]

As long as party unity ranks low in the value scale of the Labour left there will be turmoil within the party, as there has been since the summer of 1966. Early in the July of that year, Frank Cousins resigned his cabinet post as minister of Technology in protest against the government's prices and incomes policy. About the same time, thirty-two Labour MPs abstained from voting for the government's Vietnam policy, and near the end of the month, forty Labour backbenchers—including Frank Cousins, who had not yet resigned his seat in Parliament—issued a statement proposing savings in governmental expenditures far beyond those proposed by the Cabinet. Late in October, Cousins and twenty-eight Labour MPs defied government whips and abstained from voting on one of the key sections of the Prices and Incomes Act.

The new year brought no relief for, in February 1967, 100 Labour MPs signed a motion warning the government against precipitate action in joining the European Common Market. A few days later at least forty-eight, and possibly sixty-three (Labour backbenchers, rebels and party leaders disagreed over the exact number), abstained on the vote on the Defence White Paper. On this division the government's majority was thirty-nine, although Labour had a majority of ninety-six seats in the Commons. This last action by the left wing of the Parliamentary Labour Party created a full-scale crisis, for there were other Labour members who also were dissatis-

[14] Miliband, op. cit., pp. 344–5. There may be some relevance to the Labour Party in the proposition that: 'Every political party consists of discordant elements which are restrained by the fact that unity is the price of victory. The question always is *Which battle do we most want to win?*' Elmer E. Schattschneider, *The Semi-Sovereign People*, New York 1960, p. 67.

fied with government policies, but who were loyal to party leaders in the House. These members became incensed by the fact that 'rebel' colleagues could abstain from voting with perfect safety, depending on the loyalists to give the government sufficient support to prevail. Some loyalists had argued with government whips at the time of the Defence White Paper vote, and the next day they warned their party leaders in the Commons that they, as well as the rebels, had consciences. They threatened to bring the government down and thereby give the abstainers opportunity to stand for re-election in their marginal constituencies.

This critical situation brought Harold Wilson into the fray, in violation of the tradition that the PLP is run by party leaders in the Commons, with the prime minister not involving himself in such matters. Wilson was painfully explicit both toward the rebels and the loyalists, although it was the former who took the brunt of his remarks. He was quoted in *The Times* as saying:

> All I say is watch it. Every dog is allowed one bite, but a different view is taken of a dog that goes on biting all the time. If there are doubts that the dog is biting not because of dictates of conscience but because he is considered vicious, then things happen to that dog. He may not get his licence renewed when it falls due.
>
> What has happened this week is one more incident in the problems of a governing party. All of us, even the small minority who may have nostalgia for the halcyon days of opposition, want this party to go on governing. If they don't, they should not be here, because the people who sent them here and worked hard a year ago in rain and snow want this party to go on governing. [15]

The response to this challenge was not long in coming. The next day one of the rebels said: 'He has it all wrong. He does not license us; we license him.' Within the next week two other traditional left-wingers attacked Wilson: Michael Foot on television and in *Tribune*, and Sydney Silverman in a long letter to the chief whip, John Silkin. The sharp point in Silverman's letter was that the rebels were doing no more than Wilson had before he became party leader, although implicitly it was a long plaint in reaction to Wilson's personal abandonment of the left. In early April, another reaction to Wilson's candid talk to the PLP came from a Labour member who told his

[15] *The Times*, March 3, 1967.

constituency that the prime minister must govern with the full agreement of MPs of the governing party or make way for someone who would.

The Labour government's decision to apply for membership to the European Common Market in early May brought on another crisis within the PLP. On May 4, 1967, seventy-four Labour back-benchers signed a motion against Britain's joining the EEC. The entire list, together with a lengthy article stating their position, appeared in *Tribune*. A week later, on the vote in the Commons, fifty-one Labour MPs abstained and thirty-six others voted against the government. The next day, seven Parliamentary Private Secretaries who had abstained were dismissed, and Labour's Liaison Committee in the Commons was said to feel a need to identify the 'syndrome' rebels who were opposing a wide range of government policy, including Vietnam, judges' salaries, incomes policy and the Common Market. It is particularly worth noting that, within the fortnight, three constituency Labour parties had given full public support to their members in their defiance of the government, and it is possible others received such reassurance privately.

This action raises the crucial question of the relationship between the member of Parliament, the Parliamentary Party, and the constituency party. Austin Ranney states that 'ideological considerations have been decisive in relatively few Labour adoptions since 1945 . . . parliamentary discipline is so strong, most CLPs feel that how a particular aspirant stands on this or that policy question really matters very little. If adopted and elected, he will have to vote as the whip directs.'[16] Quite clearly, some of the participants in this inter-relationship have not been told the rules of the game, or else they choose to ignore them. It is also quite clear that, for all the abuse the NEC takes in regard to its alleged discrimination against left-wingers for parliamentary nominations, a substantial number were elected in 1964 and 1966. (For example, of the seventy-four Labour MPs who signed the statement published in *Tribune* opposing British entry into the Common Market, forty-seven were elected to the House of Commons subsequent to the general election of 1959.)

An article on the political attitudes of constituency party activists by Richard Rose concludes with the observation that 'it would seem that factional disputes divide parties vertically, joining some Privy

[16] Ranney, *Pathways to Parliament* . . ., op. cit., p. 210.

Councillors, MPs, lobbyists, activists and voters into a faction which is in conflict with another which also contains members drawn from all ranks of the party'.[17] This is undoubtedly true, and it underscores the crucial role of constituency parties for it is they that provide the Labour left with seats in the House of Commons and places on the National Executive Committee. Constituency parties first choose candidates such as Ian Mikardo and Michael Foot, and if they are defeated for re-election, other constituencies with huge Labour majorities adopt them so that they need never fear defeat again. The late Konni Zilliacus, twice expelled from the party, was adopted by the CLP in the Gorton division of Manchester, which had a Labour majority of almost 1,000 even in the general election of 1959, and of 8,300 in 1966. There is no evidence that established members of the Labour left who wished to resume an interrupted career in Parliament or to gain election to it were denied the opportunity. Since the parliamentary career of an able, articulate and aggressive critic of party policy is usually assured, there will always be persons who choose this alternative to the vicissitudes encountered by less flamboyant MPs.

As long as constituency parties accept only the superficial discipline of voting with the party in the House of Commons, invoking frequent appeals to conscience as rationalisations for deviant voting, the Labour Party will continue to give the impression of being at loggerheads. This situation will persist for as long as the individual Labour MP remains free to say and do what he pleases on all matters, both in and out of Parliament, voting with his party or abstaining as he sees fit. Labour leaders frequently try to make a virtue of the contention that goes on within the party. Although there is little indication that British voters place a high value on party unity, there is even less that they prefer to be governed by a brawling, unruly party characterised by abstention, opposition and a steady flow of public criticism of the prime minister and the leaders of the Parliamentary Labour Party. To the extent that the foregoing is an accurate picture of the Labour Party in recent months, the constituency parties must assume a share of the responsibility for creating it, as well as for any loss of popular support that may follow.

[17] Rose, "Political Ideas . . .", op. cit., p. 371.

APPENDIX I

*Questionnaire used
in the Enquiry*

*Interview Guide for Study of Labour
Constituency Parties
All respondents to answer*

1. How long have you been active politically?
2. Has all your political service been with the Labour Party?
3. In what other party have you held membership?
4. What party positions do you now hold?
5. What party positions have you held in the past?
6. What public offices do you now hold?
7. What public offices have you held in the past?
8. What is your age?

   0 25 or less   2 31–35   4 41–45   6 51–55   8 61–65
   1 26–30   3 36–40   5 46–50   7 56–60   9 66 and over

9. What is your occupation?
10. Do you belong to an organised religious group?
    a. Which one?
11. Are you a trade union member?
    a. Which one?
12. At what age did you leave school?
    1. 12–14
    2. 15–18
    3. 19 and over
13. What type of school did you attend?
    1. Elementary
    2. Secondary

3. Grammar
4. Public
5. University

14. a. Do you think the Labour Party should move to the right or to the left of its present ideological position, or should it stay where it is?

   b. What issues do you have in mind as you think on this question?
   Foreign Policy
   Central Planning (Nationalisation)
   Social Services

15. Do you think this adjustment would make it easier or harder to win national elections?

16. a. Do you accept, partially accept, or reject the way the NEC is administering Labour Party proscription policy?

   b. Did you support/oppose the Amendment to the Membership Clause of the Party Constitution at the 1962 Annual Conference?

17. Do you think your (MP—Parliamentary Candidate) is to the right or to the left of his CLP?

18. What issues have you in mind when you compare the politics of your (MP—Parliamentary Candidate) and his CLP?

19. Why do you think your CLP chooses an (MP—Parliamentary Candidate) who is more to the (Left—Right) than they are?

20. What are your views on:

   a. The Common Market
      1. Strongly Oppose
      2. Moderately Oppose
      3. Neutral
      4. Moderately Support
      5. Strongly Support
      6. No Opinion

   b. Defence Policy
      1. Accept PLP Defence Policy
      2. Accept PLP Defence Policy with Reservations
      3. Reject PLP Defence Policy
      4. No Opinion

   c. American Action in Cuba
      1. Strongly Opposed

     2. Moderately Opposed

     3. Neutral

     4. Moderately Supported

     5. Strongly Supported

     6. No Opinion

  d. Chinese Action in India

     1. Strongly Opposed

     2. Moderately Opposed

     3. Neutral

     4. Moderately Supported

     5. Strongly Supported

     6. No Opinion

21. Does the fact that the United States is a capitalistic nation and the Soviet Union communistic affect in any way your attitudes toward these countries?

    1. Pro-USSR

    2. Neutral

    3. Pro-USA

    4. Critical of both

    5. No Opinion

22. Is there any organised factionalism in your constituency?

    1. Are all elections to the GMC Executive, for Conference Delegate, and for Parliamentary candidate contested?

    2. Is there always controversy over the mandating of the Conference Delegate and concern expressed as to how he actually voted?

    3. Is there controversy over the passage of the resolution to be forwarded to the NEC for inclusion in the Conference Agenda?

    4. Is there controversy over the passage of resolutions addressed to the NEC on matters of current interest such as the American-Cuba and the Chinese-Indian matters?

23. What is the nature of this factionalism?

    1. Is it personal in that some local party leaders are unpopular with others in the GMC?

    2. Does it have a religious basis?

    3. Is it ideological in nature, involving questions like the Common Market, Unilateral Disarmament, and Clause 4?

24. How does this factionalism show itself in:

    1. The selection of the Conference Delegate?

2. The mandating of the Conference Delegate?
3. The selection of the Parliamentary candidate?
4. The selection of the Secretary/Agent?
5. The selection of constituency party officers?
25. To what factions do the following officials belong?
  1. Delegate
  2. Parliamentary candidate
  3. Secretary/Agent
  4. Constituency Party Officers
26. Do all factions, including the defeated ones, give full support to the Party in:
  1. Raising funds for the constituency party
  2. Campaigns for local office
  3. General Election Campaigns
  4. Recruitment of new Party members
27. What effect does local or national factionalism within the Labour Party have upon its support from the general public?
  1. Good effect
  2. No effect
  3. Poor effect

FOR MPS, PARLIAMENTARY CANDIDATES, AGENTS, SECRETARIES, AND CHAIRMEN

28. What preparations have you made for the next General Election?
29 What do you think of your chances of victory?
30. How many candidates were there in your division in 1959?
31. How many candidates do you think will there be in the next General Election?
32. What effect do you think this will have on the Labour candidacy?
33. How long have you been_____in this constituency?
34. How much time do you devote to your job? (In the case of MPS, to constituency work?)
35. What is your compensation, including perquisites?
36. Have you had experience as_____in other divisions?
  1. Yes
  2. No

37. If 'Yes' on previous question
    1. Where?
    2. How long?
38. What proportion of your time is devoted to fund-raising activities? How many hours per month?
39. Do you see any relationship between fund-raising activities and political organisation work? What is the relationship?
40. How do your constituency party leaders view your relationships with Transport House; with the PLP?

FOR MPS

41. About how much do you spend each year on constituency work?
42. What are the main expenses in this regard?
43. How is the cost of these expenses met?
    1. Personally
    2. CLP
    3. Affiliated organisations

FOR PROSPECTIVE PARLIAMENTARY CANDIDATES

44. Have you ever stood for Parliament before?
    1. Yes
    2. No
45. If 'Yes' to previous question,
    1. Where?
    2. When?
46. Were you successful?
    1. Yes
    2. No
47. If 'Yes' to previous question, what was the length of your service?
48. Have you been short-listed before?
    1. Yes
    2. No
49. If 'Yes' to previous question,
    1. Where?
    2. When?
50. How frequently have you visited your constituency since your selection?

51. a. Are you a resident of the constituency that chose you to be its candidate?
    1. Yes
    2. No
  b. Did you or your family have any connections in the past with this division? If 'Yes', what was their nature?
52. Was there a strong contest for the selection as parliamentary candidate in your constituency?
53. How many nominations were received by the GMC?
54. How many of the nominees were on Panel A or Panel B?
55. Who were the sponsors of those on Panel A?
56. How many nominations were declared valid by Transport House?
57. How many nominees were short-listed?
58. How many were sponsored, and by whom?
59. How many ballots were taken before one of the nominees obtained a majority?
60. On what date was the candidate selected?
61. In addition to biographical details on each nominee and a short question and answer period, what information did the selection conference have on which to base a decision?
62. Did each of the nominees on the short list have a champion at the selection conference?
63. Were you aware of any lobbying being done on behalf of any of the short-listed candidates?
64. If Transport House wanted a division to adopt a certain candidate, how would they go about it?
65. What role did Transport House and the Regional Organiser play in the selection of your parliamentary candidate?
66. Was there any difficulty in getting your candidate endorsed by Transport House?
67. How independent was your constituency in the selection of its parliamentary candidate?
68. What is the most important Party meeting in your constituency each year—that is, the one which attracts the most people and creates the greatest interest?
    1. Local Conference
    2. Constituency Selection Conference
    3. Election of Conference Delegate

4. Mandating of Conference Delegate
5. Annual General Meeting

69. What importance is attached to the selection of the Conference Delegate in your constituency?

70. How many times in the past has the 1962 Conference Delegate represented the constituency at an Annual Conference?

71. Is the position of Conference Delegate rotated in your division?
   1. Yes
   2. No

72. If previous question is answered 'Yes', what is the basis of rotation?

73. Is there much competition for this post in the division?
   1. How many candidates were there for the post in 1962?
   2. How many ballots were taken before the delegate was chosen?
   3. Was the meeting at which the delegate was chosen well attended?
   4. Was the purpose of the meeting more or less publicised than the purpose of other meetings?

74. Why do people want to be chosen Conference Delegate?
   Is there any honour, prestige, or other satisfaction?

75. What sort of informal qualifications must a candidate for Delegate have?

76. Is the procedure followed in the selection of Conference Delegate in your constituency provided for in CLP by-laws, or is it purely customary?

77. How are nominations made?
   1. From the floor
   2. Submitted in written form from ward or branches

78. At what sort of meeting is the selection made?
   1. AGM
   2. Regular GMC meeting
   3. Special GMC meeting

79. How is the vote taken?
   1. Ballot
   2. Show of hands

80. What sort of majority is needed to win election as a Delegate?
   1. Simple
   2. Exhaustive

81. What role does the GMC Executive play in the choice of Delegate?
82. Describe the meeting at which the Delegate was mandated.
    1. Was there controversy as opposed to discussion on any of the issues?
    2. Which issues were controversial?
    3. Were votes taken on these issues?
83. How was the 1962 Delegate mandated on the following resolutions and actions?
    1. No mandate
    2. Election of constituency members to NEC—to the Women's Section

Castle	Bacon
Wilson	Braddock
Greenwood	Butler
Crossman	Hart
Benn	Herbison
Driberg	Hinks
Mikardo	Jeger
Callaghan	Lee
Stonehouse	Stephen
Healey	White

    3. Amendment to the membership clause of the Party Constitution permitting expulsion for association with proscribed organisations.
       1. For
       2. Against
       3. No mandate
    4. Resolution dealing with the Common Market
       1. For
       2. Against
       3. No mandate
    5. Any other issues on which the delegate was mandated
84. How much discretion did the Delegate have on matters coming before the Conference?
    1. Considerable
    2. Limited
    3. None
85. Was the Delegate requested to bring his book of ballots to the report meeting?

86. At what sort of meeting does the Conference Delegate report?
    1. At the end of business at a regular GMC meeting
    2. As the principal item of business at a regular GMC meeting
    3. At a special meeting called only for the purpose of hearing the report of the Conference Delegate
87. Is the reporting of the Conference Delegate taken as seriously as it was 10 years ago?
    1. Yes
    2. No (If not, why?)
88. Does the CLP select an alternate or deputy Delegate?
    1. Yes
    2. No
89. If 'No' to previous question, what happens if, at the last moment, the elected Delegate cannot attend?
90. What remuneration is given the Delegate?
    1. Travel
    2. Food
    3. Lodging
    4. Lost wages
    5. Out-of-pocket expenses
91. Who pays the expenses of the Delegate?
    1. The Delegate
    2. The CLP
    3. An Affiliated group
92. What is the range of the costs of the Conference Delegate to the CLP?
    1. £10–£15   4. £26–£30
    2. £16–£20   5. £30 and over
    3. £21–£25

FOR PARTY TREASURERS

93. How much did your constituency party spend last year? (Not in a Parliamentary election year, and excluding by-election expenses, where applicable)
94. What were the main categories of expenditure? (Give percentage if unwilling to give figure in Pounds)
    a. Agent
    b. Rent
    c. Secretary

   d. Car or other transport
   e. Local elections
   f. Publicity
   g. Others (specify)
95. How do you raise your money?
   a. Affiliation fees
   b. Trade Union contributions
   c. Transport House grants
   d. Football pools
   e. Labour Clubs
   f. Social events—bazaars, dances, fairs
   g. Individual contributions (above 6s. dues)
   h. Others (specify)
96. How much money do you send to borough, regional, and national parties?
97. What assistance in cash or kind do you receive from local unions, co-ops., etc.?

Register of Electors, 1967
Form A

FORM A

REGISTER OF ELECTORS, 1967

(Qualifying date: 10th October, 1966; register in force for twelve months from 16th February, 1967.)

I am required by Parliament to prepare and publish each year an up to date Register of Electors. A person whose name does not appear in the Register cannot vote at either a parliamentary or a local government election. It is therefore important that you as Occupier should fill up this form and return it to me. Please do so immediately; I will give you any help you need if you apply to me.

Please enter particulars of every British subject (see note) or citizen of the Republic of Ireland whether or not he/she is already on the Register who is over 21 or whose 21st birthday falls on or before 16th June, 1967, and who will be resident at your address on 10th October, 1966, including anyone who, though temporarily absent, normally lives there. Do not, however, enter members of the Forces or anyone else on a service qualification as explained in the adjacent note on Service Voters. Do not enter aliens.

The Electoral Registration Officer.

Please complete sections 1, 2, 3 and 4 below.

SECTION 1. ADDRESS:

No. of Flat (if any)	No. of house (or name, if it is not numbered)	Name of Street or Road	Parish, or Town and postal district (if any)

SECTION 2. RESIDENTS WHO ARE OVER 21 OR WHOSE 21st BIRTHDAY FALLS ON OR BEFORE 16th JUNE, 1967:

Surname, & Style or Title (Mr., Mrs., etc) Christian names or other forenames (BLOCK CAPITALS) (Enter occupier's name first)	If occupier is over 60 enter "over 60" in third column (see note on jury service).	Enter "Over 21," or if 21st birthday is after 11th Oct., 1966, and on or before 16th June, 1967, give date of birth	If Seaman (other than R.N.) enter "M.S."

SECTION 3. OTHER OCCUPIERS OF HOUSE

Is any part of the house or flat you occupy separately occupied by persons not entered above?

Answer YES or NO ....

SECTION 4. I hereby declare that to the best of my knowledge and belief:—
(a) the particulars given above are true and accurate.
(b) all the persons whose names are entered above are BRITISH SUBJECTS or citizens of the Republic of Ireland and are over 21 or will attain their 21st birthday on or before 16th June, 1967.

Signed ....

Date ....

THIS INFORMATION IS REQUIRED BY LAW

NOTES

RESIDENCE

You should include a person ordinarily resident who is temporarily away, e.g. on a visit, in hospital, as a seaman, or as a student; and any person who has been sent away on a job unless his absence will be for more than six months.

Guests and visitors who ordinarily live elsewhere must not be included but you should include resident domestics or lodgers.

AGE

A person whose 21st birthday is after 11th October, 1966, and on or before 16th June, 1967, will be entitled to be registered and to vote at elections held after 1st October, 1967.

BRITISH SUBJECTS

Commonwealth citizens are British subjects.

SERVICE VOTERS

You should not include (a) members of H.M. Forces, (b) Crown Servants employed outside the United Kingdom or (c) the wives who are living outside the United Kingdom to be with their husbands. (Their names will be included in the Register if they have made the necessary service declaration; to do this they should apply to their Service or Department.) You should, however, include Reservists called up for training.

SEAMEN

You should enter "M.S." against the name of a seaman (other than R.N.); he will then be invited to appoint a proxy to vote for him, or to vote by post.

JURY SERVICE

The names of occupiers of property under the age of 60 who are liable for jury service will be marked as jurors in the Register. People in certain occupations may claim exemption when the electors lists are on view at council offices, certain post offices, etc., from 28th November to 16th December.

POSTAL VOTING

Anyone who thinks that he may be entitled to vote by post, e.g. because of physical disability or because of his periodic absences on business (absence on holiday is not a ground for voting by post) should apply to me for a form of application to do so. Do not wait until an election before applying, or you may be too late. Postal voting is not permitted at a rural district, rural borough and parish council elections.

M.P.R. 51-4417

210

Works Cited

Abrams, Mark and Rose, Richard, *Must Labour Lose?*, Penguin, Harmondsworth and Baltimore 1960.

Albu, Austen, "Comment on Crossman", *Socialist Commentary*, August 1960.

Alexander, K. J. W. and Hobbs, Alexander, "What Influences Labour MPs?", *New Society*, December 15, 1962.

Allen, A. J., *The English Voter*, English Universities Press, London 1964.

Bealey, Frank and Pelling, Henry, *Labour and Politics, 1900–1906*, Macmillan, London 1958.

Bealey, Frank, Blondel, J. and McCann, W. P., *Constituency Politics*, Faber & Faber, London 1965; The Macmillan Company, New York 1966.

Beer, Samuel H., *British Politics in the Collectivist Age*, Knopf, New York 1965; published in Britain as *Modern British Politics: A Study of Parties and Pressure Groups*, Faber & Faber, London 1965.

Beloff, Nora, "Where Votes Don't Count", *Observer*, August 16, 1964.

Benney, Mark, Gray, A. P. and Pear, R. H., *How People Vote*, Routledge, London 1956; Humanities Press, New York 1956.

Birch, A. H., *Small Town Politics*, Oxford University Press, London and New York 1959.

Blondel, Jean, *Voters, Parties and Leaders*, Penguin, Harmondsworth and Baltimore 1964.

Brittan, Samuel, "Unsettled at Brighton", *Observer*, September 8, 1963.

Butler, David, *The British General Election of 1955*, Macmillan, London 1955.

211

Butler, David, "The Paradox of Party Differences", *American Behavioral Scientist*, Vol. IV, No. 3, 1960.

Butler, David and Rose, Richard, *The British General Election of 1959*, Macmillan, London 1960; St. Martin's Press, New York 1960.

Butler, David and King, Anthony, *The British General Election of 1964*, Macmillan, London 1965; St. Martin's Press, New York 1965.

—— *The British General Election of 1966*, Macmillan, London 1966; St. Martin's Press, New York 1966.

Castle, Barbara, "The Anti-Socialist Community", *New Statesman*, March 30, 1962.

Cater, Douglas, *Power in Washington*, Random House, New York 1965.

Churchill, Randolph, *The Fight for the Tory Leadership*, Heinemann, London 1964; Houghton Mifflin, Boston 1964.

Clarke, W. J., *General Election Report*, Constituency Labour Party, Kemptown, Brighton, October 15, 1964.

Comfort, G. O., *Professional Politicians: A Study of British Party Agents*, Public Affairs Press, Washington D.C. 1958.

Crosland, Charles A. R., *The Future of Socialism*, Macmillan, London 1957; St. Martin's Press, New York 1957.

—— *The Conservative Enemy*, Cape, London 1962.

Crossman, R. H. S., *Labour in the Affluent Society*, Fabian Society Tract 325, London 1959.

Dowse, Robert E., *Left in the Centre*, Longmans, London 1966; Northwestern University Press, Evanston, Ill. 1966.

Epstein, Leon, "British MPs and Their Local Parties", *American Political Science Review*, Vol. LIV, June 1960.

Goldthorpe, J. H. and Lockwood, David, "Affluence and the British Class Structure", *Sociological Review*, New Series Vol. II, No. 2, July 1963.

Gruson, Sydney, "Anatomy of Britain's Labour Party", *New York Times Sunday Magazine*, April 19, 1964.

—— "Wilson Stirs Up a Whirlwind", *New York Times Sunday Magazine*, December 6, 1964.

Harrison, Martin, *Trade Unions and the Labour Party Since 1945*, Allen & Unwin, London 1960; Wayne State University Press, Detroit 1960.

Hindell, Keith and Williams, Philip, "Scarborough and Blackpool: An Analysis of Some Votes and the Labour Party Conferences of 1960 and 1961", *Political Quarterly*, Vol. xxxiii, No. 3, July–September 1962.

Hinden, Rita, "The Lesson for Labour", in Abrams and Rose, q.v.

Hinderaker, Ivan, *Party Politics*, Henry Holt, New York 1956.

James, David, "We Find That There is Some Unidentified Animate Object in Loch Ness", *Observer*, May 17, 1964.

Janosik, Edward, "Britain's New Labour Leaders", *Orbis*, Vol. iii, No. 3, Autumn 1963.

Labour Party Annual Conference Reports: 1940, 1948, 1949, 1960, 1961, 1962, 1963, 1964, Labour Party, Transport House, London.

Macleod, Iain, "The Tory Leadership", *Spectator*, January 17, 1964.

McCloskey, Herbert, "Issue Conflict and Consensus Among Party Leaders and Followers", *American Political Science Review*, Vol. liv, June 1960.

McKenzie, R. T., *British Political Parties*, 2nd edn. revised, Heinemann, London 1964; Praeger, New York 1964.

—— "The Wilson Report and the Future of the Labour Party Organisation", *Political Studies*, February 1956.

—— "Showing Ideology the Door", *Observer*, December 8, 1963.

—— "The Tories in Turmoil", *Observer*, March 15, 1964.

Marquand, David, "The Liberal Revival", *Encounter*, July 1962.

Mikardo, Ian, "Common Market", *Tribune*, September 28, 1962.

Miliband, Ralph, *Parliamentary Socialism*, Allen & Unwin, London 1961.

Model Rules, Set A, Clause XII, Section (5)—*Constitution and Rules for Constituency Labour Parties in Single and Undivided Boroughs*, Labour Party, Transport House, London sw 1.

National Opinion Polls, *Bulletin:* September 1962; October 1964.

New Statesman: June 1, 1962; June 8, 1962; June 15, 1962; June 22, 1962.

Pelling, Henry, *The Origins of the Labour Party*, 1880–1900, Oxford University Press, 2nd edn., London and New York 1965.

Pendennis, *Observer:* "Fighting for the tuc's Soul", September 1, 1963; see also issue of March 7, 1965.

Pfaltzgraff, Robert L., *Britain Faces Europe*, 1956–66: in preparation.

Phillips, Morgan, *Labour in The Sixties*, Labour Party, London 1960.

214   *Works Cited*

Pickles, William, *Not With Europe: The Political Case for Staying Out*, Fabian Society, London 1962.

Poirier, Philip, *The Advent of the British Labour Party*, Allen & Unwin, London 1958; Columbia University Press, New York 1958.

Powell, Enoch, "Little Trojan Horses", *Observer*, March 15, 1964.

Ranney, Austin, "Inter-Constituency Movement of British Parliamentary Candidates", *American Political Science Review*, March 1964.

—— *Pathways to Parliament: Candidate Selection in Britain*, University of Wisconsin Press, Madison, Wis. 1965.

Rose, Richard, "The Political Ideas of English Party Activists", *American Political Science Review*, Vol. LVI, June 1962.

—— "Parties, Factions and Tendencies in Britain", *Political Studies*, February 1964.

—— *Politics in England*, Little, Brown, Boston 1964; Faber & Faber, London 1965.

—— (ed.), *Studies in British Politics*, London 1966.

Schattschneider, Elmer E., *The Semi-Sovereign People*, Holt, Rinehart & Winston, New York 1960.

Shaw, Malcolm, "An American Looks at the Party Conferences", *Parliamentary Affairs*, Vol. xv, No. 2, Spring 1962.

Social Surveys (Gallup Poll) Ltd., *Gallup News*, No. 6, London, November 1964.

——, *Gallup Political Index*, Report No. 54, London, December 1964.

Titmuss, Richard M., *Income Distribution and Social Change*, Allen & Unwin, London 1962; University of Toronto Press, Toronto 1962.

Turner, Julius, "Responsible Parties: A Dissent from the Floor", *American Political Science Review*, Vol. xlv, March 1951.

White, Theodore, *The Making of the President 1960*, Atheneum, New York 1961; Cape, London 1961.

Woodward, Julian L. and Roper, Elmo, "Political Activity of American Citizens", *American Political Science Review*, Vol. xliv, December 1950.

Yates, Ivan, "Thunder from the Left", *Observer*, February 21, 1965.

List of Tables

Index

Acland, Sir Richard, 10, 82
Acton, Lord, 193n.
Agents: *see under* Constituency Election Campaigns
Albu, Austen, 32
Allaun, Frank, 162
Annual Conference, 2; Arrangements Committee, 45, 158, 159; Composite Resolutions and Amendments, 159; compositing, 158; composition of, 157, 160; conduct of, 159–61; impact of decisions, 2; nature of resolutions submitted, 175–8; NEC influence in, 159; organisation of proceedings, 158–9; party policy making, 167; trade union influence in, 160, 166–7; voting methods of, 26, 91, 160; weak CLPs, activity of, 175–8; *see also* Annual Conference, Unofficial
Annual Conferences: *1960*, 92; *1961*, 92; *1962*, 32, 36, 39, 42, 45—agenda, 37
Annual Conference Delegate: appointment, 162–6—failure to appoint, 164; competition for position, 164; congruity between voting and mandate, 178–9; expenses, 180–1; importance, 3, 166–8; mandating, 171–4; qualifications—formal, 162, informal, 165; reasons for attending, 169–71; reporting to CLP, 179–80; selection procedure, 162–5; voting patterns, 174
Annual Conference, Unofficial, 161–2; left-wing influence in, 161; principal speakers, 162
Attlee, Lord (Clement Attlee), 83

Balance of payments (1964), 185
Barker, Sara, 132
Bevan, Aneurin, 94
Bevin, Ernest, 185
Block vote, 26, 91, 160
Brighton Kemptown CLP, 63–84
Briginshaw, R. W., 45
Brockway, Lord (Fenner Brockway), 162
Brown, George, 65, 74, 83
Butler, Lord (R. A. Butler), 182

Campaign for Democratic Socialism, 103, 123, 136
Campaign for Nuclear Disarmament, 100, 125, 147
Candidates: *see* Parliamentary Candidates, *and under* Constituency Election Campaigns
Card vote, 160
Cartwright, John, 71
Castle, Barbara, 45, 162
Cater, Douglas, 193
Chief Returning Officer, 66
Chinese action against India, 52–5; attitudes of CLP leaders to, 52—high incidence of indeterminate answers, 53–5
Churchill, Randolph, 110
Clarke, W. J., 69, 71, 78, 80
Common Market: *see* European Economic Community
Commonwealth Party, 10
Communist Party, 10, 35, 100, 134
Conservative Party, 68; disunity, 100–12; strengths, 194
Constituency Election Campaigns: agent, 77–9; ballots, counting of, 66; candidate–agent relations,

219